# The Power of Community

**Immigration and the Transnational Experience**
Series Editors: Enrique (Henry) T. Trueba, Pedro Reyes, and Yali Zou

*The Power of Community: Mobilizing for Family and Schooling*
  by Concha Delgado-Gaitan

Forthcoming:
*Ethnography and Education: Qualitative Approaches to the Study of Education*
  edited by Yali Zou and Enrique (Henry) T. Trueba

# The Power of Community

## Mobilizing for Family and Schooling

Concha Delgado-Gaitan

ROWMAN & LITTLEFIELD PUBLISHERS, INC.
Lanham • Boulder • New York • Oxford

ROWMAN & LITTLEFIELD PUBLISHERS, INC.

Published in the United States of America
by Rowman & Littlefield Publishers, Inc.
4720 Boston Way, Lanham, Maryland 20706
www.rowmanlittlefield.com

12 Hid's Copse Road, Cumnor Hill, Oxford OX2 9JJ, England

British Library Cataloguing-in-Publication Information Available

**Library of Congress Cataloging-in-Publication Data**

Delgado-Gaitan, Concha.
    The power of community : mobilizing for family and schooling / Concha Delgado-Gaitan.
        p. cm.—(Immigration and the transnational experience)
    Includes bibliographical references and index.
    ISBN 0-7425-1787-X (alk. paper)—ISBN 0-7425-1550-8 (pbk. : alk. paper)
        1. Hispanic Americans—Education—California—Carpinteria—Case studies. 2.
    Educational anthropology—California—Carpinteria—Case studies. 3. Community and
    school—California—Carpinteria—Case studies. 4. Home and
    school—California—Carpinteria—Case studies. 5. Education—Parent
    participation—California—Carpinteria—Case studies. I. Title. II. Series.

LC2674.C2 D45 2001
371.19'09794'91—dc21                                                            2001031990

Printed in the United States of America

∞™ The paper used in this publication meets the minimum requirements of
American National Standard for Information Sciences—Permanence of Paper for
Printed Library Materials, ANSI/NISO Z39.48-1992.

for the children and families
who have inspired my joy of learning and writing

# Contents

# Foreword

This book brings a number of unusual elements together: a candid, fresh, and honest look at educational phenomena, at Latino families, and at schools. It offers the narratives of immigrant families, but these narratives would have never existed if the families had not met Concha Delgado-Gaitan and trusted her. The selection of critical incidents described and the selection of voices to be heard as a representation of many families was a delicate job done with a great deal of wisdom and care. Academic work, scholarly research, and the choice of critical incidents is for other researchers a job done with objective distance and detachment. Not for Concha.

I first met Concha in the 1980s when she was finishing her doctorate at Stanford. Her writing in the late 1980s led to her major contribution in the 1990s, specifically to *Literacy for Empowerment: The Role of Parents in Children's Education* (1990). With this book Concha began to change her behavior as a researcher. In a profound and long-lasting turn as a scholar, she adopted a Freirean perspective on theory and praxis, and began to live a new life. She produced (jointly with Trueba) a book on the culture change undergone by immigrant families, *Crossing Cultural Borders: Education for Immigrant Families in America* (1991), and soon after that she made her most eloquent statement on her new identity as a researcher. This change was marked by her well-known article in the *Harvard Educational Review,* "Researching Change and Changing the Researchers" (1993).

As Concha continued working with Latino children and their socialization into academia, she realized that literacy for empowerment had to
be translated into specific discourses. In 1996 she wrote *Protean Literacy: Extending Discourse on Empowerment*, a book that emphasized the
*consejos* (guidance) provided by elder Mexicans and parents, among others, to children as a way of socializing them into the home values and
virtues admired by the community.
Moacir Gadotti writes:

> Dialogical pedagogy, with a humanistic basis, attempted to reestablish the idea
> of meeting as a basis of education. The pedagogy of existence defended the
> autonomy of the pupil, the conviviality of the teacher-pupil relationship, non-
> directivity, and self-management. The 1960s and 1970s were the years of revolt
> against authoritarianism and colonialism in which liberation movements,
> mainly those in Africa, were involved. The political revolt against authoritari-
> anism had a profound influence on the so-called critical pedagogies which
> more recently were included in the authoritarian movement of nondirectivity.
> . . . Anyone who studies the history of education will see that educators and
> pedagogues have always conceived of education as a process aiming at the
> development of the human being, and respecting the individuality of each per-
> son. One could also say that the great majority of educators have always
> thought about developing the autonomy of the human being. (1996. *Pedagogy
> of Praxis: A Dialectical Philosophy of Education*. Translated by John Milton.
> Preface by Paulo Freire. Albany: State University of New York, 58–59)

One of the most profound and difficult challenges that we face is to
understand the role of cultural values in the implementation of a given
pedagogy. In some cultures, children learn to give up their autonomies
for the sake of engaging in intensive learning of certain skills and concepts. Chinese children, for example, exhibit a great deal of respect for
school traditions and observe to the most trivial and smallest detail, the
protocols and behaviors prescribed for them in different context
within the school. A pedagogy that would alter that value could be
perceived by Chinese teachers as most destructive. In American society, two of the fundamental values are "honesty" and "individualism"
interpreted in the pursuit of autonomous and independent academic
tasks. Concha explains how Mexican children raised in the culture of
cooperation (rather than one of competition and individual autonomy)
do not view helping each other as "cheating" or breaking any codes,
nor do they see it as a hindrance to the development of their intellec-
tual skills or their character.

So, in adapting critical pedagogy to the cultural values of children in transition one must be aware of the role that parents, family, and community play in the process of socialization. What has been perceived as a universal value in critical pedagogy may not necessarily be so. Henry Giroux has warned us about the need to understand national identity and multiculturalism in modern global societies undergoing rapid change:

> Global changes have provided the conditions for challenge to modern assumptions regarding the unity of nationalism and culture, the state and the nation, and national identity and the universal imperatives of a common culture. The historic and spatial shifts that have, in part, produced new forms of theorizing about globalization, the politics of diaspora, immigration, identity politics, multiculturalism and postcolonialism are as profound intellectually as they are disruptive politically. (1996. *Fugitive Cultures: Race, Violence, and Youth.* New York: Routledge, 185–86)

*The Power of Community,* in my opinion, is Concha Delgado-Gaitan's best work. It summarizes both the lessons she has learned in life as a scholar and as a committed community person who integrated her life in ways that very few people have ever done. To understand the basic contribution of *The Power of Community* one has to understand the life experiences of Concha and her message of hope.

Enrique (Henry) T. Trueba
University of Texas, Pan American

~

# Acknowledgments

Profoundest gratitude goes to my special friends and collaborators in Carpinteria: *Cristina Aguilar* and her family, *Magdalena Alonzo* and her family, *Javier and Lupe Alvarez* and their family, *David and Maria Andrade* and their family, *Marta Meza* and her family, and *Teresa and Miguel Gutiérrez* and their family.

I also extend my sincerest and warmest appreciation to *Robert Keatinge*, administrator and committed advocate of families and of the Latino community. I especially thank the Carpinteria School District administrators and teaching personnel for all of their cooperation during the years of my research in Carpinteria.

During the years that I conducted research in Carpinteria, I received funds from numerous sources that assisted me in completing specific sections of this project, and to these organizations, I am deeply grateful. They are: Academic Senate at the University of California, Santa Barbara; Pearl Chase Foundation; Johns Hopkins Center for Social Organization of Schools; University of California President's Award for Research Most Leading to Improvement in Education; and The Spencer Foundation.

∾

# CHAPTER ONE

# An Ethnography of Immigrants

On a warm fall Saturday morning, a white and red moving van pulled up in front of a fourplex where a "For Rent" sign was coming down. A Chevrolet pulled up behind the small moving van and parked. A Latino man, a woman, and four young children got out of the car.

"Beat you to the door!" called a boy.

"I'm faster than you!" yelled a girl.

The woman picked up the toddler and walked toward the downstairs door to unlock it, while the man went to the moving van and helped the movers begin to unload the furniture. This Latino family raised the demographic statistics of Latinos not only in Carpinteria but also in California.

Carpinteria is a community of little more than twelve thousand residents on the Central California coast about twenty miles south of Santa Barbara. While Carpinteria may appear to be geographically separate from other communities, the people are intricately connected to the economics of others in smaller towns and larger cities surrounding it. Together they belong to a state that is fast becoming home for a majority that is made up of people of color. The 1999 U.S. Census reported that (Hispanics) Latinos alone make up 31.5 percent, Asians 12 percent, Blacks 7.5 percent, and Whites 49 percent of the state's population. Non-Whites constitute a majority. California's increasing non-White population includes an ever-growing immigrant group.[1] Seventeen percent of its new legal immigrant group comes from Mexico. Although many Latinos, including Mexicans, claim generations of heritage in California and the nation, more current waves of immigrants have come in recent decades.

Immigration is not a new phenomenon for California any more than it is for the country as a whole. This country originated with immigrants who committed genocide on Native American Indians. The contradiction is that the labor of these immigrants has built horizons for other immigrants to reach. In Jay Lifton's words, the United States is "a protean nation" in the way that immigrants came, moved forward, and extended. Of course, the negative part of U.S. history is that its white immigrants suppressed native cultures as well as African American and Latino cultures, and U.S. citizens tended to foster fundamentalism, racism, and xenophobia in their attempt to maintain a monolithic culture.[2] How to express the integrity of one's particular culture is the plight of many groups that attempt to make this a culturally diverse democracy.[3] In spite of group diversity, immigrants share a common experience—their relationship to U.S. institutions—which helps us learn the importance of culture. The issue of immigration pervades all social institutions of a community. In spite of the exclusion that immigrants have faced in schools, they have been the most responsive institutions to immigrants since the beginning of public education in this country. Public schools in the United States began with a strong intention to "Americanize" various European immigrants.[4] Latinos, who are the focus of this book, are unfamiliar with that part of the history of U.S. "Americanization." During that period, the Southwestern part of the United States where Mexicans lived still belonged to Mexico.

Throughout the history of the United States, immigrants have been both credited with and blamed for the economic condition of the United States. The ebb and flow of Mexican immigration during the twentieth century has been explained by the economic needs of the United States as much as by the political turmoil in Mexico. The first part of the century saw people emigrating from Mexico to escape the Mexican Revolution. Many were rejoining their families who had already lived in the United States for generations, dating back to the times when the Southwest belonged to Mexico. Newcomers worked in agriculture, garment factories, and in the meat packing industry. The very people who worked to improve the economy of the host country became victims of discrimination by the country that once extended a hand to them. During the Depression, Mexicans were accused of draining the economy and deported. In the early 1950s California's agricultural demands spurred the Bracero program, which allowed single Mexican men to immigrate to the United States for the purpose of working in agriculture. This policy provided a tireless seasonal "cheap labor force." Although these men were required to return to Mexico after the growing season, some chose to stay and continued working year-round on smaller ranches, becoming part of the low-paid workforce in the agricultural industry.

In periods of economic downturn, anti-immigrant sentiments resurface. Through the lows and even the highs of economic prosperity, Mexicans in the United States remain overly represented in the lower ranks of the labor force and find their children underachieving in excessive numbers in the public schools. A consistent cry from anti-immigrant organizations is that immigrants who work for lower wages than those demanded by unions and the U.S. labor force steal jobs away from Whites. Increasing crime and unchecked population explosions are also blamed on immigrants. Some statistics indicate that the immigrant and U.S.-born Latino population tends to be younger; they have more children than non-Latinos. This trend urges that attention be paid to education for Latino groups.

Immigrants and refugee groups have a strong presence in the social historical developments of this country. Testimony before the Select Committee on Statewide Immigration Impact emphasized, "The U.S. influences political circumstances that create refugee and migrant flows. Repression and human rights violations are important 'push' factors . . . past U.S. actions and foreign policy interests in countries such as Vietnam, Laos, Cambodia, Nicaragua, El Salvador, Guatemala, Haiti and Iraq have also contributed to the 'push' of refugees and migrants worldwide."[5] Persistent poverty and unequal distribution of wealth in many countries will continue to push individuals out of their own countries in search of better economic conditions and job opportunities in the United States.

Latino children from Mexico and Central America have challenged California schools to deal with learning in their primary language. Most Latino immigrant families in the United States tend to be poor. The median age of Latinos in the United States is 25.5 years. Less than 25 percent of these immigrants have a high school diploma (as opposed to 77 percent of the U.S.-born adults), and less than 3.5 percent have a bachelor's degree.[6] Critics of immigrant groups fault immigrant children for crowded schools and poor educational outcomes. However, some research findings show that children of immigrants are most likely to become bilingual, speak English fluently, and prefer it to their parents' native language. By the second generation, children speak primarily English, even though they may be in bilingual classrooms.

Building understanding and communication in an ethnically, racially, and linguistically diverse community requires a strong commitment and dependable collaboration between families and schools. Ethnography offers an opportunity for researchers to study ways in which people move toward democratic organization. Carpinteria is one example of how community efforts that build on people's strengths can bridge ethnic differences through power sharing. Different communities deal differently with ethnic diversity issues.

I am conscious of the particular lenses that I brought to the research setting, which were colored by a lifetime of experience as well as learning through academic readings. Social and cultural perspectives help explain the meaning of language, culture, and literacy in people's lives. Numerous specific concepts inform the themes that emerge in this book. No single theory can explain the complex experiences of people's lives that are revealed in this story. The process of change I describe is one of empowerment, and I draw from concepts and ideas developed by intellectuals in various fields, to help me frame the many stories included in this book. Writings from several scholars inspired my thinking. Among them were Paulo Freire on empowerment of community through literacy, Robert Jay Lifton's concepts of malleability and resilience, and Henry Trueba's work on resilience in the Latino community and immigrant adjustment in a new culture. Interweaving these ideas, I attempted to depict the complexity of this community, including personal and collective empowerment, psychosocial ability, and sociocultural adjustment, while understanding individuals' personal lives beyond time and space.

Of particular interest to me is how immigrant adjustment to a new language, culture, and literacy challenges people to transcend their perceived limitations, pain, and isolation. The complex day in and day out social and cultural adjustment of Latino families in Carpinteria is driven by their dreams of working hard to provide their children the best education and promises of a more comfortable life than they had as poor immigrants. Maxine Baca Zinn's research on women helped to shape my ideas about the way that diverse families confront the realities and obstacles that all families confront. She maintains that there are no panaceas to help families surmount adversity in education, that in fact, participation in the economic and social structures is imperative. Apart from challenging their educational status, families in Carpinteria experienced personal expansion that changed their beliefs of self, their attitudes toward others, and their willingness to act on behalf of the "greater good"—a process I term empowerment.[7] Through empowerment we discover that we are much more than the cultural badges we wear. The protean self emerges with new visions that go forth in a collective journey of critical reflection and invests in the individual and the group's pliability and resilience.[8] New concepts of self frame the protean person, who is capable of bringing together incompatible elements of identity and transformation.[9]

Power, the pivotal concept in empowerment, resides in every one of us. One's potential to exercise it develops through one's life journey. For the people in Carpinteria, the opportunity to exercise their collective power was animated through their collective reflection about their common history, culture, and community. Through collective critical reflection parents forged beyond personal and social doubts and deficit thinking to focus on their strengths and shift their perception of themselves in order to continue learning; thus emerged the fundamental orientation of the group. Empowerment of individuals, families, and the Latino community at large evolves as individuals emerge from isolation into connectedness. In empowerment, moving forward, learning, and growing don't always happen in a straight line; they often move in a spiral motion, moving forward then slipping back. But such backward and forward movement doesn't constitute failure; it may be necessary for us to learn a specific step at a deeper level. When we move forward again, we take bigger steps, continuing in a spiraling motion. Every step backward strengthens our movement forward.

Issues of communication between schools and families engaged both Spanish-speaking families and educators. Both Spanish- and English-speaking communities took steps toward each other in rigorous and empowering dialogue that ultimately became the COPLA (Comité de Padres Latinos/Committee of Latin Parents) organization. In 1985 I began an ethnographic literacy study, which, unbeknownst to me, would entail mobilizing efforts by Latino immigrant parents. During my research of the families, the parents recognized their status in the community and addressed their needs by organizing COPLA, which has become a continuous Latino voice in the community. It would be easy enough to measure the growth of the community by focusing on the structural functions, policies, procedures, and merits of the COPLA organization. That COPLA continues to be a strong Latino influence in Carpinteria after fifteen years is in itself an important accomplishment. But it is the people who make up the organization that shape this book's story. How they respected each other, the language they employed, the nature of their conversations, the values that identified them with their community, and what the organization meant to them all define the human capital that contains the lessons of identity, resilience, and possibilities for us to learn.

By the year 2000, Spanish-speaking Latino families had an active voice in the school and in community politics. COPLA has been a central vehicle in bringing about Latino representation in school agendas, decisions, and community educational programs. In COPLA, Latinos have a formal agency through which they can navigate the school system, advocating for improvements in their children's schooling. Today, although pressing issues continue to exist for Latino parents to negotiate with the schools, the difference is that now an established organization is in place that serves as the voice of Spanish-speaking people. Latino families have experienced a great deal of personal and professional growth since they first began their community activism. For example, Petra Angeles, who was one of the original leaders in COPLA, has herself returned to school and taken the GED, earning her high school diploma. She has since enrolled in the community college and plans to become a nurse. After her two children graduated from high school, she set aside her own fear of being a student and realized that it was time to challenge herself to do what had always been her plea to her children—study. In her words, "One morning I just got up and told myself that I wanted to get rid of that fear that I had always had since I quit junior high school in Texas. Can you believe it? All those years I told other parents in COPLA to be an example to their children and I had my own fears about learning English. Now there's nothing stopping me, even if I'm so old that they have to push me in a wheelchair to get my nursing degree."

The ways in which people in Carpinteria have grown through their involvement in COPLA are unique to each person. Some people who were not active initially, like Petra Angeles was, have since found opportunities for personal growth by getting involved in the organization. When COPLA was first organized, Dora Rivera was married to a man who was extremely active in organizing the group and was part of its leadership for years. She, on the other hand, resisted attending meetings because she lacked confidence. A recent telephone call with her describes a different person. "I had to tell you," she began, "the high school Latino COPLA group just named me president of the organization." I congratulated her and for a moment strained to think why she would consider this a big enough triumph to call me long distance. She reminded me, "When you last met with the group down here, I was feeling so badly because my marriage was falling apart. I felt so powerless to take even one step forward to change my relationship with my children or my husband. Yet

I knew what I had to do, I had to take action. I had to trust myself and get involved with my children in their school if I was going to restore my self-esteem. So, I began attending meetings, and I found so much support from others. I felt stronger and stronger. My marriage isn't perfect now, but I feel more confident about my alternatives. I know it's been many years that I've been talking to you about this. But see, I'm taking action now and getting involved in COPLA."

Since the middle of the nineteenth century, prejudice and isolation have characterized the experience of many generations of Latinos of Mexican descent, living in Carpinteria. Mexican immigrant families who arrived in Carpinteria after 1970 have also experienced discrimination, but they live in a political climate different from that in which past generations of Latinos lived. The more recent political climate offers greater educational opportunity, as a result of the war on poverty legislation, stemming from *Lau v. Nichols*.[10] Even so, adjusting to a new country, a new language, and a different school culture is fraught with distress. The immigrants' stories remind us that in adversity there is opportunity and that rather than folding under the pressure and threat of a new system, the self turns out to be quite resilient. Longtime Chicano residents who weathered the shifts of segregated schools and social segregation, along with the more recent Mexican immigrants in Carpinteria, have continued growing and struggling to become active participants in their community and school. Their stories show how Mexican immigrant families have risked, confronted, and evolved; theirs is a story of the self's capacity for functional wisdom within the cultural framework of the family and community. In Carpinteria it is not ethnicity or culture that divides; rather, it is poverty, racism, illiteracy, and ignorance that erects fences between people. Culture, when affirmed and shared, creates possibilities for building bridges.

This book spotlights individuals and families involved in COPLA, a community collective that continues to be at the center of these people's sociocultural change. The lives of cultural brokers in Carpinteria interweave with the lives of Latino activists. I felt changed personally and professionally as a result of my work with people in Carpinteria. My role as an ethnographer expanded while I was working on this project. Commonly, the researcher and the research community are discussed in terms of an insider/outsider relationship. Without question many differences exist in the cultural experience of researcher and the collaborators in the communities who are the focus of the research. However, relationships aren't simply an insider/outsider dichotomy, because in complex societies like those found in the United States, the researcher and the focus communities at some point become actors in a common culture.

For instance, I am an immigrant Latina, whose background is similar to that of many families in the research community, but I have been educated in the English-speaking mainstream culture, an experience that differs from that of some of the Spanish-speaking families in Carpinteria. Thus, our values and practices are both similar and different. I wrote this book from the researcher's perspective, attempting to blend both the outsider and insider viewpoints. My research builds on sociocultural theories that explain the meaning of language, culture, and literacy in people's lives, making me conscious of the particular lenses I bring to the study. The point where the research ends and the community's story begins is sometimes blurred. Anthropologist Suad Joseph writes that research outcomes may differ depending on the psychosocial dynamic between ethnographers and the communities we study—class, race, gender, education, ethnicity, and specific family histories are always interactive.[11]

In this Carpinteria story, the community leaders and I lived a few miles from each other, but our lives intertwined. Our venture together was one of learning that being empowered meant learning to think and live differently. On this road, it sometimes felt lonely, but that's the purpose of community—to remind us that we're not alone.

Many of the people whose stories are included here are Spanish-speaking Latinos, immigrants from Mexico. But their story encompasses a much wider community, including Latinos whose families span generations in the United States and European-Americans. My intent is to describe several years of research involving people's lives and a process of learning a new language, culture, and literacy and their pursuit of continuity in the midst of discontinuity.[12] Through the process of working with each other, Latino families demonstrated their resilience, and, together with the school personnel, they showed malleability.

The immigrant Latino's cultural identity, language, and common historical and political experience both challenged and affirmed the beliefs and values that governed the lives in this project. As immigrants from various parts of Mexico, Carpinteria Latinos spoke Spanish and some English, worked in low-wage skilled jobs, and taught their children to value schooling. Many adults had their schooling interrupted, which made their own children's education a high priority for them. Shaped by the lessons of their own pain, parents placed their children's needs center stage, giving rise to and sustaining their activism in the community and at the same time creating the space in which this ethnography came to be formed.

# CHAPTER TWO

❦

# Cultural Brokers in a
# Growing Community

"They're hard workers," was a comment frequently made by employers of many agricultural workers in Carpinteria. Working in agriculture has been a major draw for Mexican immigrants into Carpinteria. However, not all Latinos are immigrants or agricultural workers. Perceptions of their experience in this community differed between early Mexicans settlers and more recent immigrants. The sociopolitical climate was less hospitable for Latinos prior to the recent generation. Yet those who came earlier laid an important foundation for the waves of immigrants that followed. Mexicans migrating to Carpinteria in the early twentieth century faced more relaxed immigration laws when pursuing their economic endeavors than did migrants of later generations. Descendants of this migration wave constitute the present-day Mexican American population in Carpinteria. The agricultural industry in Carpinteria was a good "fit" for Mexicans who had the desired skills and motivation or who had no other option.

But prior to any Euro-American or Mexican immigration to Carpinteria, it was the home of the Chumash Indians, who had lived there since the sixteenth century. The Chumash were hunters and fishermen, which left ample agricultural opportunities for the Mexicans. The land that belonged to the Chumash was taken over as their fishing became industrialized by major fishing companies, and the Chumash people were forced into the hills, where substandard living conditions threatened their survival.

The population of Carpinteria did not exceed one thousand residents until the mid-1940s. Predictably, employment differentiated ethnic groups, as did different geographic boundaries. The Mexicans worked in farm-related jobs and lived in neighborhoods apart from the non-Latino population.[1] Lemons and avocados were the principal crops worked by Mexicans in the Carpinteria area. By 1950 the Bracero program had brought in a new migration of Mexicans to work specifically in agriculture. Dutch, Japanese, and a few Mexicans owned ranches that employed Mexicans as laborers. Although the men were supposed to return to Mexico at the end of the growing season, many of them stayed in Carpinteria. Some married local women, while others returned to Mexico to marry and later immigrated with their wives to Carpinteria where they raised their families.

Mexican workers have always been valued for their experience in agriculture. They provide cheap labor, but that does not grant them equal status in the workplace, housing, social activities, or schools. Institutionalized segregation was prevalent in the schools until the early 1970s. According to a newspaper article from Santa Paula, a nearby town, the Carpinteria school board segregated Mexicans because they were classified as Indians, and the State of California permitted the isolation of Indians under de jure segregation laws:

> School authorities of Carpinteria have caused considerable interest in all parts of the state with their decision in declining to accept the ruling of U.S. Attorney General Webb that [states] cannot segregate Mexican, Chinese, Japanese and Indian children. . . . The Carpinteria school board takes the ground that children of Mexican born parents are Indians. . . . In Santa Paula the Mexican situation is handled in a tactful manner, school authorities believe. Many of the Mexicans are going to school in the Canyon and Ventura [schools] situated in their own sections of this city . . . the school[s] situated in their own districts take care of the majority of the Mexican children, and special courses of study have been arranged for them. They are said to be happy in their own schools.[2]

Under the guise of this legal interpretation of race, schools in Carpinteria could legally segregate Mexicans into the Weaver School, which became known as the "Mexican school." Children who attended this school at the time it was segregated recall the harsh treatment that Mexican children faced at the hands of their teachers and principals.

Javier Torres, who later became a teacher and principal in Carpinteria, had vivid memories of his earlier school experience in that community. He was born and raised in Carpinteria, and his family spoke only Spanish at home. "First grade began my career in Catholic school and as an English-speaker. In first grade I became an English speaking person. At that point I have specific images. Before then I knew I had a dog, but I didn't remember its name. The only reason I remembered that there even was a dog is because I've seen pictures of me and I am next to Smoky."

Javier's parents were strong Catholics and valued a strict education. They sacrificed financially to send him and his brother to Catholic school. "In Catholic school I apparently did very, very well. I have only positive feelings. There were some bullies there, and they made life a little uncomfortable, but as far as the classroom was concerned and the school itself, it was all very positive. When my brother and I went to the public school, in the fourth grade, was the first time I ran into failure. It was the first memory of incidents that obviously involved discrimination in the public schools, maybe because the school only accepted what was English and White. We went to Weaver School, which was the Mexican school."

Since most of the Mexican children who attended Weaver School lived in the same neighborhood, they didn't always think of themselves as being segregated. Javier recollects, "All of us living in or around this part of the town we went to the Weaver School. The other schools were the Anglo schools. Although there were Anglos in our school too, it was impacted with Hispanic kids. But my first failure there taught me a lot about possibilities that were available to us with the right support. [The failure happened with] [m]y teacher, Trini Sanchez, the only Hispanic on the staff setting me aside and having me go through a list of vocabulary words. I could read these words but did not know the meanings. And I remember being dropped from the highest reading group to the second level reading group. It was a very humiliating experience. It was the first time I experienced not being successful in school. I didn't speak English for four years and in spite of it, I was doing quite well." Javier tried hard to do his work, and his parents encouraged him daily. This enabled him to improve in later grades.

"In the fifth grade I was back in the top group, and that was not a problem until we got to sixth grade. But when all the kids came together at the junior high I faced the worst failure in my academic grades. I suddenly found myself near bottom groups from the first day of school. I had never been in such groups, and I was with the kids that I considered not very intelligent and who couldn't do their schoolwork. Now I was with them, and I was one of them. I guess I was achieving to the level of expectation. This was what we now call tracking."

Just as Javier encountered discrimination in his early school days, so did other Latino teachers when they were students. Trini Sanchez raised her family and taught in the Catholic school for a short time when Javier Torres was a student. She recounts her seventh grade experience in a Carpinteria school when she could not speak Spanish to her friends—even during recess—without being punished. "One day we were at recess and the teacher who was supervising at the time did not like it that my friends and I were speaking in Spanish. She took us to the principal's office and the vice principal spanked us all and then we were expelled. Our parents were so angry that they went to the office the next day and complained to the principal, but he wasn't there. So, they talked to the vice principal, who told them that they had no right to complain because it was the school's policy not to allow Mexican children to speak Spanish. My mother said that she felt very angry and frustrated because she had gone to talk to the principal to insist that they treat us with more respect, but she couldn't say anything because no one listened to them."

The restriction on use of primary language, compounded by corporal punishment, was not behavior specific to Carpinteria schools. Like Javier and Trini Sanchez, many Mexican students throughout the Southwestern states, where schools segregated Mexican students, lived in fear and frustration during that period.[3] Mexican immigrants in Carpinteria share a language, an ethnicity, a history, a subordinate social class position, and availability of only poor learning opportunities in Mexico. Sharing their common culture, families tell a personal story of struggle, adjustment, and endurance in their travels from Mexico to their adaptation in Carpinteria.

## An Immigrant Tradition

Patterns of hard work prevailed for Mexicans who immigrated to Carpinteria. When immigrants arrived in Carpinteria, they maintained strong ties to their families in Mexico and simultaneously made an effort to fit into a new society. David Segura and his wife, Alicia, have lived in Carpinteria for more than thirty years, but connections to family in Mexico blur the geographic borders. The Segura children, Hector, Nuvia, and Mirea, were born in Carpinteria.

David spent his childhood in Zapote, Michoacán, a small town on the outskirts of Michoacán. His parents and six siblings lived in a rancho, which required the labor of every member of the family to work the crops that fed the family. They sold the produce locally for a meager income. David completed an elementary education in Zapote, where there was no high school. He moved to Potrero, Guanajuato, a nearby town in the adjacent state, where he attended high school and met Alicia.

Alicia's family owned a corn mill where the family ground corn for others and made masa (cornmeal) for their daily tortillas. As the seventh of fourteen children, Alicia worked hard around the family's ranch and in the corn mill. As a result, her availability to attend school beyond elementary grades was limited. She was saddened when she had to quit school; consequently Alicia always envied those who were able to continue. When Alicia was sixteen, her aunt took her to Tijuana to work in a factory. She stayed for only one year until her mother needed her back at the ranch in Mexico. During Alicia's short stay in Tijuana she continued her long-distance courtship with David through writing.

David was about twenty when he made his first trip to Sacramento, California, with his mother, a U.S. citizen. They stayed with one of David's brothers, who lived and worked in Sacramento. Following a brief visit, David joined his father in Carpinteria, where the father had a job picking carnations. Shortly afterward, both of David's parents returned to Mexico. His relationship with Alicia evolved through letters and David's periodic visits to Mexico.

Agricultural employment was plentiful in Carpinteria, where David eventually made his home. During the 1970s managers hired mostly single Mexican men who left their families in Mexico. But by the mid-1970s, many families were reunited in Carpinteria, as men sent for their wives and children during the initial legal amnesty efforts that allowed undocumented agricultural workers to acquire legal residential status in the United States. Nurseries hired both men and women in the expanding industry.

Alicia and David married in Mexico, and he returned to Carpinteria without her until he could acquire enough money for both of them to live. Finally he was able to support both of them in the United States, and he sent for Alicia. Soon after arriving, she began working in a factory. David recalls how supportive the Latino community was. "At that time, one could rent a house with very little money. Rents were low, and one could live with very little money. Families frequently visited each other on Sundays. I was very involved with the religious club since 1972 that had as its purpose to raise funds for the church."

Alicia's experience differed. "When I came to live in Carpinteria, I was very sad because I did not have my family and I felt isolated where we lived in the ranch. The church had outings on Sunday, and we gathered to be united with our families. The soccer games were also an opportunity to get together with other people. David played a lot of soccer, and at those games I met Rebeca Cortina, because there the two of us played with our young sons and later we became *compadres*. She later became our youngest daughter's godmother."

David began taking English-as-a-second-language classes when he first moved to Carpinteria. He continued progressing in his English proficiency until he qualified for U.S. history classes, which intrigued him. He worked until 6:00 P.M. at the ranch, went home to have a bite to eat, and was in class by 7:00 P.M. When he returned home at 10:15 P.M., he read for about an hour, then helped around the house for a few minutes, and finally went to bed so that he could awaken at 4:00 A.M. to begin work again. "I learned so much about the history of this country, and I enjoyed all of the books, so that I began buying many history books myself—history of all the world. Eventually, I took classes that led me toward my citizenship." David's story seemed rather curious since his mother was a U.S. citizen, and David admitted he didn't know he was already a citizen by virtue of the fact that his mother had been born in the United States. If he had known, he would have only had to file a few forms. "But it was probably better this way," he said, "because I learned so much in those citizenship classes and I became interested in reading everything that was history related."

David's family applauded his accomplishment. Alicia also began to take English classes at night. When she became pregnant with their first child, Hector, Alicia attended other classes in Spanish, including birthing and child care. Representatives from Casa de la Raza in Santa Barbara notified Alicia about the classes and offered to provide her with transportation, which enabled her to learn about natural childbirth and how to care for her newborn baby's nutrition and health. Even through her childbearing years, Alicia continued working in the factory

Employment and work were not the only priorities for Mexican immigrant families in Carpinteria. Their families were also of great importance to them. Wanting to raise their families with a strong sense of respect, bilingualism, and commitment to family, Latino parents kept a close eye on the home front.

The Seguras held family in high priority. David was quite involved in the schools from the time their children began preschool. David and Alicia, however, were disappointed with the more recent newcomer families from Michoacán, who tended to isolate themselves from the community and schools. The new arrivals came from more remote ranches and had virtually no schooling. To compound the problem, they confronted unemployment in Carpinteria, which had not been the case when David and Alicia had arrived. When there is high unemployment, adults, particularly the men, take to drinking and "hanging out" in their front yards, while the children go unattended. Young people who find adjustment difficult often turn to loitering on the streets and sometimes vandalism. Solutions to the problem call for aggressive responses in the areas of education, fairness in the labor market, affordable housing, and assistance for the myriad cultural changes that immigrant families are forced to undergo. David believes that organizations like COPLA (Comité de Padres Latinos/Committee of Latin Parents) are critically important in helping families to stay off the streets. David attends more COPLA meetings than Alicia does, but she helps with the children's homework. She has become so competent in English as a result of helping her children and taking citizenship classes that she passed the exam to become a U.S. citizen. "I was quite nervous, but my children helped me to study for the exam. Now that it's over, I can spend a bit more time with the kids when I get home from work. The nursery seems to be quite slow lately anyway so that my hours have been shortened." Alicia's commitment to her children's schooling has been emphasized by example, through the advancement of her own education.

The immigrant experience in Carpinteria is characteristically diverse. Although immigrants like David and Alicia Segura have lived an exemplary immigrant experience by improving their socioeconomic condition and their children's opportunities for education and employment, other immigrant families have had a very different life in Carpinteria, making the existence of the parent group all the more imperative.

By the time that the Segura children began school in Carpinteria the political climate in the schools had changed considerably from the earlier days of segregated schools. Some of the very students who once attended the all-Mexican schools became important professionals and change agents in the community as teachers and counselors. One of those teachers, Javier Torres, is part of this study. Javier became a preschool program leader and later a bilingual teacher. In 1993 he was appointed principal of Martin School.

Another important development in educational reform occurred in the early 1970s. As a result of *Lau v. Nichols,* the federal government made funds available to create bilingual programs for limited-English-speaking students—those with a home language other than English.[4] Carpinteria used state and federal funds to create a bilingual preschool and elementary school program. The children who benefited from these programs had parents who had immigrated in the recent generation. For the most part, these children were born in the United States, but their parents were predominantly Spanish speaking.

## Cultural Brokers

For children, as well as adults, learning a new language and culture often necessitates a mediator between the familiar and the new. Someone who knows the rough parts of the road for an immigrant can facilitate the appropriate knowledge and means that will allow people to participate more fully in their new community. It is crucial to have Spanish-speaking Euro-American educators who can translate when necessary. Paul Niles, the director of special projects in the Carpinteria school district, played that role. His work with community groups and Latino families was a continual stabilizing force, especially between Latino families and the schools. He adamantly believed that the thrust in the school district was to prepare all students to make informed choices about attending a university after high school graduation. More recently, 17 percent of Carpinteria students attend a four-year college or university following high school graduation.[5] Long before Paul became the school district representative in the Latino parent group, he was a director of the Title VII bilingual program, with teaching responsibilities in ESL (English as a Second Language) classes in the middle and high schools. His commitment to working with parents and building strong ties between families and educators stems from his firsthand experience with the district's bilingual program when it was federally funded.

Challenging the traditional curriculum for Spanish-speaking students opened opportunities for Javier Torres. In 1978, Javier left his teaching position to organize the early childhood program for the district. He recounts, "I became the coordinator of all of these programs. I organized an Early Childhood Center which encompassed all of them. As the first Hispanic in that role, I began looking at how other Hispanics were performing as administrators. One of the most important things I did was to begin looking at the existing data on student achievement. No one had ever done that. They had never looked at children's entering skills when they began school. Every year the school district screened the children, but they didn't compare Anglo and Hispanic student achievement. The reason those comparisons became important was that students seemed to begin on a more even plane, but then Anglo students soared in their growth while Hispanic students didn't grow as quickly when they moved through school. Anglo kids came in with many more advantages, and language was the greatest one." These findings have been instrumental in shaping educational programs for Latino students.

Javier further explains, "Based on those findings we wrote a grant for a bilingual preschool that would allow Mexican children who spoke only Spanish at home to get their preschool education in Spanish. And by doing so, Mexican kids would have the basic skills of their English-speaking counterparts. After that they could go into a regular bilingual classroom where they were taught in Spanish and were learning English. We had done our research with other very well known Spanish-only preschools. They got excellent results. So we went for it. And we got the grant."

A critical feature of successful educational programs is hiring teachers who are well trained and know the students' language and culture. This was the goal in Carpinteria as Javier tells it. "We hired two teachers, one who spoke primarily English and the other who spoke primarily Spanish. They were to teach as a team. We thought that the two of them could bring about the program that we conceived. The English-speaking teacher made an interesting comment, she said, 'We have no business in working here with these kids in English they do not even appear to speak their own language.' Obviously she was the one with the language problem. The children spoke Spanish and that's why the curriculum was in their language. She was there to teach them English. This convinced us more that we had to rely only on their Spanish strengths and make sure that their primary language was fully developed before introducing English." The preschool directors proceeded to make the preschool curriculum strictly Spanish speaking. Javier continued to describe the program, "We followed neo-Piaget's theory of development in the program. Other preschool programs we visited showed this to be the best approach with language-minority students. Our program became nationally renowned, because the children made great gains, which made it possible for them to progress faster in school once they left preschool."

The program was visited frequently by preschool teachers and directors from across the country. As Javier recalls, "Carpinteria's bilingual program had a national reputation for its strong achievement record, which could be attributed to the enrichment focus on children's first language." While most bilingual programs constructed bilingual classes with both Spanish and English curricula simultaneously, Paul observed the value of having students immersed in Spanish and becoming proficient learners in their language before being expected to learn in English. Paul also became convinced that bilingual education truly was an enrichment for English speakers wanting to learn Spanish as well.

Paul Niles helped shape the program's philosophy and direction. His background in sales prepared him with skills necessary to present the bilingual program to English-speaking families and parents interested in placing their children in bilingual classes. With 50 percent of the bilingual class English-speaking Anglo and 50 percent Spanish-speaking Latino, Paul established an effective bilingual program, where a fluent bilingual teacher taught the entire curriculum in Spanish one day and in English the next. The English-speaking parents became strong advocates for the bilingual program, because their children learned Spanish, and the Spanish-speakers achieved as they learned English. According to Paul, the force that parents exerted to support the program was consistent with what he witnessed in highly successful bilingual programs in his prior workplace in Burbank. His interest and success in working with parents in advisory committees made his later work with COPLA all the more compelling.

Paul explained why the bilingual program flourished in the late 1970s and began to decline in its effectiveness by the early 1980s. "One important change in the bilingual program has been a shift in our population. The years that I began to collect data in Carpinteria, a new trend was being noticed; more Mexican immigrant children came from bigger cities and had schooling in Mexico prior to coming here. More recently, there are more immigrant children entering our schools who come from poorer rural areas where they have not had any education and they're not as inclined to want to learn English and to become bilingual or to apply themselves in the classes as they did twenty years ago."

Other reasons for the difference in bilingual education were that many bilingual teachers left Carpinteria School District as a result of personal mobility. Paul elaborated, "The school district had a difficult time competing with pay which excellent bilingual teachers could receive in neighboring school districts. Exhausted federal funds rendered the school district unable to continue offering expanded bilingual programs to Spanish speakers. Consequently, the direct benefit to students, provision of teacher training, and the resources of teacher-assistants were lost. All of these components supported teachers' effectiveness in working with Spanish-speaking students and teachers' assistants. The administrative reorganization by a different superintendent between 1986 to 1990 progressively moved the school district from a centralized administration to a decentralized system where principals, who had little training in bilingual education, were expected to assume responsibility for implementing their program." Hence, teachers lost their district-wide coordinator when his responsibilities diversified, forcing him to divide his attention among other programs. Still, strong efforts to address the needs of Latino students were a priority for educators who were convinced that everyone, including Latino students, were capable of learning, given a supportive, creative, and effective learning environment.

When I first began to conduct research in Carpinteria, I found that several committed educators in the Carpinteria schools reached out to Latino families and were available to them as much as possible, even before the Spanish-speaking Latino parent community officially organized.

## Building Community

To understand the present educational dynamics in Carpinteria, we need to turn back the clock to the early 1970s. The school district developed a bilingual preschool, where the teacher, Celia Marquez, changed the lives of many Spanish-speaking children in the school district. She spoke Spanish and knew the culture of the families and the community well, because she also lived in Carpinteria. She made the parents coteachers with her in a way that helped them learn to help their children in the home, and she also made them accountable to her for helping in the preschool. Most of these parents, all of whom were immigrants from Mexico, had had no more than a fourth grade education in Mexico and held jobs as agricultural workers in the nurseries.

Celia taught the parents to read books to their children and encouraged parents to converse with their children by making time to do household chores that involved children. By allowing children to help in cooking, washing dishes, and shopping, parents and children could enjoy a great deal of language interplay. The preschool teacher was the key to the successful program. She provided a rich curriculum in Spanish and created a strong relationship with Spanish-speaking families. Although the bilingual preschool program remained strong, the declining strength of the bilingual program affected the first through sixth grades.

When the children left the preschool program, however, few resources existed to help Spanish-speaking parents bridge the connection with the elementary school. As Spanish-speaking children moved up the academic ladder and learned more English, parents were distanced from their children and the schooling process. Parents reported that by the time their children reached junior high school, they felt as if they were living with strangers.

Consuelo Avila, a parent, recalled her experience with her son, Raul. When I interviewed Consuelo, Raul had just been promoted to the fourth grade. She talked about her difficulty in helping her son improve his reading skills. "Raul was in the third grade and read only in Spanish. But when he began learning to read in English, he had many problems. He was not doing well, and his teacher, Mrs. Robins, called me. She also sent home notes with Raul and told him to tell me to call him. But I felt so embarrassed, thinking that it was my fault that I just kept trying to help my son as much as possible at home by myself." Weeks passed and the teacher continued working with Raul. At home, his mother knew that he was having problems. "I just did not understand his homework. I was unable to help him because the instructions were confusing even though they were in Spanish." The reports sent home by the teacher never reached Consuelo, because Raul was afraid to give them to her. All the while, his mother felt that she was to blame. "I felt kind of ashamed that I couldn't help Raul since my schooling was so limited. That kept me from going to the school and talking to Mrs. Robins." The distance grew between Raul and his mother as well as between Mrs. Avila and Mrs. Robins. The breakdown in communication isolated everyone in a way that caused them to work harder yet minimized gains.[6]

Raul's case is typical of Mexican parents' experience in the schools, not only in Carpinteria, but also in other communities where I have worked. Although Raul's case was not an extremely urgent one, it was nevertheless a critical one, because it became increasingly problematic for parents like Mrs. Avila who remained strangers to the teachers like Mrs. Robins. As their children moved up the grades, the gap between parents and schools widened. Parents felt unable to deal with the schools, and teachers mistakenly assumed that Latino parents did not care about their children's schooling. The schism between Latino families and schools was reflected both in the children's underachievement and in the parents' and teachers' frustrations. Both sides faced structural limitations in achieving meaningful communication. Teachers were limited by their poor training in working with families from diverse communities. On the other hand, parents were restricted by their illiteracy and lack of understanding of the schooling system. Instead of understanding that the problem was one of a structural nature, parents blamed themselves for their children's learning problems. Their lack of participation was one of the underlying reasons for mobilizing Latino parents to unite under the Comité de Padres Latinos.

COPLA bridged the gap between parents like Mrs. Avila and teachers like Mrs. Robins, who had students like Raul. This organization differed in purpose from other parent groups in the school district. The Latino parents didn't intend to organize for the purpose of meeting legal mandates of the school district. Such official committees, made up primarily of White, English-speaking parents, usually organized only to deal with questions of budget and school policies. Different from these groups, COPLA parents wanted to support each other in learning how to work with the schools in an informed way and help their children in their schooling. They constructed new avenues through which the community could voice their interests, expand their knowledge, and become partners with the schools.

In COPLA meetings, parents became informed about their children's educational needs. The information came through invited school personnel or from parent leaders. When Spanish-speaking students reached the third grade, they were usually transferred from bilingual classes into English-only classes. When children make this sort of language shift, they often need much more support to make the transition. Confidence, trust, and strong academic support are vital to learning a new language. But it is at this very point when parents withdraw from helping their children because they feel intimidated by the schoolwork in English that their children bring home. The issue is not that the students are learning English, but that parents are shut out of their learning process. The distance created between children and parents revealed the power imbalance that existed between the home and the school culture. In the home-school power struggle, the school usually intends to maintain a position of power, in spite of gestures made toward giving voice to underrepresented populations. This situation called for intervention. The COPLA organization played a catalyst's role in changing the power relations between home and school. This group's approach to change differed from traditional community or educational reforms.

Other efforts had been made before COPLA entered the scene. If schools are perceived to have power and the community is perceived as powerless, then the schools and communities will remain oppositional to one another. For example, schools in Carpinteria had made numerous attempts to close the cultural gap. Because the schools usually spearheaded these efforts, they had the advantage, and the parents became the recipients of whatever was proposed. Thus, the school's power remained intact. Although people's native language and culture were incorporated into the school programs, the Latino voice remained excluded from the decision-making process of school reforms.

School links to the Latino community, including Paul Niles and Javier Torres, understood the needs of the parents and students because they knew the reality of the dismal test scores of English-speaking Latino students. Typically Latinos scored 10 to 20 percentile points below their Euro-American student counterparts, who scored in the fiftieth percentile in the school district. The 1993 student achievement scores, for example, showed Latino students clustered in the fifth percentile, while Euro-American students averaged in the sixty-fourth percentile rank.

Reasons abound as to why Latinos have been excluded from mainstream tracks in public schools.[7] Community efforts have long been a force in changing national policies. In that regard, the statement "All politics are local" has become a cliché for focusing attention on democratic participation. Major developments in school reform programs, such as bilingual/bicultural education, are rooted in attempts to provide more equal education within the framework of the Americanization of Mexicans. The Americanization of Mexican students through school has taken place in the educational system and has been tethered to the necessary reconstruction and citizenship building seen as the goal of public schools. The process has been accomplished primarily through isolation of students in Americanization programs that focus on changing the students' language, religion, dress, recreational activities, family traditions, and home lifestyle.[8] Cultural and political consciousness remain to be explored, as ethnically isolated families negotiate their silent cultural forces. Historically, schools, including Carpinteria's, have established relationships with families and communities that position the schools as the authority, but a different vision was born in a group of Latino parents.

Even before I began research in Carpinteria, community leaders had reached out to the Latino families in an attempt to involve them in the life of the community. When I began working with the Latinos, I observed their efforts to adjust to a new culture while creating a new one of their own. The Carpinteria community organized a different approach to living in a democratic society. Their intent was to integrate their Latino identity as Spanish speakers with a new cultural identity as immigrants with dreams and hopes for their children. When these people began a dialogue about whom they were and where they wanted to go, they discovered that the changes ahead for them would be internal as well as external. They were forced to challenge their thinking about the obstacles that impede their gains of resources and opportunities for growth. Unpredictable possibilities opened up for the group when the parents made it clear that they were willing to put aside their fears for the sake of their children. The following interaction took place during one of the first meetings held by Latino parents who later became the organization known as COPLA. Present at the initial meeting were Alicia Rosario, Rebeca Cortina, Manuel Peña, Rosa Martinez, David Segura, Antonia Juarez, and Juan Ramirez.

Rebeca commented, "We have many problems to confront among ourselves. That is, we cannot argue with the schools because we have neither the means nor the language with which to do it."

Antonia added, "I would say that the important thing is to want to do it and it is for that reason that collectively we can learn what we need to know to help our children."

"Well, we already know how to raise our children. Nobody needs to teach us how to love our children," argued Alicia.

"It seems to me that some Latino families here do need to learn how to take care of their children because I see their young children loose on the streets and their parents are nowhere to be seen," said David.

Alicia agreed, "That's true that some parents don't have money to pay a capable person to take care of their children. Sometimes they [the parents] leave their children with irresponsible people."

Manuel offered, "What I understand from what you are saying is that we have the ability to be responsible but there are some parents who need more help."

"Many times schools have a reason to say what they do about us Mexicans because one needs to appear confident and courageous even though we don't know how to navigate the system," observed David.

Juan shared his fears, "Well, I wasn't going to say anything, but the truth is that since we began talking about having to go the schools to talk to principals, I've lost a lot of sleep. I don't know how it is possible to do something like this, which I've never done before, except when they call me with complaints about my oldest son."

Rebeca reassured him, "You've already told us that you're afraid to go alone to the schools, and we've assured you that no one will have to go alone because we're going in a group."

"I know," Juan said, "but even though I care about my children, it is difficult to do something like this in another language when one cannot speak it."

"It seems to me that, even though we don't speak English and don't know the cultural ways of this country and of Carpinteria, we also have a beautiful language, and we are respectful and have a culture that is equally valuable. That is why we should present ourselves in that spirit," said Rosa.

Juan agreed, "Well you're right. It's true that we do have a language with which we can communicate, even though it's different than English."

"I appreciate what Mrs. Martinez says because at times we feel inferior since we don't speak English well, but we're not inferior and we need to be proud of what we can give our children. All of Mexico's history is part of us—even if we live here," added Alicia.

Juan agreed, "Yes, Mrs. Alicia, but why are we made to feel inferior by teachers and principals who say that our children aren't important to us because we don't attend meetings or because we arrive late to meetings and numerous other criticisms they make?"

David questioned their behavior. "Well it's true because many of us act as if we're afraid of life. Why is it that we don't go to the schools if our children matter to us? We need to change those habits that impede our presence in our children's schools. Like Mrs. Marquez always told us when our children were in preschool, these are our schools so we should act responsibly."

"How do we change those habits?" Juan asked. "How can we learn to speak English which is so difficult?"

Alicia suggested, "It isn't easy to change our habits. It is necessary to talk and discuss how we think. That is why we are here to help each other—it's not easy but there is strength in unity. We should note, for example, that even though we need to learn English, that we must also make the schools communicate with us in Spanish. My children have been in these schools many years, and even though they're in bilingual classes, I never see any notices sent home in Spanish."

Critical reflection in conversations among these community members raised their awareness of their strengths, which collectively began an empowerment process in the community, their families, and in their personal life.

## Shifting Power

How power manifests itself in our daily life often eludes us, but without question, power is the fluid energy that supports our actions. Power resides within each of us, individually and collectively, meaning that power is always at play no matter the activities in which we participate. No, we don't consciously wake up each day and decide how we're going to exercise our power, but make no mistake, the results of our actions or inactions can be explained in terms of internal and external power. Admittedly, my research initially did not account for the analysis that later dominated my theoretical framework. My extensive academic reading included works by Paulo Freire, Michael Apple, Henry Trueba, and others from Cornell University, whose research and writing were oriented toward changing power relations. However, I didn't initially see the underpinnings of power in Carpinteria until I got a picture of these people's history and culture and how change occurred through language, social interaction, and in particular, day-to-day literacy activities.

Change occurs in a medley of ways. Commonly, the times and locations of connections among families and schools are associated with structured events, where the school defines the interactions of the actors. In those settings, educators assume a position of knowledge over the parents or community members. Transactions result in parents having to adhere to the school culture to support their children in school-related tasks. Cultural borders created by structural conditions are rigid boundaries enforced by school policies and practices. In this mode, the pedagogy of change is learned through school-defined structure. Latino families as well as other ethnic and poor families who have been underrepresented in schools, continuously cross borders between their cultural knowledge and that of the school's to a limited end. In contrast, organizations like COPLA create a forum for ongoing conversations where new ideas and relationships are born.

On one of the many home interviews I had with the Garcias, I got to see the respect and kindness shared by the children and their parents. Lupe Garcia greeted me at the door, holding a baby less than a year old. She and her tall, dark-haired husband, Leo, who waited in the living room, motioned for me to sit on the couch. I sat down, preparing to begin my formal interview with the parents, when I noticed them signaling to their three young children, who peeked curiously out the bedroom door. The children stood in front of me and took turns shaking my hand as their father introduced them. The oldest daughter, about fourteen years old, excused herself and walked to the kitchen, then came out carrying a tray holding one cup filled with coffee and sugar and milk. She sat it on the living room center table saying, "For you, *maestra* Delgado." I smiled warmly and thanked her. The father dismissed the three children and told them to take the baby with them to their room, and we began the interview. I listened with admiration as both parents shared stories of their children's triumphs in improving their school studies and about their concern for the youngest one, whose persistent behavior problems in school continued in spite of the help he received at home from his parents and siblings. His mother routinely visited the school to meet with her son's teacher, but no remedy for the situation had yet been found. Hours later we finished our interview, but I felt so comfortable that I didn't want to leave.

Three weeks after my interview with the Garcias at their home, I saw Lupe Garcia at a community meeting of Latino parents. The parents had organized to discuss what kind of teaching was being done in the schools where their children attended and how they could best support their children's education. They invited me to attend the meeting because they wanted me to see how parents worked with each other. At the parent meeting, one parent, Sara Vega, acknowledged my presence by explaining to the group of parents that I was a professor at UCSB. She added that I was working with their community to learn about family and community literacy; furthermore, she hoped that I would consider joining them in their effort to learn about the schooling system and to organize themselves for their children's education. Sara Vega looked in my direction and shared her conviction that education, whether for young or old, begins in the heart. Then she quoted Cervantes, "La experiencia es la madre de la ciencia" (Experience is the mother of science). I couldn't have agreed more. I knew then that our common work on literacy in the community would stretch beyond my initial perceived limits.

Of particular interest in the parent meetings was how they interacted with each other, the language they used to discuss issues of children, literacy, learning, and culture. What became apparent was that parents exhibited the same values of respect and trust for each other that I had noticed in the many family interviews I had conducted. The qualities displayed by the people in their interactions demonstrated strength born of what could only be love. In their presence, I was heartened that I had the opportunity to collaborate with people who conducted themselves in a respectful way with one another and whose commitment to growth was tenacious. They tapped into their own power, and together they began shifting their collective power as Spanish-speaking Latinos in their community.

# CHAPTER THREE

⚬

# Forming a Collective Voice

On Friday evenings Latino families could be seen arriving at Weaver School for parent meetings. Parents walked their children to the kindergarten classroom for child care and then went to the school library for their meeting. When relating to each other about educational matters, Latino adults placed the children center stage. The child as their primary focus defined COPLA's efforts from the start of the organization. A dialogue ensued between parents and between Latino families and schools. Since its inception, COPLA has undergone numerous phases of development, resulting from organizational expansion in size, direction, and influence. Three major phases identify COPLA's development: Phase 1, defining COPLA; Phase 2, expanding COPLA; and Phase 3, re-creating COPLA. Throughout their work, COPLA members, parents, and educators developed an ethic of respect in the way that they addressed each other, listened to each other's voices, and spoke of children's needs. Usually the people who attended meetings represented themselves until the organization officially decided to have the schools elect representatives. COPLA moved forward and called itself an organization, its only criteria for membership being that people be involved with some level of schooling in Carpinteria. Although ethnicity or language were not requirements for participating in COPLA, the meetings were conducted in Spanish because the majority of the people who attended them spoke only Spanish. If English-speaking school personnel or Euro-American parents attended, they sat next to someone who could translate for them.

As an organized group, COPLA expected to create a visible presence in the schools.

## First Phase: Defining COPLA

Latino parents began an open conversation that distinguished COPLA as an organization. They respected each other and each other's dedication and commitment to their children. In this initial stage of their organizing efforts, their dialogue influenced the way in which parents and schools related. COPLA parents and school district personnel communicated more frequently. School personnel began translating their written communication with Latino parents. Parents reached out to each other through personal and written forms, effectively improving their relationship. Specific changes in schools, principally in Marina and Weaver Elementary Schools, tailored their programs for inclusion. Prior to Latino parent advocacy, Spanish-speaking students were excluded from gifted programs and received little English language development in the classroom.

Spanish-speaking parents began to attend more meetings in the schools and became increasingly active in issues that directly affected their children. Some parents began to attend large meetings, while others developed more trust with their children's teachers, resulting in more personal contact. Their level of participation varied because the experience they brought to the group differed. For example, Vicky Flores describes how she grew through her participation in COPLA, "I didn't feel that I needed to know who my children's teachers were because I trusted that they knew what they were doing. I didn't know what my children needed because I didn't have much schooling in Mexico, so why should I question what they were doing in the classroom? I'm not the one that was educated to be a teacher." Her position about the school altered after attending a few COPLA meetings. She tells how her understanding of education changed. "At first I didn't see why other parents felt that it was necessary to learn about schools, but I kept attending meetings because my neighbor insisted that I go with her. Finally, in one meeting I asked them why as Latinos we should have to know all of the information that was being presented to us. Suddenly they all began explaining how Latino children were left behind in school and they received less attention if we as parents didn't get involved. My neighbor told me that her son was having problems reading and when she went to talk to the school the teacher gave her materials to help her son. I know I should go talk to the teacher because my youngest daughter, Angie, tells me that she is having lots of problems." Vicky Flores took one step at a time toward supporting her daughter's schooling. "When I got my confidence up, I went to talk to the teacher, and I was very scared, but she knew that I wanted to help and she made me feel very comfortable while she showed me what to do to help Angie."

Increased communication between parents and teachers also raised teachers' understanding about Latino children's potential. This became the heart of COPLA's success.

Many parents attended the district COPLA meetings as well as the local school meetings. During the first two years of their mobilization, fifteen parents regularly attended the district-wide meetings; the leaders included Maria Rosario, Rosa Martinez, Antonia Suarez, Ofelia Torres, Rebeca Cortina, Ramon Méndez, Roberto Rodriguez, Manuel Peña, Juan Ramirez, Beto Ruiz, Lalo Robles, and Mario Soliz. Other active leaders were school personnel, including, Paul Niles, Ramiro Marquez, Principal, Weaver School; Kay Patton, Principal, Morton School; Sally West, Principal, Marina School; Kevin Lane, Principal, South High School; and John Sosa, Migrant Coordinator.

In meetings, people usually addressed each other by their first name. Initially, however, parents addressed school personnel by Señor (Mr.) or Señora (Mrs.), and the reverse was the practice until a few months later. Then, both parents and school personnel addressed each other by their first names. A few parents, however, still addressed the other parents by their formal titles.

**COPLA Meeting**
Weaver School was the usual meeting place for the district-wide COPLA meetings. The group met for about ninety minutes each time. At the district COPLA meeting, on December 12, 1989, eight people were present, including two administrators. During the meeting parents dealt with the issue of not being informed enough about their children's reading program to understand how to assist their children at home. Señor Méndez read the agenda for the meeting and noted that the first order of business was to discuss the question of teaching parents how to deal with children's reading when they did not understand classroom curriculum. Señor Marquez, the principal, commented that Marina School should be doing more of that kind of training for the families because there are no problems with the reading program at Weaver. He added, "The problem we have here at Weaver is one of English. Our students in the fourth through sixth grades need more help with math and English."

Manuel suggested, "If we could read the books the children are reading at school, we could help them."

Maria noted, "But all parents don't have the skills and abilities to read the difficult books, or to comprehend them. What can they do if they don't know how to manipulate the meaning of the story and the words? Actually, maybe that's what we as COPLA leaders can do, help the parents to understand how to help their children with those tasks."

"Here at Weaver, we're trying to get the teachers to work with the parents of their own English and Spanish-speaking students," explained Mr. Marquez. People listened attentively and after Mr. Marquez spoke, two others raised their hands, and Ramon acknowledged both by saying, "We'll hear from Mrs. Cortina, then from Manuel Peña."

Rebeca Cortina proposed, "Maybe we should meet with the Marina School principal and the teacher can meet with COPLA parents to present to them the classroom reading curriculum." Rebeca, like some other parents, understood terms like *curriculum* and certain steps to take, like meeting with the principal, because she had been active in the schools.

Final comments were made in a process that the group called "once around." Paul Niles suggested the process to them as a way for everyone to think about what they'd learned in the meeting or to share some feeling or thought they had about the meeting. At the end of every meeting, members spoke about something that impressed them, and some offered a critique. I found this process quite revealing as parents critically assessed what they had learned and how the meeting had progressed. Their comments told me that they had been attentive to the issues and that, although they held strong positions, they were willing to concede and compromise when the group needed to unite on an issue in order to proceed.

During the first phase, COPLA made changes in the school district programs. The Carpinteria School District accepted more bilingual students into the Gifted and Talented Education program (GATE). After lengthy discussions between program leaders, principals, and parents of Spanish-speaking students, they agreed that bilingual students would be accepted into GATE based on teacher recommendation, waiving the English IQ tests required by district policy.

Cultural knowledge of COPLA leaders informed their organizing strategies. Years of working with them inspired me with countless stories of *their visions.* One cool, summer, Friday evening, I met with a group of parents as they decided on a method to mobilize other parents and to elect a leader. Parents arrived directly from their workplaces—nurseries, factories, and housecleaning. When the entire group had gathered at the Weaver School parking lot, we realized that the administrators had forgotten to open the building for our use. This didn't discourage the parents. Although it was a few years ago, I can still feel my foot cramping under me as I sat more than two-and-a-half hours in the parking lot. Parents discussed the qualities they wanted in a leader and various ways to recruit other Latino parents to become active. Their fears and pride about raising children in an unfamiliar culture dominated the conversation.

Still sitting in the parking lot, Carmen Arambula convinced the group to think about how valuable they were to their families. She felt strongly that Latinos should organize because as she put it, "Venemos porque podemos, *NO* a veer si podemos." In essence, she said, "We've come here because we can, not to see if we can." This became the quintessential motto of COPLA parents. In effect, this was their theory, and every person they met was their practice. Rather than electing a president right away, they operated as a district-wide committee and rotated leadership. This group had clear priorities—they listened to each other and respected each person's input. The Latino parents formed an inclusive group that allowed everyone (Latino, non-Latino, Spanish-speaking, and English-speaking) to participate. All were welcome. Their power emerged from the bottom up. A special note here—a few years into their activism COPLA did draft bylaws, but not until they had experimented with a few leadership forms. Even now they do not use Robert's Rules of Order.

A small group of parents expanded to include all Latino families in the Carpinteria schools. They continued to empower themselves, employing cultural tools like their shared language and history. Systematically, the leaders work with principals and teachers in each school to organize parents—one school at a time.

Each time parents organized a meeting, I observed the strategies they employed to mobilize. I wondered how long would their movement sustain? But, these were the wrong questions. They were way ahead of me. There was no failure where they were concerned. Parents continuously reassured each other that even a few parents in attendance were important.

Once the district COPLA group was more formalized, Latino parents began to organize local school-site COPLA groups in each school. The satellite groups were clearly in place, but had more visibility in two elementary schools, Marina and Weaver. Progress was slower in Morton School, as well as in South High School and West High School. Some

Latino parents who were not active in COPLA criticized those who were, accusing them of being "busybodies" with little else to do. This confirmed the need for organizations like COPLA to assist Latino parents to become more knowledgeable about their role as advocates for their children. The irony, of course, is that even the children of critics benefited from the initial efforts of COPLA.

Two high school Latino parents convened a meeting and invited teachers from English-as-a-Second Language (ESL) classes. Their end was to establish a COPLA committee. Kevin Lane, the principal, grilled "carne asada" for more than fifty parents who attended. He also made a green salad and asked a couple of parents to bring Mexican rice and tortillas. This was the largest gathering of Latino parents ever seen at the school. Dinner was served at six o'clock and by seven, Ramon Méndez, president of the District COPLA Committee, began the meeting by introducing himself and admitted being nervous about addressing a large group of people. But he said it was encouraging to see such a large number of Latino parents attend a meeting about issues related to their children's learning.

"We who work with the District COPLA Committee have had to learn how to do many things. Even if many of us have not been schooled, we have supported each other in learning to address Latino parents and to encourage them in getting involved in the schools. Our children need us, and we need to be as informed as possible about the way schools operate here and how to help our children."

He introduced three other members of the District Committee and the two teachers, Becky Hill and Connie Johns, who would make the presentation about the high school's curriculum for Spanish-speaking students, including the school's expectations regarding absences, class grades, tests, and high school completion requirements.

In their presentation, the teachers outlined the various courses offered in the ESL track, designed for students who were limited in their use of English. They made a number of strong points about the parents' need to stay aware of their children's school attendance. But parents also shared their concern about the school's failure to notify them that their children were skipping classes. That night, parents and teachers united on this topic. They both learned that they had to find a way to communicate directly with each other, not because the students were incapable of being honest, but rather they needed assurance that their parents and teachers were united on the goals and standards for them. Adults in that meeting spoke to this issue and began to break down the barriers between them.

They realized that both teachers and parents had to address the students' needs and problems together, supporting students to adhere to school policy and procedure. Parent responsibility for getting students to attend class every day was futile unless teachers also showed caring and personal interest in the students' daily activities. Rosa Martinez epitomized their sentiment. "If we don't know where our children are at 10:00 P.M. at night, then it's our responsibility to make sure that they are home getting ready for bed and for school the next day. If you're a teacher and don't know where the student is when she or he should be in your class, then it's up to you to do everything possible to find out why that student does not attend your class. But because they're both of our responsibility, we must all work together to communicate with the student and let them know that we're both on her or his side."

## Learning Leadership

Early efforts to organize parents challenged those who were not accustomed to speaking to school administrators or to large groups. At a meeting at Marina School library, February 3, 1989, the District COPLA Committee, Paul Niles, the School District Director, Marina's principal, and a first grade teacher, attended, as did thirty parents. The meeting was held to assist Marina's COPLA committee to elect officers. Prior to the meeting, Ramon Méndez, a Marina School parent and president of the District COPLA Committee, met with the principal to set the agenda.

Mr. Méndez addressed the Spanish-speaking parents at Marina. He began the meeting by thanking people who attended, and he apologized for being nervous whenever he spoke to a large group of people. He presented the goals of the organization by talking about parents' role as the children's first and most important teachers.

"We know our children best, and have a great deal to offer them as we work with them. In COPLA we are trying to learn from each other. We're trying to resolve differences between parents and teachers and to cooperate with each other. One of the goals is to name a committee to lead COPLA at each school. That is why we are here at Marina School tonight to assist you in electing a committee to work with the principal to organize activities in Spanish for Latino parents. We're wanting to teach parents about educational programs offered to our children and to obtain cooperation from other community agencies."

Mr. Manuel Peña from the District COPLA Committee suggested to Ramon Méndez that they ask the parents if they understood. When Ramon asked them if they had any questions, a father raised his hand and asked if Marina School had a representative in the District COPLA Committee. Ramon answered that they had some parents who had children in Marina like him, but as of yet they did not have a person who had been elected by the parents in Marina. And parents' vote was necessary and important in COPLA. One parent asked about the kind of activities that Ramon meant. Ramon gave invited guests as an example. "You can invite people to speak about a theme which is of interest to the parents." Kay Patton, who had followed the proceedings of the meeting through translation, said that it could be someone to talk to the parents about reading.

Maria Rosario called Ramon's attention to the time. It was now almost forty-five minutes into the meeting, and they still had to hold an election. Mr. Méndez asked the parents to nominate people for three positions—president, vice president, and secretary. He explained that the person who served as vice president would work closely with the president during the first year, so they could assume the president's position the second year. Parents said that they did not feel comfortable nominating people because they didn't know other parents well enough. Others commented that they didn't feel experienced enough to assume such leadership responsibilities. Maria Rosario assured the parents that COPLA did not require previous leadership experience and that what was important was commitment to work with the aim of helping the children to receive maximum support in their schooling.

Rebeca Cortina reiterated that what people need to know to work on the COPLA committee is revealed to them each step of the way. Rebeca again reminded them not to allow the word *president* to scare them, because what they needed was willingness and interest in learning as much as in helping the children. Manuel Peña suggested that parents write their nominations on a piece of paper, and if those chosen accepted the nominations, their names would be written on the board and everyone would vote. Vicente Rosales told the parents, "All of you who say that we don't know each other, well here's the chance to get to know each other by working together."

By now the meeting had lasted an hour and a half, and the group continued to discuss strategies for electing their COPLA officers. Rosa Martinez proposed another idea for nominating and voting for people, by suggesting that the names be put in a hat and someone could pick out the names. Ruben Simon objected to the suggestion because it would not constitute an election. He felt that people needed to vote for the candidates. Antonio Vasquez, a parent from Marina School, felt that already too much time had been spent on the election process. Three people stood up and prepared to leave the room, claiming to have other meetings. Another woman raised her hand and told the group that she would have to leave soon because her child-care provider had to go home. Other people stretched their backs away from the small wooden library chairs and shifted their positions. People sighed and looked around the room. Ramon agreed that too much time had been spent electing the COPLA committee and that maybe they could just go ahead and vote for the candidates and learn from the process. He proposed that they list the eight names on the board and that people write down the name of one person and that the top three votes would become president, vice president, and secretary, respectively.

Nine names were submitted, and of those, only one person declined the nomination. Those remaining were Antonia Suarez, Manuel Peña, Vicente Rosales, Jose Santos, Martina Romero, Fidel Ramos, Rosa Martinez, and Juan Ramirez. Manuel Peña became president, Fidel Ramos, vice president, and Martina Romero, secretary. Two representatives to COPLA were also elected. Ramon reminded them that they would all attend the monthly District COPLA meetings. And the meeting continued. Ramon told the group that two items remained on the agenda, to discuss communication in Spanish and to respond to parents' questions about their children. On the topic of communication in Spanish, Ramon emphasized the need for the new COPLA committee at Marina to deal with the issue of school communication to Latino parents in Spanish.

Ramon presented the last item on the agenda as a critical mission of COPLA in learning and supporting each other. People were invited to submit a concern regarding their children. A woman raised her hand and explained that her daughter in the first grade didn't pay attention, and she felt that the child was more advanced than she demonstrated and that possibly her inattention was due to the teacher's low expectations. Another woman spoke about her daughter in the third grade also being in a classroom with low expectations. She suggested that what Latino parents should do is to visit the classrooms and check to see what materials are being used with the students and to make sure that a challenging curriculum is taught. "Furthermore," another parent added, "we as parents also need to work closely with our children at home so that they know that we care how well they read."

Kay Patton, the principal of Morton School, expressed her desire for parents to communicate directly with teachers about those questions. She further suggested that possibly as a COPLA activity, the bilingual teachers could meet with the parents and explain the literature program as well as other curriculum. Mrs. Patton had prepared a text written in Spanish with the help of Paul Niles to read to the parents, "I'm very happy to see that you're interested in your children's education. I want to talk with you more. Your questions are very important, and we're here to help you address them."

Parents acknowledged her statement by applauding, and then a parent asked if COPLA could sponsor a drawing contest for kids. The question was not answered, and Maria suggested that the issue be raised at the next meeting. "That's it. We should end the meeting," suggested Maria.

Ramon apologized for the long election process and reminded everyone that they were all still learning and said, "It's all for the kids, so we can stand to be patient." He thanked everyone for attending, and the meeting ended. People lingered and talked with each other about how tired they were and how late it was while they hoped that future meetings would be shorter. Others continued the meeting by making comments about their children and the need to talk with the teachers about the books that they read.

Before COPLA began, Latino parents had been active in their children's education in a variety of ways, through migrant education committees, preschool advisory committees, and parent-teacher conferences. In the first phase of COPLA, parents garnered the existing knowledge and provided a context for parents to expand and develop their skills as advocates to enhance their children's education.

## Second Phase: Expanding COPLA

It took a great deal of rereading of my field notes before I realized that COPLA had crossed from a first to a second phase. This was partly because I had expected a finite conclusion to my study. I hadn't planned on staying in Carpinteria for years, studying family and community literacy. Latino parents in Carpinteria expanded their sphere of influence in this second phase out into the broader community. The nature of the dialogue with the schools marked COPLA's success as an advocate organization in this second phase of mobilization. Parents' interactions with each other and with the school personnel identified COPLA as a supportive community leadership group that delivered results. Often, parent organizations are mired in the politics of the school, making it impossible for them to assume a proactive role. COPLA realized the importance of reaching out to other community services that could assist in their development.

Some Latino parents had personal experience with various agencies in Carpinteria, Santa Barbara, and other neighboring communities. When they got involved with COPLA, they contacted these agencies and invited them to speak to the organization about services available to the Latino families. Building communication between the Latino community and the schools was COPLA's purpose. Calling on members of other organizations to meet with them, school level COPLA groups held informational meetings and brought out more Latino parents to become acquainted with their children's schools. Of course children were important, but parents were also in need of social services that could help them and their children.

The district COPLA agenda for the November 2, 1991, meeting revealed how reaching out to inform the Latino parent community was a successful mobilization effort. The COPLA satellite school committees reported on how they reached out to connect with community organizations. Mario Fernández, president, opened the meeting at the high school. He reported that two weeks prior the high school COPLA had a successful meeting where sixty parents attended in addition to fifteen Latino students from ESL classes. Teenage alcoholism was the topic, and the Klein Bottle organization came to discuss the subject with the parents, who had requested their service.

The parent representatives from Weaver School reported that twenty-five people attended the last meeting, where they worked with staff from a popular community newspaper from the Santa Barbara area that wanted COPLA schools to contribute interviews and articles about their efforts to organize Spanish-speaking Latinos. COPLA parents also agreed to devote three meetings to the topic of children's self-esteem, led by a bilingual psychologist and a bilingual teacher. The Family Math Project was also adopted as a project for Weaver families. Members from the UCSB Math Department research project on family math would assist the parents in the workshop on helping their children with math. Weaver School COPLA parents had connected with the university and local community agencies to expand their knowledge about ways to help their children succeed in school.

Marina School representative, Manuel Peña, reported that more than one hundred Latino parents attended the school COPLA meeting the previous month. At the meeting questions were directed to the principal about school programs and objectives for learning. The student discipline policy raised the most concern. Parents wanted to ensure that school personnel enforced fairness and firmness.

Manuel also reported on the questions raised by parents at the end of the meeting. Individual problem solving began with a father who wanted to know where he could find children's literature books written in Spanish. Neither the public library nor the stores had books written in Spanish, and because he was unable to get interesting Spanish books for his children, he couldn't meet the school's request to read regularly with his children. The school, which did not allow books to be taken home, perpetuated the problem. Other parents shared his concern. They told him that the problem was quite real. He was directed to a small bookstore in Oxnard that sold children's books written in Spanish. Parents discussed the possibility of getting a catalogue or a list of the books available at the store and organizing carpools to make trips to buy books. The parent who raised the problem circulated a paper to collect names and numbers of interested parents.

At the end of that Marina School meeting, a mother asked for assistance in ways to deal with her kindergartner, who was afraid to go to school. She was guided by the COPLA leadership to first speak with the child's teacher to find out what the teacher might know about the source of the girl's fear. If the problem was not resolved, then she was to speak with the principal. Ramon Méndez, also a representative from Marina School, said later that he had tried to follow up to see if the woman had attempted to reach the teacher. Apparently, the woman, accompanied by a friend, did go to the school and met with her daughter's teacher about her learning problems. Both the teacher and the parents felt that it was an important first meeting. Ramon reiterated that parents at the COPLA meeting guided and supported each other so that, in conjunction with the schools, they could solve problems involving their children. By sharing personal experience they helped others to overcome obstacles. But more importantly, the purpose was to teach parents how the schools operated. The goal was to have parents become knowledgeable about how to resolve their family and educational problems.

The Morton School representative, Roberto Rodriguez, extended the discussion of specific individual problems raised by Morton School parents. Latino parents seemed to have concerns with some teachers who were not bilingual and were consistently insensitive to working with Latino children and their parents. Parents of a fourth grade boy complained about their son's failing to return homework. They were aware that the child did his homework because they helped him with it, but the teacher never received it. The parents wanted to have a meeting with the teacher but were intimidated because in past meetings, the teacher had become quite angry about their son's presumed laziness. Roberto and Antonia, of the school's COPLA committee, suggested ways to approach the teacher. They reminded the parents that in a case where they did not feel satisfied with the results of their meeting with the teachers, they should contact the principal. Someone from the COPLA committee usually contacted the parents who raised concerns at school meetings as a means of following up.

At that November 2, 1991, meeting, four of the five schools reported on their respective school's COPLA meetings. Conspicuously absent was the middle school report. The parents in charge of organizing that school had difficulty convening regular meetings because the administrator was disinterested. It would take more than three years before Latino parents would have a collective voice in the middle school.

Following the school reports, the main topic on the district COPLA meeting's agenda was the presentation by a UCSB representative. He wanted to talk with the COPLA group about meeting with Latino parents in the high school to inform Latino students about the opportunities to attend UCSB. He introduced himself, "I'm Mario Ramirez. Tonight I want to speak to you about the program which we have to qualify Latino students for the university."

Ramon welcomed the guest. "Thank you for your visit. Yes, we're very interested in your presentation, because our Latino families are meeting to become knowledgeable about programs that benefit our children."

Maria said, "I think that our children need every opportunity to take classes that will prepare them for the university. And I know that many of our children don't know how to get into those classes, and our program accepts only Latino students who have taken the required courses to enter the university. Some of them qualify but because they speak only Spanish, they can't take classes like chemistry and physics. I go to argue with the high school principals, who should have classes for bilingual children, but obviously they don't think it's important."

"Our program accepts only Latino students who have taken the required courses to enter the university," explained Mr. Ramirez.

Rebeca said, "I would say that it's important to talk with Latino students in the high school because some of them are bilingual and they've learned English to a point that they can enter more advanced classes."

Juan agreed. "I feel that any information about college that our Latino students can receive would be important."

Another member, Manuel, said, "It seems as though Mr. Ramirez needs our permission to present to the Latino parents in the high school.

It's true that our students can benefit from this program, but I also agree with those who have noted that this is an urgent issue for us to consider. We need to learn how we can best prepare our students to enter classes that the universities require, not only the University of California, Santa Barbara."

The guest responded, "I know that other Latino communities also think the same and they worry about the high school students."

"I'm on top of the classes that my son takes, which are all in English, and sometimes he doesn't feel prepared for certain mathematics and history. When that has occurred, he has taken classes in the summer to advance himself and to feel more in control of his subject. Wouldn't it be possible to have such a plan for Spanish-speaking students?" asked Ofelia.

"I very much like the idea of proposing this to the school district." Rosa said. "Our children also have to support one another just like we're doing. The students can help each other in summer programs to have an advantage in their fall courses. That makes sense to me."

Manuel said, "That's true and maybe we can discuss this issue with more time in another meeting. But today I understand that Mr. Ramirez from the university can't resolve this problem. He can only help to advance Latino students who, as we say, are already high achievers."

"I could speak on behalf of the school district," said Paul Niles. "And everything that's been said tonight regarding the appropriate bilingual classes is important. One of the problems that we have found is that we don't have the numbers of students that we need to offer history, physics, and other subjects taught in Spanish."

"We understand the problem which the district has but meanwhile our children who can benefit from such bilingual classes don't have the opportunity," added Maria.

"Well, I don't have children in high school so I don't know much about what you've discussed here," said Ramon. "But I do know that the important thing for us to consider here is what's important for our children. Therefore, it stands to reason that the district has to provide us ways to advance our children in the high school. Also what I see is that it is necessary for Mr. and Mrs. Fernández, who are the COPLA representatives in the high school, to deal with this question as something urgent, and they should invite the Migrant Education students and director, Mr. Sosa, to more openly discuss our students' needs. Right now, it seems that as president I have to beg your permission and see if we can come to some agreement about the purpose of Mr. Ramirez's visit, which is to work with the high school COPLA committee."

Celia Marquez proposed that they invite Mr. Ramirez to the next COPLA meeting at the high school. "I think they should also deal with the issue of bilingual classes for advanced subjects. Mr. Fernández and myself also have children in the elementary grades, not just the high school. I think that all parents should benefit from this information on scholarship for the university. They can learn how to advise their children from the beginning in elementary grades."

Ramon agreed. "Yes, it would be good that we open the discussion with Mr. Ramirez to all interested parents."

Ramon closed the meeting, which began at 6:30 and ended at 9:00 P.M. In their once-around process, parents took turns commenting about their impressions of the meeting. Most parents commented that they felt frustrated by the reality that, although some opportunities for scholarships were available, issues of language, bilingual classes, and underachievement of Latino students had yet to be resolved in the Carpinteria high school. Although COPLA was cooperating with a community that also supported Latino students, parents were finding that resolving some problems only served to create others. In other words, there was no end to the problems that confronted them. But my observations showed that problems didn't deter them; they tackled each challenge with firm determination to stretch and grow beyond their organizational parameters. Parents didn't limit the agenda topics; they discussed whatever issues had to be addressed that would expand their advocacy for their children.

COPLA increased its visibility through linkages with other community organizations and strengthened its connections with the respective schools. The talent and skills of its members were spotlighted. When their children were in the Spanish preschool, some parents had learned to stand in front of groups and teach classes on material with which they were familiar. Now in their role as COPLA leaders, they stepped up to the challenge and commitment to support others. These parent leaders reached out to the community through the workshops. Rebeca and Ofelia scheduled a workshop entitled "Communication among Parents." But it didn't happen without preparation on their part, as Ofelia explains. "Rebeca and I met three times on Saturday to plan our workshop. I was so nervous that I had to write out everything that I was to say. She was more confident, because she liked talking to people in public. I'm so shy that I felt like dropping out of the workshop, but Rebeca kept telling me that I could do it and that worked until we did the workshop."

The conference was held in the Weaver School. The gray, cloudy, cold day in November did little to discourage conference participants from attending. More than one hundred parents from the five schools registered for the conference, which was to begin at 8:00 A.M.

Ofelia and Rebeca led a workshop on communication. Maria and Ramon led a workshop called "Helping Children with Homework." Other workshops by Celia, the preschool teacher, and representatives from community agencies included, "Alcoholism," "Discipline in the Family," and "Sexuality." Information about the conference and preregistration forms went out to the parents from the Migrant Program. Parents selected two workshops from the five and attended one in the morning and the second one after lunch. With the assistance of two students, I videotaped the two workshops led by COPLA parents. We set up the camcorder on a tripod in the back of the room, and periodically, I removed it from the pedestal and walked around to capture the participants' expressions.

**Parent Communication Presentation**

Ofelia and Rebeca's topic demanded an interactive format where the presenters could engage the parents in discussing their needs and ways to form social networks that could be resourceful in their children's education. They had about twenty people in both of their workshops. Rebeca and Ofelia confessed feeling nervous, as parents began to enter the room for the workshop. But they managed to walk to the door and greet the people, inviting them to take a seat while they took their positions at the front of the room. After introducing themselves, they explained that their work in the COPLA organization led them to take an interest in teaching other Latino parents how to support their children's education. They presented the topic and format for their workshop.

Collectively, the parents formulated a list of obstacles, which they felt prevented them from advocating for their children.

We don't speak English.
We don't have transportation.
We're afraid to go to schools by ourselves.
We don't know how to help our children with homework.
We don't have child-care services.

Ofelia then elicited comments from the parents, and Rebeca listed the rights that they knew parents had in the schools.

The right to question.
The right to comment.

The right to participate in making decisions in the school regarding their children's education.

The right to know.

The right to communicate with our children in our own language—Spanish.

They seemed to understand the importance of parental presence in the school in spite of having detailed their obstacles. After discussing each of the rights, on a large, clean sheet of clipboard paper, they began listing responsibilities that they felt parents had in their children's education.

Responsibility to advocate for our children.

Responsibility to help our children with homework.

Responsibility to speak with the teachers.

Responsibility to seek assistance for our children when we're unable to assist them.

Responsibility to learn English to enable us to communicate with our children, since they're learning more and more English and forgetting Spanish.

Ofelia and Rebeca connected with the parents, convincing them that it was possible to overcome their perceived limitations by joining with other parents for mutual support. Parents recognized that COPLA provided them with the opportunity to join with others who had similar historical and cultural experience to examine their current community environment and possibilities for change and development.

**Schoolwork Presentation**

Maria and Ramon presented on the topic of homework, and twenty-one parents attended the session. Eight of the people were couples, and in addition, four men and nine women made up the group. The objective was to raise concerns about their children's homework that parents shared. Maria and Ramon introduced themselves as interested parents involved in COPLA. Maria identified the areas to be covered in the workshop: "problems doing homework" and "strategies to resolve homework problems." Parents raised many problems that haunted them in trying to help their children to do homework—adults' lack of formal schooling; excessive amount of homework without sufficient instructions; children reluctant to do homework; teachers who refused to help parents do homework; and teachers penalizing too harshly for errors made on homework tasks. Ramon wrote the list on the flip chart, as Maria elicited comments from the parents, and they embellished each other's statements. Participants sat in the small classroom desks leaning toward each other corroborating each other's comments with stories that conveyed frustration.

A woman who had brought her ten-year-old daughter with her said, "My daughter is receiving so much homework that she's unable to play with her friends. And then she feels discouraged when the teacher just collects the homework without giving her any feedback. So, she doesn't know whether or not she's doing the pages correctly."

Another parent expressed a similar problem. "Teachers often assigned too much work that really has such little meaning even if the instructions were clear." She looked around and noticed others nodding in agreement, and she continued. "I know that teachers want students to practice their subjects, but it's not possible when they don't have sufficient explanation about what they have to do. Homework turns out being work only to frustrate children and us, the parents."

While concerns and problems were quickly forthcoming, Ramon and Maria also encouraged the parents to talk with each other in pairs to explore possibilities for action. Workshop participants advanced ideas for dealing with homework that had interaction between parents and teachers at the center. Parents wanted teachers to provide more instruction on how to do homework tasks. In addition to how parents could communicate with teachers, Maria and Ramon also helped the parents to think about ways to advocate for their children by uniting with each other. They succeeded in getting their important message to the parents, which was: parents were responsible for seeking resources other than their formal educational background to assist their children with homework. Although they felt frustrated about their children's homework situation, parents realized that it was possible to think differently about their ability to help their children. One parent said, "I don't think that we should blame ourselves for not knowing English. I would say that we should find someone who could help them and oftentimes it could be the teacher, but it requires me to communicate with her." Ramon and Maria underscored her comment, emphasizing the importance of meeting with other Latino parents in COPLA who had similar experiences with their families and their children's teachers. The meetings helped Latino parents realize that they weren't isolated. Discovering the need to work effectively with others for their children's education led many parents to actively work in COPLA.

At the end of that Saturday afternoon, my research assistants and I packed up our camcorders and spoke to the parents about their day. Driving home to Santa Barbara, I welcomed the opportunity to discuss the day's event with my students. The workshop sessions had a very pragmatic mission, to raise parent consciousness on communicating with others and with their children, thus breaking isolation. COPLA leaders intended the participants to realize their potential as individuals and as a community. Their message was clear: there are different ways to deal with problems, as an isolated family or as a united group.

During the second phase of development, the COPLA satellite groups became stronger in each of the schools. Their particular forms of operating depended on the principal's ability to work with the Latino community and the specific educational needs of the children in the respective grade levels. Joining forces with other community groups expanded COPLA's advocacy for Latino families and education of Latino students. Among these organizations was the Latino for Better Government (LFBG) group, which is made up of professional Chicanos in Carpinteria who also have as their focus increased success of minority students and the hiring of Latino personnel in the school district, especially teachers and administrators. During this phase of its development, COPLA joined efforts with other organizations and became a recognized voice in the schools. Their perspective was solicited when hiring school personnel. This was a new development—recognizing the importance of the Latino community voice in hiring school personnel. Latinos in both organizations, LFBG and COPLA, were involved in the selection of the new superintendent, Dr. Pablo Seda, who was hired during the summer of 1991. Although their perspectives were not in conflict, they differed, since as individuals, they lived in Carpinteria during different historical periods. Serving on the selection committee became an opportunity for these two groups to talk about their common interests.

Shortly after Dr. Seda was hired, LFBG and COPLA united on a common issue. A united Latino voice became important in the community council. A problem involving Latino families was brought before the City Council in the spring of 1992, which ignited the English- and Spanish-speaking Latino community. The council voted to enforce a city ordinance that had been on the books but had not previously been strictly enforced, which called for the imposition of a fine on households that had unused cars, or even parked cars, in the front of the house. According to Carpinteria Latinos, part of the ordinance included penalties for households with a large number of residents. They felt that the Latinos were being targeted, because they were the largest poor population, forced by economics to house extended families in small apartments and houses. More accurately the issue was affordable housing.[1]

When the problem began to unfold, I was only able to get the details by phone interviews and newspaper articles, since I had moved back to the Bay Area to teach at another university. Not until the summer was I able to travel down to Carpinteria to talk face-to-face with those involved. A leader in the District COPLA group described the situation. "Unfortunately, it's true that many Latinos—above all, young people—stay out late outside in their front yards or whatever. And some Latinos are fun loving and smoke at their outdoor parties on Saturdays and Sundays when they have barbecue. So Anglos don't like to see this and they don't like so much noise and they want to raise the rents. Then, other people with more money want to buy the places that are higher priced. Some councilpersons who are in favor of enforcing the ordinance argued that a great deal of child abuse was found in households where large numbers of people lived. It's true there is child abuse in some families, but that issue should be handled legally and separately because there are many more people who are just poor and need a place for their family to live."

Representatives from Latinos for Better Government and COPLA met to decide on ways to respond to the Community Council regarding the issue. At the council meeting, a member from LFBG presented arguments against the ordinance, and hundreds of Latinos attended as a result of COPLA's organizing efforts. While the City Council failed to resolve the issue with any concrete decision, it appears that the Latino community formed stronger linkages on behalf of justice. COPLA also seized the opportunity to ask the school district for more training in the area of child development. Dr. Seda, the superintendent, proposed and funded a series of workshops for the Spanish-speaking Latino families. The plan was for Dr. Guillermo Santana to train COPLA leaders, who would in turn train other parents on topics of child development.

Phase two in COPLA's evolution expanded its networking strategies to better educate and support Latino children. Parents formed stronger connections with each other as their problems were addressed in local COPLA meetings. As they learned to share their experience with each other for their children's gain, they collectively developed informal and formal leadership skills to the point where they were able to head school-site committees, encouraging more involvement in children's education.

## Third Phase: Re-creating COPLA

Reaching across institutional boundaries was COPLA's mission. Negotiations between COPLA, the schools, and the district administration brought about improvements in the educational programs, including the hiring of Spanish-speaking personnel. The middle school finally hired a Spanish-speaking secretary for the front office. Two Latino principals and a Latino superintendent were hired during this phase, but as Latino influence grew, outreach to new Latino families in the community declined. Reevaluating their priorities became necessary for COPLA in order to continue being a viable group.

By hiring Dr. Pablo Seda as the superintendent, the district's central administration made new commitments to work with the Latino community, as well as with other parent groups. As part of this new commitment to parent involvement, the district administration hired Dr. Santana to train COPLA leaders on child development and finding the strengths in individual families. The leaders who trained with Dr. Santana organized other parents to extend their training. The second tier of trainees then selected a third group to train.

In spite of the programs and policy changes that included more Latino staff in the schools and increased participation of Latino parents in their children's schooling, new dilemmas surfaced in COPLA. The district COPLA leadership faced the problem of decreased parent attendance at the local COPLA school meetings. COPLA parents shared different reasons for this. They critiqued the organizational directions, activities, and their leadership as well as the school's expectations. After examining their organizational commitment, they offered two pointed explanations for the apparent decline in attendance at meetings. One was that the focus of the organization had changed from awareness to actual practice, and many parents had become more active in their children's schooling. They had become directly involved at the level of parent-teacher communication. Another interpretation was that the COPLA leadership had neglected to educate new families in the community. COPLA was spending much of its attention linking with other community organizations. Meanwhile, they were not paying as much attention to activities like the "problem-solving" part of the meetings. Low attendance also went unchallenged, and personal outreach to families was replaced by written reminders of the meetings.

Leaders spoke to the urgency of the issue of restating their objectives for working together in an organization for parents focused on improving their children's educational opportunities by enriching their own. In the autumn meeting, parents raised critical questions that would direct their future work as an organization: How can COPLA continue existing as an organization? What are the most important objectives? What are the obstacles that preclude COPLA from achieving its goals? How do we propose to deal with them? What are the most important things we've accomplished during the past five years? Although they raised these major questions for themselves, they did acknowledge that they genuinely wanted to continue growing and learning how to help their children with their schooling.

COPLA continued reaching out to parents in the local schools. While the local school committees met and remained quite active, they drew fewer people to the meetings. Strengthening COPLA participation meant revisiting the group's initial vision to teach each other and to connect with other families in the school district. Although COPLA temporarily neglected to reach out to the isolated Spanish-speaking families in this phase, they never abandoned their primary focus, which was the child. In spite of the low attendance at meetings, teachers and parents reported more connection around children's daily concerns in the classroom. Principals also became more engaged with their respective school's COPLA group. This community building was aggressively supported by Superintendent Seda's objective to bridge the school, family, and community. In his evaluation of the school principals, he held them responsible for instituting strong family and school relationships. Together, school personnel and parents had a greater task ahead of them—to reach out to Latino families who felt isolated and convince them that they, too, could be leaders. In their efforts to get more new families active in COPLA, Latino parents quickly learned that a bigger problem hindered parent participation. Around this time, all educational communities were beginning to face hard crackdowns by California politicians who wanted to deport all undocumented Mexican workers. These threats created much fear, holding many Mexican families hostage in their homes and minimizing their contact with institutions unless absolutely necessary. "How can we ask them to risk getting sent back to Mexico?" asked Rodolfo Alvarez, who had talked to some families in his neighborhood, encouraging them to get involved in their children's schooling. Although many of them wanted to get involved in their children's schools, their wish to stay in the United States and keep their children in U.S. schools was greater.

In the third phase, COPLA leadership facilitated the bringing of community resources to a larger number of students while gaining political voice across the district. Some of the leaders began organizing after school groups for youth. Rebeca Cortina organized a folkloric dance group with the assistance of a dance instructor from Santa Barbara who offered classes to the children. To keep the dancers performing, Rebeca held fund-raisers, including community dances on Saturday nights, to pay for the children's costumes, lessons, and transportation to activities. She also solicited Carpinteria businesses to sponsor the children's performances. Parents whose children danced in the folkloric group also often attended COPLA meetings.

The parents who helped organize the folkloric group reminded their children, "We don't want anything for ourselves, it's all for you. We can only teach you what we know."

Rebeca added, "The dance group has worked out very well. The same girls who are now the dancers are the same ones who used to wander the streets. Now they don't have to hang out in the streets. There are some girls who I used to encounter on the street and I would ask them what they were doing out so late and they would tell me that they were out walking. But it wasn't a time when girls should be out walking. Now they go to the dance and from there they go home. They don't need to be on the street. Their parents also know where they are dancing. One of the mothers who never cared where her daughter was came to visit the dance class last Thursday to watch her dance, and she said that she was very pleased that her daughter liked dancing."

Girls in Rebeca's dance group paid five dollars a month to dance. Local Mexican stores sponsored four to five months of dance classes for children who could not afford the classes. While some young boys held their hands behind their backs and danced around young girls in the folkloric group who swirled their long skirts, other boys found soccer more to their liking. Ramon organized a soccer league for young children of three age groups—8–11, 12–14, and 15–18—but he got his brother-in-law and other people to coach, because he was still quite involved in the COPLA leadership and had also assumed parent directorship of the Migrant Education Program.

## Challenging the School Culture

Their love for children connected Latino parents in forging a united, supportive group. Collective knowledge, language, culture, and shared history sustained the parents' and educators' focus on children as the impelling force of their work. Even as the organization proliferated, the parents remained sincere about their primary goal of working together on projects for their children. And that commitment returned them to their original goal, to reach out to isolated families and support them in learning about the school and obtaining resources for their children's education.

By constructing new discourse norms in a common space in this specific historical point in time between the schools and families, Latino parents created a voice for themselves. Latino parents organized and joined with others to share their life experiences, the need to cooperate with the schools, and improve programs and policies situated in the culture, language, and politics of the community. This awareness led to continued dialogue between the schools and the families.

Six key features of COPLA framed its identity: the participants had mutual respect for each other; continuous critical reflection engaged the leadership, allowing for systematic growth; parents and school personnel held the child central to its activities; an egalitarian mode of interaction allowed for shared power between parents and the school personnel; parents addressed multifaceted social needs that impacted the family, classroom, and community at large; and, continuous dialogue extended beyond the crisis issues, making the organization flexible, but with defined boundaries.[2]

COPLA is one context in which Latino Spanish-speaking families built consciousness about their rights and responsibilities. These were changes I observed in Latino families in Carpinteria, involving parents in reflection on the improvement of education. Most significant was the transformation of families' interactions in the home and the relationship between them and the schools. Underrepresented people, including women and ethnic and linguistically subordinate groups, of which women constitute a significant portion, must participate fully in all facets of society. Their participation figures prominently in the history of a given community. People's language, values, traditions, roles, and beliefs are indispensable to creating change and equality.

Integral to the discourse of change is the critical reflection process, which raises people's experience and concerns to a conscious level, as Pablo Freire wrote. Through continual dialogue, parents and school personnel transformed practices and policies related to Spanish-speaking Latino children. Inherent in this process is the conviction that all individuals have strengths and that learning new roles occurs through negotiation and participation in new social arrangements.

The critical reflection process that engaged Latino families in Carpinteria as a supportive network enabled them to become a recognized presence. Three key changes occurred: parents changed their view of self, they changed the way they saw each other, and they acted to change conditions and empower themselves. Empowerment, for this community, was a process driven by changed individual perceptions that motivated people to alter their circumstances. The change that ensued through collective and personal awareness accounted for changed local policies, improved programs, and continued growth for the individuals, their families, and the community. They acknowledged the social and cultural distance between them and dealt with the problems at hand. Fears were conquered as parents and educators together discovered their strengths and a voice.

CHAPTER FOUR

∾

# Dynamic Connections

On a cool, windy Tuesday, Rebeca Cortina parked her car and went into the aluminum factory where she worked on the assembly line. When she entered the building, a woman coworker came up to ask Rebeca a question, "Maybe you who know much about community organization can help me."

"What do you need?"

"My niece is having problems with her husband, who is abusing her, and she doesn't know how to keep him away from the house without him getting violent."

"There is one organization in Santa Barbara that she can call, and they have counselors there that are professionals who can help her," Rebeca said.

"Here, can you please write down the name for me?" asked the woman, handing Rebeca a small piece of paper and the stub of a pencil.

Rebeca wrote down the name of the organization. "I'm sorry about your niece," she said, handing the paper and pencil back to the woman.

"It's been hard because I'm her only relative here. Her mother is my older sister, she's in Mexico," said the woman.

"I hope she gets the support she needs."

"Thank you. I appreciate it."

Despair and opportunity often coexist. Immigrant families in Carpinteria learned about community resources through their social network. The exchange between Ms. Cortina and her coworker were commonplace for COPLA leaders in any context I observed them in. Although information flowed easily among Spanish-speaking Latinos, many families endured tough times. Community groups, including Guadalupeños in the Catholic Church, Sunday soccer teams, and COPLA, united Latinos interested in those areas. Latinos actively participated in these organizations. Families connected socially, emotionally, intellectually, even economically, through these networks. Maintaining a healthy, conflict-free family is only temporarily possible in this world. This meant that some families had difficult obstacles to overcome. At some point, most immigrant families faced very difficult times. Some transcended their isolation through their participation in COPLA, but others still needed more time and support to find a way out of their pain. I met and worked with numerous others who felt stuck in pain as a result of their feelings of hopelessness. They lost their jobs. Many lived in crowded apartments with large extended families. Some households were filled with fear as a result of an alcoholic father or mother who abused the family. Members of these families lived with a gag over their mouths because of the shame and isolation resulting from poverty and lack of education.

For many children who live in families where the support they need is absent, going to school is their only outlet away from a fear-filled environment. Yet, their ability to be comfortable enough to learn in school is often impeded by their emotional stress, compounded by unresponsive schools until this cycle is interrupted. Angel Moro, a parent, tells of the importance of the right support. "Getting the appropriate help is so necessary for students when they get to school. If they can get someone who takes an interest in them, they can get beyond whatever failure they experience."

Families, too, transcend oppressive difficulties and find their sources of strength and power. How to tap into the strengths of those involved in order that they can confront their stressful situations and connect with a supportive person or group to redirect their pain outward rather than inward is a major question.[1] No simple formulas exist for becoming an empowered individual, family, or community. But what is true is that strength and power reside in everyone regardless of color, religion, socioeconomic standing, place of residence, ethnicity, or educational attainment.[2] Families in Carpinteria tapped that potential through family, social, workplace, and religious networks.

Familiar social and cultural ties are the safety net for families. Most conversations I heard in the years that I spent in Carpinteria gave every indication of the value that family held for all. The Sosa family, along with other leaders involved in COPLA mentioned earlier in this book illustrate how families tap their strengths. They harnessed their ability to confront stressful situations related to their children's connectedness with others in a supportive situation and have managed to redirect their pain outward rather than inward. Parents found support in dealing with problems of schooling their children by being active in the COPLA group.

What we know about the psychosocial dynamics of families that are active in groups like COPLA is that people can't always find their power when their lives feel out of control. But their experience of isolation and oppression are not necessarily unique when they are shared with others. Collectively our potential for changing our lives increases. The possibilities for change are revealed in relation to the larger community or on a much more personal level, such as smaller social units like family or other social groups.

Social networks provided opportunities for people in Carpinteria to become connected with others around common issues and to learn that they were not alone in dealing with their problems, as overwhelming as they might have seemed. By joining with others we gain a different perspective on problems, which then enables us to become proactive. Mrs. Mata noted, "We get to open doors and see the possibility of solutions by reaching out and finding our way to those resources that lead us to new opportunities. That means we get to have more and more love within our families and community." Shortly before making this comment, Mrs. Mata had sought out counseling services for her nephew, who had been having truancy problems at the high school since his mother died. Mrs. Mata and her family had taken the nephew in to live with their family.

Various avenues existed for families to communicate with each other and to maintain and to confront their issues about their common and different values within communities. Building community among COPLA families included intimate family gatherings, church social organizations, Alcoholic Anonymous (AA) meetings, soccer games, or team matches and workplace-related socials. Families shared information about family and employment resources, including children's educational options. To the extent that families were able to socialize around their personal interests, they had a means of supporting each other's cultural values, even redefining them through the process of change.

## Elena and Her Family

Most families I met in Carpinteria made education the principal goal for their children. Leadership among Latino parents, focusing on how their own families were impacted by activism, provided a deeper sense of the commitment, determination, and love, which the leaders brought to the Latino community organization. Elena Rosario and her family were one of first families in Carpinteria with whom I made contact. In 1985, her youngest son was in preschool. In my observation of the bilingual pre-school parent meetings, I couldn't miss Elena's eloquent and caring statements on whatever the topic was discussed. She soon became a valued collaborator; her insights about her life, her family's life, and the life of the community propelled the study in Carpinteria. I trained her, along with other community members, to assist me in data collection, involving specific interviews throughout the years of research.

When I first met Elena, her husband, Alfredo, and three children, Raul, Gloria, and Armando, lived in a one-room recreational trailer, which was parked in a lot for recreational vehicles on the outskirts of Carpinteria. When the children were younger and smaller, the Rosarios managed much better than when the children grew taller and bigger and their need for privacy became crucial. They creatively added more space for their oldest son by erecting a small tool shed adjacent to the trailer. This angered the lot owner to whom they paid rent, and he tried to evict them. Unable to afford an apartment or home, the Rosarios were forced to re-move the fixture until the owners forgot the incident. They attempted erecting the shed repeatedly. This was just one of many strategies that the Rosario family used to help make ends meet on their two-person income, which was barely sufficient to cover food and rent.

Alfredo, Elena's husband, had a steadier job than she had. A printing company employed him, and there he has continued to advance. Elena's employment record, on the other hand, was irregular. After arriving in Carpinteria in 1982, she worked at McDonald's but left the organization when she got tired of conflicts with the manager, who insisted on throwing away extra food. Elena wanted to take the excess bread to poor families she knew were hungry. Thereafter, she worked part time in a community preschool, where she began to apply her training in developmental psychology, which she gained at a university in Mexico. Although she had only spent one year at the university, she always wanted to resume her studies.

Elena's involvement in COPLA later helped her to meet school personnel who recognized her skills and knowledge about children, which helped her get a job as a part-time teacher's assistant in a bilingual classroom. Elena loved working in the classroom with children and she understood them so well. Through working with her family, I learned that her work in the classroom was an extension of her love and caring for her own children. Elena's childhood had been filled with books and the expectation that she would learn and nurture others. She was the eldest of ten children, four boys and six girls, all born in Mexico City. Her family was of modest means, but her parents managed to provide Elena with a loving home life that held high expectations for her to be educated and to follow a career.

"My parents always wanted us to study, and they supported us with books. We had many literature books in our home. All of my brothers and sisters also loved to read and study. One brother is a lawyer, and a sister is a physicist, and I want to continue my preparation to become a teacher."

When Elena and her family immigrated to Carpinteria she believed in the dreams and hopes of economic success through education for all of her family. Soon after her children began school, critical incidents convinced her that the road that led toward her dreams was going to be rougher than she imagined.

"I was very scared, because I was unfamiliar with the system and the language. My children had the good fortune to begin school immediately, and I was happy about that. But then I discovered that my oldest son, who had started school in the fourth grade when we came from Mexico, had problems. The school called me, and I went to see what was happening. When I arrived at the office, I felt imprisoned by my fear because no one spoke my language except for the principal and one other teacher whom I did not know at the time. When I spoke with the principal, she couldn't prove that the boys whom she said were in trouble had done what they were accused of doing. What I learned was that she, the principal, did not pay any attention to students who did not speak English. There I began to think about ways for us Latinos to be heard—at least in the schools."

When Raul was in high school, Elena found that she was spending a great deal of time in school helping Armando negotiate his classes so that he could get the teachers she knew cared most about students. What Elena learned through trial and error and through the assistance of Paul Niles about how to help her son later became gifts she brought to COPLA as Latino parents organized. Raul graduated from high school and went to work in the same printing company as his father. Many parents with children in high school had problems similar to those Elena had with Armando.

Elena's middle child, Gloria, presented the school and her parents with problems that made Raul's seem almost pleasurable. When she was in sixth grade, Gloria began having problems with some classmates who kept challenging her to defend herself physically, and so she struggled with giving in to their taunting. Finally Elena helped Gloria to rise above the issues that kept distracting her from her schoolwork. Elena reinforced her unwavering love and trust in Gloria as a person.

"I assured her that we are here to help her and that she has to trust in us because we love her. I tell her that she has to follow her heart and stop listening to those friends who misguide her. I constantly remind her that friends who want her to take drugs or do wrong are not really friends."

Gloria's academic and social problems in school seemed manageable to Elena, until one night when she found herself driving her daughter to the hospital to have her stomach pumped, because she had taken an overdose of pills. After extensive counseling, Gloria appeared to feel better about herself and her studies, or so it seemed to her mother, until she found Gloria intoxicated and again had to call the doctor.

Meanwhile, Elena continued her daytime job and took on an additional part-time job selling natural products. She hoped to save enough money to buy a larger trailer, or maybe even buy a small house of their own, and so put an end to the daily squabbles they were involved in at the trailer court, not to mention alleviate their congested situation. Years passed, however, and Elena and her family remained in the trailer court, because life crises interfered with the family's ability to accumulate enough money for a down payment. Elena occasionally made comments that led me to believe that her tenacity had roots deeper than her dreams. She explained, "When we lived in Mexico City, I had heard that here in the U.S. one could enjoy a better life and education for the children. What no one told me was that it would cost me many tears and suffering."

Elena's collaboration with other parents and her work in the schools provided her with a voice to express her knowledge and experience of family and with a belief in possibilities, even through the daily strife of poor immigrant life in Carpinteria. Her and Alfredo's struggles with family problems were such that she was forced to minimize her participation in COPLA events. Although she attended few COPLA meetings, she continued her commitments to the organization by serving on the committee for the selection of a new superintendent, which eventually hired Dr. Pablo Seda. While this level of participation on the superintendent selection committee was difficult for Elena, as one of the representatives from COPLA, she believed it was necessary to involve herself in the selection of the school district's key administrator. She was still feeling the pain of earlier discrimination in the schools she had experienced as a result of the absence of non-Spanish-speaking personnel to communicate with Latino families. Elena's commitment to children and communication between families and schools made COPLA a viable unit in which to collaborate with others.

"In my experience with my children in their schools, I have had many problems with personnel who don't speak Spanish. I think that all other Latinos have also had that problem. What I don't understand so easily is why it is that parents don't take action like they should for their children's rights. I've become aware of the absence of participation of Latino parents in school.

"Not only in COPLA but also in all of my other work, I have dedicated myself to asking other parents as to the reason for their apathy regarding their school-related meetings. Before COPLA, many parents responded by questioning why it was even necessary for them to go to any meeting. They had no problem saying that they preferred staying home to eat and rest after working."

Honesty, responsibility, and presence characterized Elena's involvement in COPLA. She critically questioned Latino parents' absence in the schools. Communicating with the school was just as much the parents' responsibility as it was the school's to communicate with parents. Elena was adamant about the importance of having a presence in the school.

Her three children are the source of both her pride and her pain. Her oldest son, Raul, graduated from high school and is working in the printing shop where his father works. Gloria, the middle child, graduated from high school and preferred doing clerical work in a local company, deferring college without any specific plans. Armando, the youngest, finished high school. He loved playing football in high school and continued to play in college. His ambitious plans to transfer to UCSB were unfulfilled, as he quit college to become a professional boxer. Elena assessed his academic strength. "My youngest son has had better luck in his studies because he has had good teachers since the beginning in preschool. He has been fortunate to be more advanced in his classes. He gets good grades in almost all of his classes. I have a lot of hope that he can get a good career." But in the fall of 2000, she was still hopeful that Armando would soon come to his senses and return to college. Although Elena feels hopeful that one day he will return to school, she admits to being heartbroken that he was such a good student and took such a wild turn in his career plans.

Elena attributes Armando's academic achievement in school to his successful start with Celia Marquez, who taught the bilingual preschool.

Elena believes that if Raul and Gloria had been able to have Celia as their teacher they would have received a stronger foundation in their education. Elena and many other parents have credited Celia with compassion and have praised her belief not only in students but also in their families. Celia's strength has always been her habit of making the parents coteachers with her.

Although Elena's hopes for her own children's education did not manifest, except in the case of her youngest son, she continues to be committed to the education of all children, both in the primary grades, where she is and has for years been a bilingual teacher's assistant, and in later grades as well. Out of school, she assists the families of students she befriends. One case stands out above the others.

Elena tutored a young third-grader who was disabled, and because she had missed a great deal of school, the student was quite behind in her academic achievement. Most of the time, the little girl, Sonia, used a wheelchair, but at home she could not use it because they lived in an upstairs apartment. Her sister had to carry her up and down the stairs and around inside the house. During Sonia's time with Elena as her tutor, they became friends and Elena became her confidante. Sonia kept Elena informed about her home life and the problems her mother faced trying to keep food on the table and a roof over their heads. Sonia's father had abandoned the family, and her mother had finally found a job. And to help the family financially, Sonia's mother had invited her brother to stay with them. Sonia did not like her uncle because he was mean and yelled at her and her older sister when he was intoxicated. Sonia's older sister cared for her at home. She helped bathe her and cooked her meals while their mother worked. Elena tried to help Sonia deal with her anger about her mean uncle; she even visited Sonia's mother to relay Sonia's fears about him. The mother was quite aware of the difficult situation in which they were forced to live, but she did not see a way out of the predicament.

Elena gave Sonia's mother information about community agencies that were affordable and employed Spanish-speaking staff who could help her deal with her problems at home. Elena noticed improvement with Sonia's emotional and psychological frame of mind; she seemed more stable, which enabled her to concentrate on her schoolwork.

One day, Elena noticed that Sonia looked quite disheveled and unkempt. Sonia told Elena that she thought her uncle had molested her older sister. She had heard all of it from her room, where she spends most of the time when she's home. Elena inquired in great detail about the incident and went to visit the mother, who became enraged when she heard about it. The mother called the police and had her brother arrested. Sonia was unable to concentrate for days afterward but eventually stabilized so that Elena believed they were finally able to make real progress in her reading.

Elena knew that the ordeal wasn't over when Sonia showed up to the tutoring session and announced that her sister was afraid she was pregnant. Elena could not stay quiet about this either, so she visited the mother again. The mother was overwhelmed about the problem but felt powerless because she had no money to take her daughter to the doctor. Elena gave the mother the name of a clinic in Santa Barbara where she could receive free services if she wasn't in a position to pay. Within days they learned that Sonia's sister was not pregnant, although she did have anemia and other health problems that caused her debilitation.

Sonia continued her tutoring sessions with Elena, and Elena noticed that Sonia progressed more steadily as some of the more severe problems abated. Eventually Elena was assigned to assist in the preschool and discontinued her tutoring assignment with Sonia. However, during the time that Elena tutored Sonia, her faith in Sonia's ability to learn kept her in close touch with the family. Elena explains how her work and interest in the families overlapped. "Since COPLA mobilized, the school district in this city has improved, and it continues to improve. Now we have bilingual educators, we can count on staff using our language in the schools; students enjoy benefits that they didn't have, with advisors and tutors in various subjects. More scholarships have been given to our students, and we have also seen more Hispanic students graduate from high school and enter college.

"Where my family is concerned we have more communication among ourselves, and my husband is more compassionate with my children. He's more involved in their education. Sometimes what gives me great satisfaction is that my husband has progressed in his work and is thinking of studying for a career."

At last, Elena feels quite satisfied as a teacher's assistant in preschool. Her most exciting accomplishment is having been able to clear some of her evenings so that she can attend classes at the community college that will lead toward a teaching credential. She feels particularly hopeful that with her teaching credential, she will be able to remain close to children and families and continue to help them broaden their personal and political consciousness and thus continue contributing to the community. Elena's family was finally able to save up enough money to buy a small two-bedroom house. It has a large backyard with a small toolshed. Of course, her oldest son, Raul, quickly converted it into his own space.

Daily complex problems defy simplistic, formulaic answers. The Carpinteria activists provide many lessons. Most salient are those that teach us to expand our inner and outer worlds. By working collectively, listening, and engaging in open conversation, they discovered both their internal and their external resources and were able to bring about desired changes in their lives while sharing their experiences with others. Work inside and outside of the home and in the community, in addition to family demands, consumed the lives of Carpinteria Latino activists. But their spirit prevailed as they reached out more and more to those who needed information, support, or just a helping hand. For some, the caring they provided others made their home life stressful. The demands on their time kept them away from home a great deal.

Religious activities in Carpinteria centered around two Catholic churches. The largest one—St. Joseph's, on the east side of the freeway—drew its membership from both sides of the freeway. At baptisms, First Communions, and funerals that I attended, services were conducted in Spanish at both churches. Choices of where families worshipped had more to do with personal traditions and preference, but the west side church was much larger.

Petra Angeles taught a Saturday morning class for children preparing to make First Communion at St. Joseph's. One of the reasons she enjoyed working with COPLA was that she had such a difficult time working with parents in the church. According to Petra, some parents did not study with their children, yet expected them to make their First Communion, even when they did not know their lessons. She recounted a situation that occurred with one of the parents in her class. Petra had a class of twenty-six children, ages six and seven. Parents left their children at 9:00 A.M. and picked them up at 11:00 A.M. Petra decided that it was time to confront the parents on the question of taking more responsibility for helping their six- and seven-year-olds. She contacted the parents and asked them to attend a meeting one Saturday at 11:00 when they picked up their children. Of the twenty-six children, only three of their parents came into the room, forcing Petra to cancel the intended meeting. Petra decided that the following Saturday she would ask the parents or whoever picked up the children, about helping them read their lessons and prepare for their test, which was to be given the following week. Petra warned them that if the children did not pass their tests, they wouldn't be able to make their First Communion.

About twenty parents—fathers, mothers, and a few older siblings—came to pick up the children from Petra's class. The children looked on as Petra reminded the adults that the time for First Communion was approaching and all of the children had to pass the test that would be given the following week. This called for a commitment on the parents' part to help the children prepare for the test. Although Petra was able to secure the cooperation of all of the parents, she could not guarantee that all of the children would pass the test.

As the other parents left, one parent remained behind to talk with Petra about his daughter's problems with reading. Petra began by telling him ways to help his daughter remember her lessons for the First Communion test. The parent said he felt confident that his daughter could probably pass the First Communion test, because it was oral, but his concern had to do with her reading problem at school. He said his daughter used to like reading, but her mother had died during the year, which caused the daughter to fall behind in her learning. Now, he said, she's quiet most of the time and doesn't even want to try. He said her sisters and brothers were also having a hard time, and he had thought about sending them back to Mexico to live with their aunt, because it was difficult for him to do it alone, even though they had some friends from their hometown who helped them daily. Petra directed him to the Migrant Education teacher in Marina to help his daughter with her reading, but she also suggested that he attend COPLA meetings so that he could become more informed about resources at the school. Petra said that it might be a good idea for him to take his children to a counselor who could help the family to deal with the mother's death. She suggested that he identify this need to the priest, who could help them find someone to help the family in that specific area.

Before the next COPLA meeting, Petra called this parent and encouraged him to attend. He said his car had broken down and he needed a ride, so she went by his house and picked him up. He thanked her for taking such an interest in his daughter's schooling and informed her that his daughter was beginning to like school again since she passed the test and was able to make her First Communion. Petra asked about the other children and whether he had sent them back to Mexico. He said he would wait until the end of the school year to evaluate the situation again, and that maybe he would ask his sister to come to the United States to help him instead of sending the children back to Mexico. He didn't want them to leave their classes while school was still in session, because, as he remembered, his wife had always made education a strong priority for the children.

Through her teaching of the Saturday First Communion classes, Petra formed linkages with families and between families and appropriate agencies. Latino parents related to one another through their day-to-day encounters at the Laundromat, the grocery store, soccer games on weekends, at their places of employment in the nurseries, in spite of the scrutiny of other employers who were usually Euro-American.

Interaction between Spanish-speaking Latino and Euro-American families was limited in Carpinteria. Their language differences distanced them. Although most contacts were cordial and inconsequential, sometimes something as innocent as children's recreation brought the English- and Spanish-speaking communities into unfriendly interactions. One case involved two Latino children, a boy and a girl, who played tennis at the middle school playground. Several times during the early months of 1992, the police were called frequently by a neighbor who saw a number of children in the playground. She expected the police to investigate the threat to her safety by these Latino students, whom she claimed were disturbing her. The neighbor accompanied the police to the playground and watched them interrogate the children about who they were and whether an adult accompanied them. The Latino counselor who usually accompanied the children had to identify himself repeatedly. He said that he was a counselor in the school and that he brought the children to the playground to help the children practice their tennis. The neighbor woman told the police that although the children were not a problem while they played tennis, she thought that Latinos should all be sent back to Mexico, because they occupied too many jobs and cost the country too much money. Latino leaders who were apprised of this occurrence went to complain to the police, citing that the police were condoning these kinds of racist harassment against Latinos. Afterward, the police stopped responding to this kind of calls. This type of contact between Latinos and Euro-Americans in Carpinteria made relationships hostile, at best, since Latinos, especially the children, feel confused about being unjustly blamed for things they didn't do. Adult Latinos complained of becoming more isolated as a result of tense confrontations with Euro-American residents.

In spite of the cultural differences, poor Spanish-speaking Latinos and Euro-Americans coexist in much of their daily activities, including shopping in the same grocery stores and doing their laundry in the same Laundromats. Occasionally, usually around planning times or school carnivals, attempts were made by Euro-Americans to contact Latino parents about school issues. Interest in working together began quietly when COPLA was organized. Euro-American parents attended COPLA meetings to learn how the group was organized and how they defined their activities. They were impressed with the efforts of the Latino parents, but they did not continue attending because unless someone translated for them, they couldn't understand what went on in the meetings. Although the English- and Spanish-speaking communities did not come together in meeting form, the dialogue between them had reached a new level. The existence of proactive Spanish-speaking Latinos in Carpinteria as a strong community was undeniable.

## Work and Play

My job as a researcher meant finding every opportunity to have conversations about family activities. To get a close-up of work and play in the lives of Carpinteria Spanish-speaking Latinos, I followed several adults to their workplace. On weekends, I brought my camcorder and audio-recorder to family gatherings, picnics, and other social events. Many women activists in COPLA worked in nurseries, schools, and factories alongside those who were not as aware about schooling in the United States. For example, during a work break a coworker approached Alicia Segura about the problems her children encountered in school. The parent hesitated to go to school when the teachers called to complain about her daughter. Alicia suggested that she meet with other women and together they could go talk with the teachers. Her coworkers used to tease her about caring too much; they believed that teachers should know how to do their job. Alicia explained how necessary direct communication was between parents and teachers. After a few years she gradually convinced them of the importance of getting involved in their children's schooling. They stopped teasing her, but they still didn't attend COPLA meetings. Neither does Alicia attend meetings. Her husband, David, began attending while she helped the children with their homework.

Leisure activities offered another meeting ground for Latino families to support each other on matters having to do with their children. One day after a children's soccer game, a mother of one of the players stopped Alicia to ask if she knew about a school where they could put their teenage son, because no school wanted him. He had been suspended from school so many times that the school district authorities refused to accept him again; the principal suggested that the child attend the county alternative school in Santa Barbara. Alicia advised them to speak with the administrators and to find out as much as possible about the alternative school and about their son's rights to return to his former school. The boy's parents accepted her advice and spoke with the principal, from whom they learned that the district did not have an obligation to accept the boy back unless it could be shown that he had made exceptional progress for at least one academic year at the alternative school. But even then, he would only be accepted on a probationary basis. This interaction was exemplary of how Alicia, as well as other COPLA leaders, made every event an opportunity to share their knowledge with their social network and to encourage people to pursue education even when it would be easier to give up.

Working in and outside of home was commonplace for Latinas in Carpinteria. Traditional gender roles generally remained unchanged regarding where the adults worked in the agricultural industry before immigrating to the United States. Although they work full-time jobs and raise children, women continue to manage the household, thus at least doubling their workload.[3] Responsibilities that were once unchallenged became an open dialogue as Latinas got more involved in community leadership. COPLA provided a context for that conversation to take place.

Although not all adults involved in COPLA were convinced of the need to reorganize the gender-defined roles in their households, the issue had been raised. Latina leaders in COPLA more readily found the need to openly discuss with their husbands' questions regarding evening meetings, children's homework, and adjustments to their share of the division of labor. Some husbands increased their chauffeuring duties as wives worked longer hours to help support their children. Other husbands accepted more responsibility in tasks like doing the family laundry more often as women attended afternoon meetings with their children's teachers. Women like Rebeca Cortina complained about their husbands' unwillingness to help around the house. Rebeca's husband hurt his back at his job and was on disability for two years before he was strong enough to resume work, although he was forced to change his employment because he was unable to lift heavy loads. When he was home, however, Rebeca expected him to at least wash dishes and do light work like dusting and occasionally boil potatoes, but he refused, using his disability as an excuse. During that period Rebeca was vice president of COPLA, and she was working two jobs to pay for a computer and flute that her daughter, Gloria, needed when she got into the high school GATE Program classes. What Rebeca did not anticipate was Gloria's refusal to attend college beyond the first year. After her first year she went to a trade school and studied computing, which helped her obtain a job in a local computer company. Rebeca lamented her daughter's decision to leave college, but praised her for at least completing the trade school program. She also held optimistic thoughts that Gloria would return to college when she got "working" and "earning money" out of her system.

Rebeca managed the ordeal with her husband's disability and his reluctance to help her around the house. Shortly after he returned to work, she was able to convince him that his assistance with housework was just as important to the maintenance of the family as her employment outside of the house was to the economic support of the family. Admitting that he felt stronger and could help with light housework, he now washes dishes and occasionally performs other minor household tasks. Rebeca was quick to give her husband credit on issues of supporting the children in their schooling tasks. He always encouraged their children, Gloria and their son, Miguel, to do their best in the academic arena, and he actually assisted them in their homework when he could. He even coached Gloria on her baseball technique so that she could make the team and gave Miguel special attention when he went out for soccer. Rebeca, nevertheless, had most of the responsibility for meeting with teachers and teaching other parents to work with schools.

By fall of 2000, neither her son, Miguel, nor her daughter, Gloria, had returned to college, but Rebeca was as proud as could be about herself. She had returned to adult night school to improve her English and complete her high school diploma in the GED Program. With her sights on becoming a nurse, she enrolled in the community college to begin a nursing program. Meanwhile, she continues her work as a housekeeper and is determined to complete her career goals even if, as she says, "my hair is snow white. I won't care. I'll be a very good nurse no matter how old."

The Cortinas' story mirrored the experience of other activist women in COPLA, while the activist men told a different story about their experience with teamwork to educate their children. Ramon Méndez and his wife, Chela, learned to work with each other's demanding schedules by dividing the tasks related to their children's schooling and the household chores. Chela felt more comfortable with helping their children, Pablo and Mona. Chela had achieved only a second-grade education in Mexico and felt rather insecure about communicating with schools but could understand some of their children's homework when they were in kindergarten, first, and second grades. Once Pablo began to get more English curriculum in the third grade she deferred to Ramon, who had completed the equivalent of high school in Mexico. Pablo sometimes waited for help with his homework until late at night when his father was at COPLA or other school related meetings. There came a point when Ramon's meetings kept him out of the house so much that Chela taught him to heat his meals and even make some quick snacks for himself because he came home too late to expect her to get him something to eat. Also there were times that he came home and left for meetings before she ever got home from work, so he had to prepare something quick to eat. Ramon brags about his terrific salsa, "Chela taught me to make a good salsa to eat with my tortillas or to put on whatever I heat in the microwave. I just chop a bit of tomato, chile jalapeño, onion, a bit of salt, and a few cilantro leaves. Then I put everything in the blender and it turns out very tasty. She's a very good cook, and sometimes I'm running around so this way I don't go hungry."

Standing by the kitchen counter, turning on the microwave to heat some tortillas, Ramon laughed when he spoke about how far he had come—to have become so active in educational groups that he can make salsa. He recognized that, although he and Chela agreed that he would take the lead in the involvement in their children's schooling and in organizational leadership, his wife still handles the most difficult of all household jobs—the family economics. In spite of their division of labor with respect to schooling and household matters, both Ramon and Chela agree on the importance of raising and educating their children. They both want their children to learn all they can and become bilingual people with a vision for exploring the world and helping others to do the same. Ramon's and Chela's appreciation for learning through collective endeavors reflected their hopes for their children's futures.

Parents often asked themselves and each other what they should expect from their children in the way of academic performance. Adult leaders in COPLA reported shifts in their family relationships as a result of their participation in COPLA. They became aware that their own low educational achievements in Mexico need not interfere with their high expectations for their children's education. But they also realized that high expectations were not enough to make it happen. Hard work was required. Accepting new responsibilities in their children's education meant adopting new practices within their families.

Elena Sosa's feelings epitomize those of the other parents. "The most that we can expect of our lives is that our children take a good road and accomplish more than we have." As parents became more active with each other and with the schools, their relationships with their children changed. They realized the importance of communicating their worldview to their children in their own language. Speaking to their children in Spanish about their family, history, and traditions was deemed worthy as parents forged a community dialogue and support between families and relatives and their communities.

At first the parents worked only minimally with their children on school-related tasks. Homework and parent-teacher conferences were always given top priority in these households. Other educational activities were only occasional occurrences, not part of regular family activities. After working in the leadership of COPLA for a couple of years, parents extended their list of activities that promoted their children's schooling. Homework occupied a great deal of parents' time with their children. Parents of high as well as low achievers made great efforts to help their children with homework in spite of their own limited academic skills. Some helped their children by sitting down with them to complete their nightly tasks, while others just asked the children to report to them about their studies upon completion. Contrary to what many teachers believed, parents of underachievers spent hours helping their children with their homework. It is important to point out here that parents with children at all levels of achievement made efforts to assist their children. The difference between the parents' ability to help their children usually had to do with their experience in communicating with the school. More importantly what we need to understand from these people's experience is that the tedious, busy homework that was assigned to the children set those parents who had had more school experience apart from those who had less.

Parents were frustrated by the fact that the children couldn't complete much of the work without parental intervention or the use of special tutors. This is the argument raised by those who oppose the assignment of meaningless quantities of homework. The question of equitable access to the necessary resources for students of all socioeconomic classes and gender groups to complete their work in a competitive way was also raised.[4] Children's schoolwork can be quite demanding, especially if they're in gifted and talented classes. Manuel Peña said, "I have learned that I need to sit with my son who is now in fourth grade in the GATE program. I want to know what he is doing. It's not that I don't trust him, it's because I want to know what curriculum he's assigned. I didn't attend school in this country, and I barely completed primary school so while I'm helping him, I'm also learning. I want to be on top of what my son does. Even though I've learned a great deal from COPLA, I also know that I cannot spend all of my time at meetings because I want to spend time with my son. My wife does not attend COPLA meetings, but she talks with my son's teachers and she communicates with them and then tells me what Roberto needs to study."

Like the Peñas, other parents couldn't always help their children with the complex tasks assigned as they advanced through the grade levels, even though they had been able to help them in the early primary grades. Leo Garcia, who had only earned a fifth-grade education in Mexico, prided himself in helping his sons in high school by finding words in the dictionary. He commented, "If I can, I sit with my sons and I help them with their questions or I help them look in the books for the examples they need."

Homework was only one arena for parent-teacher connections. Other contacts were made through parent-teacher conferences, parent initiated calls, and parent- and teacher-initiated written reports. Parents observed that their children made a great deal of progress as a result of their participation in COPLA.

Jesús Lopez talked about his son in tenth grade. "It seems to me that my son tries harder and pays more attention to what I tell him. And that makes me feel good."

Jessie Alonzo described how her fourth-grade son and seventh-grade daughter had benefited from her activism. "I've noticed that my children have benefited from my attention to what happens in their school, and they like it that I go to their school to watch them work."

Graciela Hernandez believed that her son's work in tenth grade had improved some due to her participation in COPLA. "I call them to wake up in the morning and prepare their breakfast. With respect to their homework, they now try to get ahead in their work."

Some parents, like Mr. Morales, have seen their children bring home higher grades. "The most important thing is that they bring home good grades and they tell us about problems, whereas before they did not communicate. As a result we have more communication in our family."

Other parents who had seen significant changes in their children's education resulting from family support commented about the progress they had witnessed in their families' communications. Enrique Mendez was particularly elated about the developments within his family. "Now that I've been participating in COPLA, I've made it known to my children how important a good education is. I communicate with my son's teachers so I can work with the children and to let them know that they're a part of our lives. I try to make them know that I'm interested in everything they do. I motivate them to give all that they can in school and to help other children, too. For example, my son likes to share his knowledge, and I encourage him to somehow transmit to others what he knows. I encourage him to read stories to his little sister and to teach her to count, to color, and so on. By doing so, he can feel important."

Students enjoyed having their parents involved in their education, both in and out of school. Both their grades and their communication with their parents improved. Even in difficult and challenging situations, parents realized that their presence made a real difference. Antonia Suarez's son had been sexually molested, and she had been trying to find ways to help him deal with his emotional distress around the incident, which affected his entire life, specifically his schooling. She explained, "My son has become more responsible and takes more interest in participating in school events. He is happier now that I'm more involved in the school. In my first year in COPLA he improved tremendously. Within such little time I have seen good results. I believe that it has been so difficult for him and all of us that I'll continue helping him in whatever way I can. I'm confident that he'll continue moving forward."

Reflecting on the importance of a well-organized home, Rosa Martinez verified a point that I observed in the homes while documenting the small details that unite a family.[5] "The point I want to make is that in one's home there should be 'rules'—time to get up in the morning, time to eat breakfast, time to prepare and to leave for school. Time to return from school, time to do homework, time to watch a bit of television, and time to talk and to read a while."

Parents have motivated each other and their children to make sense of a system from which they previously felt alienated. Most significantly, Latino families turned their attention inward in order to learn more about their children, about their schooling activities, and about the various means of connecting the family and the school. COPLA had a different impact on parents who participated more actively. For some, COPLA provided a forum to discover more about the schools. For others, like Luis and Lucia Ruiz, COPLA provided a means to more effectively assist their children at home about school issues. They were quite active in COPLA; Luis Ruiz always participated in the meetings, and it seemed that he was quite knowledgeable about how to best take advantage of the programs the school had to offer. Both credited their activism in COPLA, sharing with other parents about their children, for their increased consciousness. However, Luis revealed an interesting vignette about his expanded awareness. "I want to be sincere with you because I could deceive you. But I would only be fooling myself. I haven't helped my children at home at all. It has been my wife who takes all the responsibility. I have a great character defect, my bad temper. But little by little I am beginning to talk with them, and I have promised them that I will change. Now I tell them that education is the only legacy that's worth anything."

The Ruizes were able to reach out to their children in more meaningful ways than they were aware of before they joined with other parents. The Ruizes shared their mutual history with other Latino parents while they struggled to make sense of their children's schooling.

❧

# Malleable Identities

In the fall, the warm mid-afternoon sun shone bright in Carpinteria. Rosa Peña walked across the street with her oldest son, Beto, by her side. He had just been asked to leave the junior high school and not return for two days. For the first couple of years after arriving in the United States, Beto found himself having chronic disciplinary problems on the playground. Rosa was silent until they got into the car. "You can't keep misbehaving this way. I want you to do your best because that's the only way you'll get through school. You're smart and you don't need to get into fights." Beto remained quiet for a while. But his mother continued, "What do you expect to do to change your behavior?"

"I don't want to be here, Mother. I don't want to be in this school, this town, or this United States."

"That's not a choice, Beto. You are here and the only choice you have is to make it easy on yourself, or you can keep making it hard. You've got your father's and my support to help you in every way possible. But, son, let me tell you, if you insist on making it hard on yourself, you're the one who will suffer the most. And you have a choice on how to manage your anger in the playground. We'll take you to a counselor, but you're the one that has to do the work to change your behavior." Rosa drove into their driveway.

Beto broke down crying, "I don't want to be here, Mother, and I don't know what to do. I'm trying my best, but I just don't like it. But I don't want you to be mad at me."

"Son, it's not easy, but we'll get through this together. We're here for you, so don't be afraid."

Rosa kept her promise to support her son through his turmoil. Personal stories of people like Rosa tell of the complexities of cultural change and transformation on the individual, the family, and the community. Many Latino immigrants in Carpinteria began their lives in the United States focused on improving their children's educational opportunities, but they weren't always that clear. The lives of Juan Ramirez and his family illustrate that life does not happen in a straight line.

In the context of an unwelcoming U.S. society, where fear of immigrants abounds, the Ramirez story of identity reinforces the notion that belonging and connectedness are cast within power relations. Our cultural history provides a broad canvas on which we construct the self—meaning that the self is never separate from the context.[1] In this light, the stories of these individuals reject any idealization of family or community; they shift between discourses, restating a major position in this book—that no action has only a single effect. People's individual identities resist closure because identities are amazingly complicated, shifting, and assume new and multiple facets in the process of living. Nothing has made this clearer than the stories of individuals from communities in which I have researched and taught. Carpinteria is no exception.

Community activism extends from the individual's personal values and history, which motivate their concern for their children's opportunities, for extended family networks, and for other community members. In their story, which follows, Juan and Andrea Ramirez share meaningful events that reveal possibilities for expanding their potential.

## Juan and His Family

The Ramirez family, especially Juan, the patriarch of the family, received many awards celebrating their endeavors. On one dining room wall of the two-bedroom Ramirez condominium, hang four plaques of commendation for Juan's activism in the Carpinteria community and schools. In 1991, COPLA awarded him a plaque with the inscription "En Reconocimiento a su Magnifico Labor Como Presidente de COPLA 1989–1991" (In Recognition of Your Magnificent Labor as President of COPLA 1989–1991). Three other plaques had been given to him: by the director of special projects, Paul Niles, and Superintendent Pablo Seda in 1992; by the director of migrant education in 1993; and by Dr. Mario Solis in 1992 for his participation in leadership classes on families in society. These awards praised his contributions to families and schools of Carpinteria.

Juan's achievements had grown along with him over the forty years of his life, which began in Zacualco de Torres, Jalisco, south of Guadalajara in route to Manzanillo. His family worked in agriculture, growing beans and corn on their small ranch to feed their family and also ran a small tortilleria (tortilla factory). From the time he was eight years old, Juan helped on the ranch before and after school. School began at 9:00 A.M., but before he went to school, Juan had to sweep up around the house or help at the corn mill.

An industrious Juan helped in the family tortilleria on weekends for a couple of years, until he began to sell Popsicles. Up at dawn, Juan prepared his pushcart for selling Popsicles. He pushed the cart from 6:00 A.M. to 5:00 P.M. and earned about twelve pesos for each day's work, which at that time was equivalent to one dollar in the United States.

School was Juan's real interest. He especially liked math since he had quite a bit of practice in the streets as a young entrepreneur. At the age of ten, Juan made small gelatins to sell. He bought the gelatins for $0.20 each and prepared them himself. He put them in small plastic cups and sold them for two pesos each, resulting in a good profit. In the absence of refrigeration, he was pressured to sell them the same day he made them. He eventually expanded his business to include cookies and candy.

Zacualco, a town of approximately fifteen thousand, was just a bit bigger than Carpinteria. It had a primary school, one high school, one business institute that taught typing, and eight Catholic churches. Because Juan liked math and had become familiar with computation tasks by selling treats, his uncle offered him the opportunity to work in his store. Although he was still in high school, Juan worked at the store five hours a night after school. He became so engrossed in his uncle's business that he abandoned his high school classes. This decision displeased Juan's uncle, who gave Juan an ultimatum: either go back to school or quit working at the store. Reluctantly, Juan returned to high school and graduated. In retrospect, Juan appreciates the fact that he was forced to go back to school and graduate. Although most children in Zacualco finished elementary school, because it was compulsory, many had to drop out of school in third grade because their families needed them to work. Such children lost their initiative, and they lacked the much-needed support required to complete even elementary school. Juan received high grades in most of his school years; he was a model for his younger brothers and sisters. The only time that his grades dropped was when he went to work in his uncle's store.

"When I began working with my uncle, I didn't succeed like I used to in math and Spanish and writing. But from that point forward, I only attended classes and was barely making it through biology and physics. Chemistry was more difficult. In Mexico, I think that I needed more of a push than what I received as a student to make me feel more important. We only dealt with what concerned the town. We couldn't see beyond what we had in Zacualco. That was our entire world."

In retrospect, Juan recognized that he wanted someone to stimulate his imagination. "What happened was that the teachers couldn't help us to see opportunities that we had around us. It was always, how would I say? They dedicated themselves just to their material and they don't prepare you to go into a vocation, or to find something to help you. They only taught classes, and though they were good teachers, it was always like a vision was missing."

After completing high school, Juan had the distressing task of notifying his parents, who had counted so much on him for the family's economic support, that he planned to leave town to study at the *preparatoria*, which is the equivalent of a community college in the United States. Juan's uncle who owned the store where Juan worked offered him a loan so he could open his own store, and Juan took him up on it and stayed in Zacualco, working in his own small store for two years. Juan later became interested in attending the university in Guadalajara and was accepted along with ten of his friends. But he failed to convince his parents, who didn't support his decision to go to the university.

"My parents said that they barely had enough for household expenses and they would not be able to help me. My father said, 'Why should I help you? I'll allow you to go, but I won't be able to support you with money.' I believe that sometimes because there are no economic means or sufficient money to help, parents deny children their support. But the truth is that sometimes parents didn't know and they didn't believe that it was important to study. They thought that by teaching us to work and to earn enough to help the family, that it was sufficient. That was the mentality at the time. And, it still is."

Juan believed that his parents did not know how to support him in what he wanted to do because their primary concern was daily survival.

Much like Juan's parents, Andrea's parents were also forced to make monumental shifts in their understanding of their children's independence and education with Andrea's youngest sister, who wanted to be a teacher and needed not only their emotional, but also their financial, support. This was particularly difficult for Andrea's parents because they had always worked hard just to keep food on the table. Juan recalls that when he first met Andrea's family, for years their meals consisted of only cucumbers and beans, which the family grew on their small family farm.

"Andrea was the third of ten children in her family. And they're very poor. It's a poverty that keeps you working every day. And there isn't even steady employment. You might have something for a week or two. You may eat today, but you don't know about tomorrow."

Juan admired Andrea's tenacity and her creative strategies to work her way out of destitute poverty. He credits her with breaking her family's poverty cycle, which consisted of working, marrying another poor person, having many children, and then caring for ill parents. But Andrea persevered through the hunger that the family faced almost on a daily basis. She pursued her interest in working in a restaurant away from home.

Juan describes how some people remain caught in the vicious poverty cycle while others choose to leave in order to be able to help themselves and others. "I see two different visions. One way to perceive our situations when we're poor is to try and hold back our children like my parents did, because they didn't want to support me to go to the university. They did this because they couldn't support me financially. Consequently, they discouraged me. And in Andrea's family, the parents didn't want her niece to study because the girl's parents needed her to help the family in the fields. So, Andrea and I, well, we had to leave our homes to learn more and to help ourselves. I came here to the United States, and she went to work outside of her townhouse in the *taqueria* because she liked the food and restaurant business."

Although Juan and Andrea faced financial difficulty in Carpinteria, they knew that their family in Mexico was in greater need. Andrea explains, "I think that we now are in better position to help our families and others than if we had stayed on the ranch with everyone."

Just as Andrea found the strength to leave home, so did Juan, when he followed his father to the United States. As the oldest of nine children, seven boys and two girls, Juan lived at home on the ranch or in his small store and helped raise the younger children until he was nineteen, when he left with his father to work in agriculture in California. Juan's father came to work in the Sacramento area with the Bracero program after working in Arizona. He stayed and became a citizen and brought Juan with him to work for a short time.

His father's brother-in-law, who came to work in Los Angeles, paved Juan's route to Carpinteria. About that time Juan was feeling a bit restless in his hometown of Zacualco, where his small business was successful to some degree. Still he wanted to try something new, and so he joined his family members working in Los Angeles, and when his cousin came up to work in Carpinteria, Juan followed him.

Juan recalls enjoying his early business experience, but he felt torn by the people's poverty and their inability to pay. "When I was in the store which I bought from my uncle, the business was good. I had paid the debts I owed to my uncle. I was quite solvent in my expenses. But there was a great deal of poverty. In the town, there is lots of poverty and one has to . . . well, the townspeople went to the store, to the market, and they had little money and sometimes they needed just the basics. Sugar. Rice. Beans. And, they don't have money. Some because they work in the fields and its seasonal work and the pay is not good, and, others because they spend it on alcohol. So many want credit. They asked, 'Can you loan me some food on credit? I'll pay you. I'll pay you soon.' They always said, but they wouldn't. And that's the way it went. My heart isn't very tough, and I gave them things on credit, and many times they didn't pay me. I was doing well, but it was my vision to have a larger store and to have a bit more money."

It was that dream of stronger economic stability that brought Juan to the United States. "My vision was to work only one year, earn some money, and return to work in my store. But the place wasn't my own. I had to pay rent and by then, the owners were asking for the place because they saw that I had built a business there. The owner said, 'You pay me or leave the business.' I didn't have a contract; it was just month-to-month. But, that was my intention, to stay a while in the U.S. and then return to the store. As you can see, my plans changed. We've been here twenty years."

After being in the United States for a while, Juan got a fifteen-day vacation, and he returned to visit his family in Zacualco. At that time Andrea worked in a restaurant, and she and Juan spent nine days together before he returned to Carpinteria. Zacualco, Jalisco, was a long way from Carpinteria, and it seemed even farther to two people in love. Andrea recalls that Juan sent an average of one letter a month, not nearly what she wanted, but at least they were encouraging in that he said he planned to return to visit her.

By the time Andrea met Juan, she had already experienced many difficult times in her early childhood. She left school in second grade because her parents did not have money to send her to the doctor for recurring headaches. Andrea finally got tired of not being able to read and write in school and at home. Her absences were frequent. She left school and helped her family by working on the ranch. Without money, her parents could not take her to a doctor. Andrea's mother convinced her that the headaches were merely excuses Andrea made up to avoid going to school.

"I didn't leave school. I quit because of my headaches. The only thing my mother said was, 'If you don't want to go to school, you don't have to go. I won't insist on it. It's up to you.' But she did say, 'School is very important,' and now I see it's true. Sometimes my son asks me things, and I can't help him. But there wasn't money to cure oneself when I was a girl with those problems. When I was older I was able to go to Guadalajara, and I got fitted for glasses."

A couple of years after leaving school, Andrea began working—sweeping and mopping—for a woman who owned a café. "The woman's café opened for dinner. That's where I began working as a child. I was about eleven years old when I began working there, cleaning the place. She paid me a meager amount, but it helped my family a bit. Later, I began working in a *tostadería* (*taquería*-like place where they made tostadas). I was there for a year making tostadas. I never liked working as a housekeeper doing housework in people's houses. I used to say that I would not go into any house to work. I liked working in businesses. I stayed about a year, and from there I stayed at the owner's house for a brief time. At the age of fifteen, I went to work at the restaurant. I worked there eight years, and at twenty-three, I left to get married."

Andrea felt pleased to have had the opportunity to work, even though it was difficult for her at times, since the hours were long and the pay was low. Most of the money she earned went to help her parents, but she was able to keep a little bit for herself. She felt that it was important to keep at least a small amount for herself, because it made her feel more independent. She was also grateful that she did not have to contribute all of her money to her family, as did all of her older brothers and sisters.

All of her siblings had to work on the family corn and bean farm and to get by, still had to work outside the home. By the time Andrea began working, there were fewer children living at home, and although they often went hungry, the situation was less severe than what her older siblings had faced. With tear-filled eyes Andrea recounted some of the most austere times she experienced as a child.

"Sometimes there was nothing to eat. Then at one point, my father became ill when a snake bit him, and he couldn't work. He spent two years sick in bed. There was always more poverty for the oldest ones than for us because they had more of us to support. When I began working, there were only four of us kids living at home, two girls and two boys. By then, my father was able to work again and our hungry days were fewer. Our home was ours because we inherited it from my grandmother, who built this one-room adobe house and left it to my mother. At least we didn't have to worry about a home. I told myself daily, 'If someday I marry or whether God wants me to marry or not, I'll just remain working. I don't want to end up like my brothers and sisters with one kid here and another by the hand, and holding another one in the other arm.' That's hard. That's a hard life. My brothers and sisters agreed with my mother who used to say, 'All children come with their own food.' But they've learned the hard way that it's not true."

A desire to improve their economic and educational opportunities drove Juan and Andrea to Carpinteria, where they both worked in the agricultural industry and became legalized citizens when the amnesty law was enacted. Twenty years after Juan and Andrea's arrival in Carpinteria, work, marriage, and three children—Miguelito, eleven years old, Mona, eight years old, and Marcos, three months old—occupy their time. Juan continues to work in a nursery in charge of outdoor plants. Andrea works in a factory making dried flower arrangements. And while Miguelito and Mona have experienced a great deal of academic success, their parents have learned along with them how best to help their children in school.

Andrea feels limited by her lack of formal education and admits to feeling shame when Miguelito asks her why she is always encouraging and urging them to value school when she herself didn't even go to school. "I explain to him that I left school because I couldn't study due to my headaches."

Returning to school is in Andrea's plans, but at present her time seems committed to caring for Juan and the three children and working full-time to help pay for a mortgage, which they encumbered themselves three years ago. Although it sounds as if she feels powerless about her situation, that is not the case. Andrea reads self-help books in Spanish and tries to study English. In fact, it was Andrea's tenacity and ingenious skills with finances, planning, and discipline that enabled the family to save enough money to buy the small, two-bedroom condo where they now live.

Juan credits the stability of the family to Andrea, who spends a great deal of time with the children while he's at night meetings. She also helps her niece in Mexico with money and support to study psychology at the university in Guadalajara and to prepare to become a teacher. Juan also credits Andrea for maintaining the emotional warmth of the family, which was a part of her own family's way of relating to one another. Juan feels that the family has a lot of faith in God and especially appreciated the conversations that took place in Andrea's family, which occurred to a lesser degree in his own. He did remember his mother telling him she loved him. But when Andrea's family gets together, Juan says, "One knows that they speak with their heart."

Andrea revels in the love that she and her children share, but she also feels strongly that sometimes poor parents expect too much of children because they worked hard as children and later want their children to support them. Andrea believes that such expectations create too much pressure for children and may disillusion them from studying in school. She comments, "I want to do it differently from that of my family and many other families. Some parents expect their children to support them when the children start working. I don't want my children to support me when they grow up. I only want them to study and to become well-educated individuals and to devote themselves to a career."

Juan's participation in COPLA inspired in him a new way of thinking, about himself, his family, and community, such that he has committed himself to the mobilization of Latinos. He believes that people must engage in their local settings to improve conditions for education of children and to build a supportive community. He attributes part of his newfound political and social consciousness to a personal search, part of which has been revealed to him in the workplace. He has grown through conflicts in the workplace, and in turn, the workplace has improved as a result of Juan's tenacity.

"I think that one of the things that has helped me to adjust to American culture rapidly has been my questioning about something. And, here in Carpinteria I feel like I don't have to depend on anyone for my worth. Before, I felt like my worth depended on what I had, rather than who I am as a person. I feel validated for who I am and what I want to do. I appreciate the freedom to do what I want without fear. I believe that's what has influenced me the most. I have learned a great deal from Mrs. Rosa Martinez, you know her, and from people in the schools and from my wife's friends."

Juan was grateful for what he had learned from supportive people around him. He also credits many of them for helping him break addictive behavior. As he recalls, "everything I've learned from all of you has helped me to stop drinking and to study and to find more resources for my children. I've spent most of my time at my job, it's true that I've had some difficult times. For example, the supervisor put a lot of pressure on us and didn't want us to communicate with the managers. But I saw a change in the supervisor when I went to school and learned English and then I could communicate with the top boss. Things have changed around the workplace. Even the supervisor seems like a different person. Maybe he understood that he was doing wrong. Also in soccer I think it's been very important for me. I think that is where I have had the most influence. Before, the majority of the adult players drank; now they have stopped drinking. I no longer drink. It's been a while now. Before, I drank, and then I stopped. That got the attention of other friends and acquaintances who also drank. Many of them didn't think that they could stop. A few have stopped and it's made me see how important good models are."

Although soccer has been both a learning and a healing experience, Andrea continues to struggle with Juan because of the time he spends away from home while she's left at home with all of the household responsibility and the family. She's aware that Juan has improved opportunities for their family and others in the community. However, some of his commitment to the community has shaken their personal stability.

Andrea began talking about her feelings of emptiness and being alone, which were magnified when she found herself alone at the hospital delivering her third child. Evidently, she went into labor on Saturday and couldn't find Juan, because he was a part-time gardener on weekends, and she didn't have his phone number. Fortunately, her sister-in-law drove her to the hospital. Andrea had the baby within forty-five minutes, and Juan didn't arrive in time for the birth.[2]

Soccer game, migrant education meeting, COPLA meeting or not, the Ramirez family usually made time for a couple of weeks during the summer to visit their families in Mexico. Their families look forward to Juan and Andrea sitting and talking with their children because they get so much from them. Yes, the material support is always welcome, but more importantly, the family looks to them for guidance and advice. An ongoing issue with the family in Mexico has been the question of Andrea's niece attending the university, when her parents need her to work and contribute to the support of the family. During one summer vacation in Zacualco, Juan talked with his brother-in-law, telling him that the family had to support Chayo, Andrea's niece.

"I told him that the most important thing that he could do was to give to his daughter his confidence. I told him that she wants very badly to develop herself, and even if you can't help her economically, you can help her with moral support. I said to him, to help her, support her, support her. I tell them that they won't regret it. Find a way."

Andrea and Juan both take money down to their families. Usually it's money that Andrea has managed to save during the year. She told some humorous anecdotes about taking clothing down to their families. Andrea has observed the children's involvement and connection to the trip.

"Miguelito and Mona have lots of things they share with their cousins in Mexico. They take toys, clothes, and some school materials, but one of the funny things is that Miguelito, who's eleven, says something like, 'Thanks to God we have so much and we can give some things to my cousins.' Mona, on the other hand, is younger and a bit more resistant to giving. She'll say to me, 'I've already given you lots of things and you're leaving me without any clothes.' I tell her that I'll buy her some more dresses, but she says, 'No don't take these, they're pretty and they're mine. I like them so leave them here.' That's the way she is, but anyway we take plenty to our relatives."

Both Juan and Andrea feel very blessed for the privileges that they have in the United States and feel even more grateful that they can share them with their families and friends in Mexico. Just as they are quick to acknowledge their opportunities to give to others, they are equally grateful to others for what they have received from them. Juan expresses his gratitude to those whom he believes have influenced the changes in his life.

"We have learned a great deal from others in this community, especially since we've become more involved in support organizations with other Latinos like in COPLA. People like you, a researcher, have had confidence in me, and that's worth a great deal. It has opened my consciousness to know that I could do whatever and to know that I needed to remain positive because we all have our own strengths. And that's the way I have continued learning from Mr. Niles. I've stayed open to all people and have become more sensible and a better person. I feel so much stronger."

As president of the Carpinteria School District Migrant Education Parent Committee, Juan held the group to a high level of integrity. His goal was to get people to collaborate with each other on behalf of all children in the school district. His specific advocacy for Spanish-speaking Latino students, who have continued to be overrepresented in the lower academic ranks, was the mission of the group. Juan's commitment to this group was no different from his commitment with any other group; he was totally absorbed. Although he spent a great deal of time away from home at school and community meetings, his top priority was always his children.

When Miguelito was a sixth grader, he waited up for Juan to return home on weeknights to help him with his homework. He was known to wait as late as ten. He prefers to wait for his father, because he's sure that he'll get the answers right. Andrea monitored him so that he doesn't get too tired, but she knows how determined Miguelito can be. While Juan doesn't encourage him to stay up late, he loves coming home to help Miguelito with his homework.

When he was trying to complete his homework in elementary school, Miguelito could not imagine how much fun the payoff would be when he was in high school. After completing three years of French by his junior year, he received a scholarship to travel to Paris, France, for ten days with the French club. Thanks to his mother's encouragement, that same year, Miguelito applied for a scholarship to travel to Washington, D.C., to visit the government offices with the Migrant Program.

As a senior in high school in the fall of 2000, Miguelito took honors English, calculus, and social studies classes as part of his college preparatory curriculum. With his sights on a four-year college, Miguelito received a great deal of academic support from the Upward Bound program. While in high school, many Latino and other students from working class families attend summer academic programs at the University of California, Santa Barbara.

At home in the evening, if the Ramirez children have completed their homework by the time Juan gets home, he enjoys reading a bedtime story to the youngest one, as he once did to the older children. Andrea also reads to the children, but says that her stories are shorter, because even with glasses, she still gets bad headaches when she reads more than a few pages.

Juan and the children have a favorite story about the relationship between a mother and her son, which Juan reads in Spanish. The story tells of a mother who sang to her son and rocked him to sleep from the time he was an infant. As the son grew, regardless of how old he was, she would sing to him and rock him to sleep. When he became an adolescent, she tolerated his loud music, crazy friends, and odd-looking clothes. But when he came home late, she walked into his room and sang to him and rocked him to sleep. The mother continued her devotion for her son even when he left home and married and had his own children. When she became old, her son visited his mother and when his mother could no longer finish the familiar song that she sang to him, he finished it for her. And on the day she died, her son took his mother in his arms and sang to her and rocked her, and then he went home and walked into his little daughter's room, just as his mother had always done with him. And, he took her in his arms and sang the same song he had heard his mother sing throughout his life. He rocked her back and forth, back and forth, just as his mother had always rocked him.

The story spoke to Juan of the continuity of life, of the kindness of family, and of extending the love we receive. He admits that of everything he has learned in his years of community activism, his connection with his children has been the best gift of all. Even though in his own school years he did not appreciate reading very much, as a parent and family advocate with the school, he recognizes the value of family literacy and the importance of sharing time together. The repetition of language in this story conveys rhythm, not only in language, but also in the love and care shared between parents and children.

Gender opportunities and family decisions were often the source of stress for families, especially when the parents felt lacking in the necessary skills to help their children. "I thought we had gone through the worst part when we had to help the kids to do their homework when my husband and I didn't have the academic skills they needed. But now that they're making decisions on their careers it is far more difficult than a stack of homework!" exclaimed Ofelia Torres. Communication between parents and children was unquestionably strong in the Latino households of the active COPLA members. Their children's futures became more concrete as they tailored family conversations around the exploration of plans for college, employment, and even marriage. The Torres family of six, including four children and the parents, Ofelia and Marcos, faced the tensions and joys of their children's decisions for careers. As a family, they had always shared their dreams and hopes with each other. Ofelia made every effort to maintain a strict schedule, which would bring the family together every night for dinner, followed by a homework session where they all sat together at the kitchen table and the living room couch to help each other. Although both parents assisted the children in their work, only Ofelia provided direct assistance, because Marcos could not read the written curriculum. However, both Marcos and Ofelia held the children accountable for completing their work and getting themselves ready for school. Most of the work fell on Ofelia, because she coordinated everything the children needed, including clothes, books, and taking them to medical appointments. Marcos made sure the children got to bed at a reasonable hour and helped them to put together a meal when Ofelia was not home.

From the time the children were in elementary school, both parents listened to their dreams of what they were "going to be" when they graduated from high school. The Torres parents did not impose their choice of profession on their children. Their only wish was for their children to get an adequate education, which would prepare them for a job beyond what they themselves had with limited schooling. Ofelia was pleased about her children's expectations and plans for careers. Marcos, the oldest son, wanted to go to college to study law. Cecilia talked about plans to become a teacher. Mario, the next youngest was interested in art and thought about including it in a career somehow. And Celia, the youngest, who was in middle school at the time this text was written, had begun inquiring about beautician work.

Shortly before Marcos's graduation day, he came home, and before dinner, he asked his mother and father to sit down, because he wanted to talk to them. They sat at the kitchen table, and he announced to them that he was seriously considering going into the Marines after graduation. Apparently, one of Marcos's friends had enlisted in the Marines and had been sent to fight in the front lines during the Persian Gulf War. Marcos believed that he too should enlist and do his part in the service while getting a free education. Mr. and Mrs. Torres expressed their ambivalence to Marcos about his decision. First his father shared his thoughts, and then his mother spoke about her fears for him. "Son, I don't like the idea about your going into the Marines. I thought you had planned to go to college here. Your mother and I worry about you because this is a big decision. At least you are here in college nearby where we know how you are. But if you're so far away and in so much danger, how will we know how you are?"

Marcos responded, "Father, I know that what I want to do is dangerous, but I feel that it's my duty. And in the Marines, I can take classes toward my career. I would like to do something that has to do with government service. I'm not sure what that means or how much training I need, but that field interests me a great deal. My grades aren't strong enough for me to get into a college or university, and this way I can study at the same time."

His mother commented, "Son, I'm very scared by your decision. I don't want you to go, even though we've always given you the freedom to make your own decisions." Tears well in her eyes. "But—oh—it'll be so difficult for everyone, dear."

Marcos tried to comfort his mother, "I know, Mom." He moved his chair next to her and put his arm around her shoulder. "But it's also an opportunity to study. I told the Marine recruiters that you would sign for me to enlist in the Marines."

Neither Marcos senior nor Ofelia wanted to sign the document that night. Marcos admitted not wanting to see his son leave for a faraway land, whether he was sent to fight in the war or just stationed in a faraway state. However, a few days later, they conceded and signed their permission for Marcos to enlist in the Marines for two years, but not before Ofelia dealt with the torment she felt about Marcos's decision. For the days that followed, she talked with her workmates about young men they might know who had enlisted in the armed forces. She was not consoled much by their stories about how much their sons or nephews had matured when they went into the service. More than feeling sorrow over her son's decision, she was emotionally torn because she had always told her children to respect their inner direction and to follow their hearts. Now she did not approve of his leaving home to join the service because it would be dangerous. What if he were sent into the front lines of the war? Ofelia admitted visiting a priest to ask for some advice about allowing Marcos to pursue his intentions.

In spite of his decision, Ofelia felt some reassurance that Marcos had learned decent values having grown up in their family. And she believed that if he was so intent on joining the service to pursue his education, then he must be making the right decision, even if it was hard for her and his father to accept. She also considered that the family couldn't afford to pay for his college education and that Marcos was convinced that he could pursue the profession of his choice while in the Marines.

When Marcos left home to begin his two-year term of service, the family missed him terribly and Marcos senior and Ofelia had a change of heart about his decision. They were proud of him and his achievements in the service. His letters and phone calls to Ofelia and Marcos convinced them that he was happy and benefiting from the educational programs offered by the government, although he did complain about the rigorous routine that woke him up at five o'clock every morning.

The year after Marcos left home, the Torres family faced a different conflict when Cecilia began dating a young man who was a few years older than she, who wanted to marry her. Ofelia and her husband didn't wait for any announcements from Cecilia. Rather, Ofelia anticipated surprises and sat her daughter down to let her know that she supported her in her plans to attend college and prepare to become a teacher. Cecilia was in eleventh grade at the time, and her mother had already admonished her to spend more time on her studies and less with her boyfriend, since her grades, although quite average, were not representative of her ability. In her own defense, Cecilia said that most of her time was spent working at McDonald's, and she felt that it was unfair to restrict her from seeing her boyfriend when he actually supported her. Ofelia decided to have a mother-to-daughter talk; the designated Friday night finally arrived. Cecilia returned from her part-time job at McDonald's, still reeking of onions and French fries. Her mother was dressed for bed. Both sat down at the kitchen table and sipped soft drinks as they talked. When Ofelia talked with Cecilia, she had only reassuring words for her, as she made her expectations known.

"I don't want you to get married right now. I want you to work and earn money and to graduate from high school. Your father and I thought that you wanted to study to be a teacher. That requires you to go to college. Doesn't it?"

"Yes," Cecilia responded. "I know that I need to go to college. But, I have to have some freedom for entertainment."

"We want to do what we can for you, dear," Ofelia said. "It's not that we want to limit you. You need to know that you're very important to us and we don't want you to get married until you have a career for yourself."

Cecilia and Ofelia accomplished what they wanted in their brief conversation on this critical topic, and Cecilia held to her word. She went to college after high school, except that she began at the local community college; she didn't have the funds or the grades to leave home and attend college. After completing her two years at the community college, she deferred college so that she could continue working, with the intent to save money to go to a four-year college.

Although little research exists on family socialization of Latina girls where educational values and support exists, Carpinteria families provide a window into parents' feelings about educating their children according to gender differences. Latinas have long been underrepresented in the educational ranks from early years of schooling to the university graduate level. The Torres's, as did many Latino immigrant families in Carpinteria, expected both their sons and daughters to have a good education. They believed that girls, as well as boys, should have the opportunity to pursue their dreams to the extent they desired.

The Torreses represented one side of Latino family beliefs about gender distinction in their children's education. They wanted all their sons and daughters to continue their education beyond high school. When they first became active in COPLA, some parents believed that boys should have more education, but they changed their minds through their participation in COPLA. Educating "all of our children" was a topic raised from the initial meeting of the organization. The message was explicit—that both sons and daughters deserve their parents' dedicated attention and encourage-ment in advancing their education. Bringing this issue to the forefront in the education of Latino children remains to be fully explored in COPLA and the Carpinteria School District. This dialogue was especially important, since other parents who were not involved in organizations like COPLA believed that their daughters didn't need as much education as their sons. For the most part, though, education was considered the most accessible way to a successful future for all young people.

## Bonding Generations

Educating her daughter was such a high priority for Ramona Ortiz that whenever her daughter found herself in crisis she knew she was not alone. During the years I interacted with Ramona Ortiz's family on nu-merous community projects, their family inspired me in many ways; most amazing were the three generations of women who shared space, a lan-guage, and common conflicts in spite of their children. Here the three women tell about their lives. All three spoke in different interviews, but all talked about one central topic—how literacy affected their lives as Lati-nas compared with those of the other two women in their households. My last conversations with them were held in the family's small home.

### Ramona

"My parents always valued our education, and so we studied as much as we could. As a child in Mexico my parents always wanted us to study, and they supported us with books. We had many literature books in our home. All of my brothers and sisters also loved to read and study. My younger sister is a physicist, my younger brother is a businessman, and my other brother is an attorney. I studied psychology and finished *preparatoria* [the equivalent of community college]."

Ramona cut short her formal schooling in Mexico to join her husband in the United States. Her dream to have her children schooled in the United States almost made up for her having to cut short her own career training in Mexico.

"When I got married in Mexico and immigrated to Lompoc, Frank, my husband, had already been here legally, working for some years. At that time, I believed with all my heart that we were doing it to provide the children we would have with all the opportunities to great eco-nomic and academic success. It didn't take long to realize that every dream had a price."

The price that Ramona speaks of is the disappointment of unfulfilled dreams that she had for her children and for the education she hoped they would receive.

"I was very scared when I first had to go in to the schools because I was unfamiliar with the system and the language. My children usually did very well, but once, when my oldest son, Carlos, was in the fourth grade, he had problems; I went to see what was happening. When I arrived at the school, I felt imprisoned by my fear because no one spoke my language except for the principal and one other teacher whom I didn't know at the time. I asked them both about the problem involving my son, and the principal, who was a woman, did not know anything about my son, or the other boys involved in the incident. It was clear to me that neither the teacher nor the principal cared about these Latino boys. They couldn't give me any details of the problems surrounding my son and the other boys. The principal and teacher really didn't know what the issues were, and this angered me terribly. Not so much because I was taking my time from work without pay to go meet with them, but because they were ignorant about these boys and who they were. And I believe they were ignorant about the situation because the boys were Latino and for no other reason. I think they didn't expect me to ask questions about their complaints. They just seemed so aloof about the boys, yet they complained about them, but had no evidence about any wrong-doing. They didn't realize that they had created a watchdog."

Monitoring her children's education became Ramona's priority, juggling her work while keeping an eye on her children's classrooms. Although her schooling had been stunted, she didn't surrender her confidence, skills, and hope to continue learning.

"After that ridiculous meeting with the teacher and principal they couldn't get rid of me. I showed up unexpectedly and observed in the classrooms, even if I had to leave my job at the nurseries without pay. I made it up cleaning houses on weekends. Then I applied for a teacher assistant (TA) position at the preschool when it became available. That made me one of them, on their turf, looking over their shoulders every day, making sure that I learned everything about teaching, who was good and who wasn't. Soon, all of the Spanish-speaking parents came to me for information about what they should expect from their children, from the teachers, from the principal. That almost became a second full-time job. I was very tired, but it was very gratifying. I felt like I was making a difference to change some things for Latino kids. Still, I wasn't doing the work for other parents, I was just sharing information that I had. I told parents that they had the responsibility to talk with the teachers and that they must visit their children's classrooms to see what's going on in there. They've got to become informed about the teachers who teach their children. That's everyone's right and responsibility. If parents haven't been in their children's classroom to observe what's going on, they have no right to complain."

Not only was Ramona adamant about her own involvement in her children's schooling, but she also held other parents to the same high standards. Even when a parent knows what is happening in her children's classroom, it is not a guarantee that all will be well. However, Ramona learned that staying on top of her children's schools was critical when dealing with problems that arose in their schooling.

"I was already a TA in the schools when Celia began to have problems at school, so in some ways I was closer to the situation because the teachers knew I worked in the schools and kept me informed on a regular basis. Yes, Celia was being defiant, partly because that's her temperament, but also because she got caught up with friends who misguided her. My husband and I assured her that we are here to help her and that she has to trust in us because we loved her. We told her that she has to follow her heart and stop listening to those friends who steer her wrong. We've tried in so many ways to show her and her brothers that we're on their side, but she has had a difficult time believing it and finds herself relying on friends for approval. We've told her that friends are those people who want the best for us and that if someone tells her not to study or wants her to take drugs or do wrong that person is not a friend.

"My husband and I felt like we were losing control of our family during those years when Celia was so rebellious towards us, but pained too, because she was having troubles in school, and for two years between the fourth and sixth grade were heartbreaking to me. It's hard to explain why all of that turmoil was happening for her except that she might have been teasing the boys and other kids also and then they picked on her in a very cruel way because they ganged up on her. We took her to counseling and tried to talk out those things as a family and although I knew that she was feeling hurt by it, I was caught totally unprepared when she took an overdose of Tylenol. First I felt horrible guilt that I hadn't protected her enough, then I was angry that she would do this after all the time we had spent guiding her and how much we loved her. I was shocked that something like this would happen in my family. I felt so stigmatized that I had worked so hard to do as much as possible for our children so that they would succeed in school and for me to get the job in the school, and then she did this. It was such shame for her and for us."

The language Ramona uses to describe her distress with the situation reveals how dramatically different this situation was compared to her expectations of schools. Teasing and taunting from peers can be quite cruel for children, as Celia learned. Ramona and Frank's decision to take Celia to counseling seemed appropriate in light of the emotional stress she endured. They used their resources in the school district to find a counselor.

"A friend in the school district gave us a referral to see a counselor in Santa Barbara. We all went, her brothers and us [her parents]. It was very helpful. The first few times, she and I just cried, but then it was easier to talk about the things that threatened her at school and at home. She said that she felt like we expected too much of her. Funny, I always thought that expecting too little was the error that most parents made. It seemed reasonable to expect the best from someone, especially my children. I studied psychology, but I'm not a psychologist, so I can't pretend to be an expert, but it seems to me that it's other pressures that Celia is reacting to, and they're things that her parents can't protect her from. Maybe what she was saying was that she expected us to protect her from the painful things that were happening to her, but when our involvement didn't help her, she was left to fend for herself. Or is that just my rationalization? I don't know. Celia says that we want her to be too good, but if wanting her to be a good student and to be a loving sister and respectful daughter is expecting too much, then I guess we do expect too much. I don't think I can expect anything less. We give her a lot, not material things, but as a family we love each other a lot and spend lots of time together, singing, reading, and going to the park."

**Rita**

Ramona's mother, Rita, lived in Mexico, but she traveled frequently between Carpinteria and Mexico. She had a close-range look at the family dynamic and had strong feelings about the changes that she witnessed in the Ortiz household. "It never seemed like a good idea to encourage my family to emigrate to the United States. Unfortunately, my two daughters were the ones to leave. My youngest lives in Massachusetts; she married a professor, and she herself is a physicist. I don't see her very often, because her husband has such control over her that she has to account for every minute of her time. He doesn't even like her to speak Spanish, because as he says, 'you're in the U.S. now, so speak English.' I'm not sure what good education does at that point.

"At least Ramona and her family visit me more often. Nevertheless, it's still very difficult to be so far from each other, especially when there is illness and death. My husband died last year, and for the last two years that he was seriously ill, Ramona had to come and go often, trying to help my sons and me to get the best care for their father. It's still difficult for me to be alone and to have Ramona so far away. My sons are wonderful, too, and so are their wives, but one's daughters are so special. When they got married, I knew I had lost part of them, but being in another country has meant lots of heartaches for me. Although I talk to them often, I get to see them so seldom. And sometimes the reasons we see each other are painful reasons."

Distance did not fray Rita's relationship with Ramona and her family. In fact their relationship was close, and while it was important for Rita to maintain the strong family ties, it also meant that she shared her daughter's torment from afar. This grandmother's pain remained etched in her heart as she watched her granddaughter struggle through such difficult emotional turmoil.

"I'll never forget when Celia had to come down to stay with us one summer, after this young beautiful girl who at such a tender age tried to harm herself. Such despair. Oh, I know that her problems were in school. But, that wouldn't happen in Mexico. The rules are clear about the way girls and boys are supposed to behave. Those schools have no limits on their students. They allow children to be so wild. They're afraid of children. They don't know how to teach them good behavior or respect. So children like Celia who come from good respectful homes are side by side with those who are taught to be irresponsible. I'm not saying that Celia does everything right, but teachers need to set limits for all the children not to allow them to harm others like they did with Celia.

"And things got even worse for my dear young Celia when she got pregnant. If schools are supposed to be so superior in the United States, why are so many young girls like Celia getting pregnant? This is a massive cultural sin. To think that these schools cannot keep young ladies interested in studying instead of giving them the license to run around doing what only married people are supposed to do. This is all beyond my comprehension. When her husband brought her down here with the baby, he kept her from seeing us. He and his family were such low-class people who treat women like servants and keep them locked up so they won't see the light of day. As long as they keep the woman pregnant at home, they can run around with others.

"It was so upsetting to think that my lovely Celia was over there held captive by that horrible family. She's an American citizen and that husband of hers wasn't, so he wanted to keep her from her family and make her his servant in his family's house. He tricked her into coming, telling her it was a vacation, and then he wouldn't let her return home. Well, we finally had to get my son, the attorney, to help get her released to go home. I don't know how he was able to talk them into letting her go, but both her and the baby were brought to my house. She was too emotionally tired to talk about it, so I didn't want to upset her any more. I just cooked for her and helped her with the baby until her father came to get her. I would love for them to live there with me, but these kids are American, even if their parents are Mexican. They would never be happy living in Mexico. They belong with their parents and friends."

Rita believed that the difference in cultural values between Mexico and the United States was to blame for the problems that Celia faced.

"In Mexico, we protect young girls. Yes, we let our daughters go out with their friends, but they usually had chaperones, either their brothers or older sister. I know that in this country you people think that's old fashioned, and I'm not saying that everyone in Mexico is chaste. I'm just saying that girls are given stricter limits. Maybe we just know better how men behave."

**Ramona**

Like most mothers, Ramona wished the best for her children. But because her own education and career plans had been cut short in Mexico, her expectations for her children were even greater. "Ever since my children were born, Frank, my husband, and I made sure that they studied and learned all they could. At home, we read to them every night before going to sleep. They loved having us read to them, and we loved it too. It seems like just yesterday that I held them in my arms and sang bedtime rhymes to them in Spanish. Some of the best times we've all enjoyed as a family is reading our favorite storybooks in Spanish. Each of the kids had their favorite stories, and we took turns reading from their books on different nights.

"Frank and I always talked to them about everything they needed to guide them, including Catholic values. We wanted them to trust us, to talk to us about things that bothered them at school or with friends or teachers. Just like my Celia's trip to the hospital when she was still in grade school turned our family inside out, again when she was sixteen and a junior in high school, we had to deal with another major shock— her pregnancy. True we knew she liked this boy, José, a lot. He was a few years older and had graduated from high school, but was not in college; he was working full time. I had noticed that he did not encourage her much in her studies, and of course, she needed little in the way of discouragement."

Both father and mother were watchful of their children's activities, which made Celia's relationship with her boyfriend more suspicious. They tried not to be strict, but as Celia fell behind in her schoolwork, all indications were that she was spending too much time with her boyfriend.

"One evening José came over, and Celia said that they wanted to tell us something. I felt my stomach turn because I sensed that something unpleasant was going to happen. When she told us that she was pregnant and that she wanted to get married, Frank and I looked at each other in disbelief. He, Frank, seemed relieved that they wanted to get married. I was furious because she had already made one mistake, to get pregnant, and now she wanted to get married. Immediately I said, 'You don't have to get married, Celia.' She lowered her head, and José said, 'But we want to be together.' I reminded her that she needed our permission because she was a minor. She said, 'I know, that's why we're telling you because we need your permission even if he's of age.' José tried to encourage us by telling us that he had a job and could support them. All I could think of was her schooling. I asked her, 'How do you plan to finish school?' 'I don't know.' she answered. I was just as angry at her father who seemed to be so complaisant. I knew I was taking on quite a bit, but I just didn't have the heart to let her go off and live with this strange boy and raise a child. So I told them that I wanted them to stay with us until the baby was born so I could make sure that she was getting the proper care. That was a real trick because we were in that tiny little trailer, so we bought a toolshed and set it up next to the trailer. They stayed in the toolshed. They paid all of their expenses, because they were married, but I was able to keep an eye on them."

Ramona's dreams of having her daughter graduate from high school and go to college were shattered when Celia became pregnant, not only because of the interruption in her schooling, but because she would now be a parent to a child when she herself was still a young girl. Ramona reflects about the way that the situation was temporarily relieved and how she grew to love the baby.

"Fortunately, just before the baby was born, Frank and I were able to buy this little house, finally, after so many years of living in that trailer and saving as much as we could with four or five jobs between Frank and me. Now we still have to work just as hard to make the house payments, insurance, and every repair that this old house needs.

"When the baby was born, I began to let go of some of my anger towards Celia. I even felt sorry for her, going through the pain of childbirth and still a child herself. And, I became a grandmother; I couldn't have been happier. I helped deliver my tiny little grandson, Anthony; he was the most beautiful child I ever saw. He helped me to see how easy forgiveness was with the love of a child. Anyway, after Anthony was born, they continued living with us in this tiny little house, and I watched Celia get more and more tired taking care of her husband and her son. At nights I heard her get up every time the baby cried and when the husband coughed ever so slightly, he would ask her to get up to get him a glass of water. The child was worn out. I couldn't interfere in their marriage, but I did try to help her with the baby and teach her how to do things so it wouldn't require as much work. Of course, I worked in the schools during the day, so I couldn't take care of the housework for everyone, which fell on her."

While Celia took care of her family, Ramona tried to take care of Celia, but the situation took a different twist when José announced his plans to visit his family in Mexico. Ramona talks about this period as the worst time of the entire ordeal.

"After the baby was about three months old, José said that his parents in Mexico wanted to meet his family and that the three of them were going down to visit. This seemed reasonable, although I knew I'd miss that little bundle. I had grown so attached to him; we all had. Then one day I received a call from Celia, from Mexico. She was crying, telling me that she was tired of being there, because his family was mistreating her and calling her names since she had gotten pregnant before she got married. Then she said that José was refusing to make return reservations, saying that he didn't want them to return. This call made all the past problems with her feel like a snap. A cold empty chill took over my body, then I began to cry. How could she do this to me, marry that awful boy then go down there to be with his family? Couldn't she see that he didn't want to raise the baby in the United States? I was out of my mind; I didn't know what to do. Here at home by myself I began to pray. I called my husband, Frank, in his office, and he told me that he'd be through with work soon and come right home.

"It took us several calls to Mexico to get through to José's family. We spoke with the parents, then with José, and they all blamed Celia, claimed that she was hysterical and didn't know how to care for the baby. Of course we didn't believe it. We knew they thought that they could convince us that they were the ones who could take care of the baby. So I called my brother who is an attorney in Mexico. He, of course, was very busy with his own work, but agreed to visit José's family."

Feeling powerless, Ramona kept busy to keep from worrying about Celia and the baby at José's house in Mexico. "I had to work and to a point, it was best that I go to work because I could stop worrying. But the minute I stopped working, the worrying began. Nightly I called my mother or my brother to see if they had been able to negotiate anything, but days passed before I got any news. My brother finally said that he had been able to negotiate with the family to release Celia and the baby to come with me, because José did not want to come back to the United States. Part of me felt relieved, but we were raised to stay married, and so when I could talk with Celia I tried to convince her to work out things with her husband, maybe go to counseling after they returned home. She was convinced that he wanted no part of returning to the United States and that if I left, then that would be the end of it all. I told her to come back, and that maybe once he was home they could mend their relationship."

Back in Carpinteria, Celia tried to recover, but according to Ramona, just having her baby wouldn't be enough. "Well it wasn't that easy because she felt very depressed about their separation. She wanted to be married, not single, of course. She wanted her whole family. The boy, José, came up to visit her and the baby, but she was afraid to be with him or to let him see the baby unsupervised. We helped her talk to an attorney to see what their rights were. The attorney told us that we had to let the father see the child, but we could be present while he visited with the baby. During that visit Celia and he agreed to get a divorce. He wanted to live in Mexico, but wanted to visit the baby whenever he came to the U.S. Celia agreed to it, but not without pain. She became depressed after his visit, I guess it was the loss of the short marriage, so I tried to help her focus back on caring for the baby and getting back to school."

The high school had a special program to help girls who got pregnant to complete their coursework and graduate. But this wouldn't have been possible without a great deal of support from Ramona.

"Fortunately, she had been wanting to return to high school and get her diploma in adult school. Finally, it seemed that I would see my little girl finish high school. Maybe there was still a possibility to see my kids get the education I so much wanted them to have. Of course, that meant that I had to take on more responsibility for the baby. So I cut back my hours at the school where I worked. This allowed me to stay with the baby while she was at school. To make up the money I was losing from the cutback, I took on more work with Shaklee sales. That helped a bit because we sure needed the money with the loss of José's paycheck. I would have done anything to make sure that Celia finished high school. Now it seemed that I kept a tighter watch on my youngest son, Eric. He was my last hope to see my dream of having my children finish high school and go on to college and get a successful career."

The problems Ramona encountered in trying to help Celia define her direction in life just kept getting more involved. She describes how disciplined Celia was in doing what she needed to complete high school, but her decisions regarding a career caused more stress for Ramona. "Not only did Celia finish high school within six months, but then she announced plans to get her college schooling through the army. What can I say? Would this child ever do anything easy? Every turn she took was hard and complicated. She claimed that way she could get a free education, but what would she do with her child? Oh God! There's no way she can take care of the baby while she's stationed in some other state, working and going to school. But Frank thinks that she needs to be more reasonable and think of the child too, maybe by going to college here locally. There are a few good colleges around here, and she can work to pay for her expenses. Leaving her child and going off to the army is a foolish idea according to him. He thinks I do too much for Celia and the boys. Maybe he's right, but what am I supposed to do? I have trained them to do a lot for themselves and to be independent where their eating needs are concerned and also to manage their time so that they do their homework or housework when I'm not here, and that takes a lot of time and work. They are good kids, and I'm trying to hold it together for the family. I've had my opportunity as a young person, but now it's their turn and they should have all the support possible within our means and what we can afford doing for them. You know that doesn't mean that I've stopped studying. Before Celia's baby came along I was finishing my teacher assistant certificate in the community college. At some point I'll finish my credential to become a teacher. But right now it's the kids; I want to ensure that they do well and get their lives on track so that they create more opportunities for themselves. I know it sounds as though I'm just complaining about Celia's choices. That's not really how I feel about her. I love her more than anything, she's my daughter. I'm actually very proud of her for being so young and having such courage to endure all of the difficult times she's had. Probably the thing that I'm most proud about Celia is that she has tried to be responsible for her actions."

## Celia

Throughout her troubled years Celia spoke candidly about the twists and turns in her life. She talked to me about her early experience in Carpinteria schools and how she responded to the alienation that she felt. "In the early years of being in the bilingual classes, I was a good student. I didn't hate school until I got to the fourth grade. Kids began to make fun of me, and I didn't know what to do. My mother tried to help me and so did the teacher, but it just got worse and worse. The boys especially were mean. They called me names in class and on the playground. Pretty soon, I couldn't concentrate on my studies either at school or at home. Then one day when no one was home, I took lots of pills—Tylenol. My older brother found me and called my mother at school where she worked. She came and called an ambulance because I didn't respond. My mother called the doctor, and she forced me to start walking and to drink lots of milk. But I still wasn't very awake, so she rushed me to the hospital and pumped my stomach. I didn't know what was happening, I just felt like my stomach was going to explode and couldn't move. I don't even know why I did it accept that I was tired of all the stupid kids in school and my mother was tired of going to the school to talk to the teacher and I felt bad that she was always upset at me and at the school. I used to think about dropping out of school, but I couldn't do it until I was sixteen and that was too far away. I just wanted to stop it all. And a friend told me that she had taken lots of Tylenol to try and stop her pain, so I that's what I did. She didn't tell me how much or anything like that, but I did think I would end my pain and my mother's and everybody's. I just hated everything."

Celia returned back to school, and for a while things quieted down. Reflecting about her confusion clarified how important it was to have the support of her family, especially when she felt lost. "When I went back to school, it was all right for a while. The kids left me alone, then the school year was over. But I still hated school. My mother sent me to my grandparents' in Mexico that summer; that was fine. My uncles and cousins were very nice to me, and they took me lots of places. I wanted to come home, but I still didn't want to return to school. But with my parents there was no way out of it. To them, school is everything, and I better be getting good grades and staying out of trouble, otherwise, they show up there at the classroom door as fast as they can. Don't get me wrong, I'm glad that they care about me and my brothers, because I see lots of kids at school where their parents don't care about them or whether they stay in school or not. I just didn't want to cause any problem for them. For sure I was confused; I didn't fit in anywhere. Even my friends didn't really feel like friends. I was very unhappy. My mother and father really did try to do a lot for us; they did so much for me and my brothers especially because I know that they don't have a lot of money.

"Even when things were OK in school and they liked my friends, Mom never wanted to see me stay home by myself. Or if she knew I was alone, she'd be calling every five minutes to make sure I was OK. Now that I have my own son I can understand what she was trying to do, but it bothered me a lot at that time."

In retrospect, having her own child contributed to Celia's understanding of how parents feel protective of their children. Although she's not remorseful about getting pregnant, she realizes the pain it caused her parents. "It came as quite a shock to both of my parents, especially to Mom, who really tried to protect me when I got pregnant. I don't think she'll ever get over that disappointment. But at the time, my boyfriend, José, was the first thing that made me feel good in a long time. And I just let things get out of hand. Yes, I did want to go against my parents because I felt like they were trying to suffocate me. Now, I realize that they just wanted me to have self-respect and to get a good education. I know what I did hurt them and that it wasn't the right thing to do, maybe I could have waited, but I didn't mean to hurt them.

"José and I thought that if we got married we could fix what we had done wrong and that way my parents wouldn't be so hard on me. I never thought that having a baby and getting married would be so much hard work. Before that, I only had to help my mother get dinner for our family, but now as a mom and wife, I had to think of three people all the time, to feed, to wash, to take care of all the time. I was tired. I'm still tired, but since it's just the baby and me, I don't have to take care of him. I thought I loved him before when we were first going out; he took care of me and we went out and had a good time, but after the baby was born, everything changed. I had to do everything. He just got to play with the baby when he got home from work. The rest of the time, I had to take care of him, and the baby. Then when we moved here to this house, I didn't see any of my friends, because they lived far away. I felt so bad for my parents who were working hard to help us that I didn't have the nerve to complain."

Celia believed that going to Mexico would be as wonderful as her past visits had been when she stayed with her grandmother. But she couldn't predict the events that would unfold once she and José arrived in Mexico with the baby. She got to experience firsthand the complexity of cultural values about women, children, and marriage.

Celia recalls, "When we went to Mexico with the baby, I was really expecting something different. I used to love going to Mexico when we went to visit my grandparents. That was always a lot of fun. We played with my cousins, and we had parties at their houses. In fact, my *quinceñera* [fifteenth birthday] was so much fun. I think Mom showed you the video, which Dad took. Well it was everything but a party at José's family. At first they were nice to the baby and me, but then José began to change. He wouldn't let me out of the house. He said women weren't supposed to go out, that taking care of their babies was all they were supposed to do. But he didn't even take me out either. So, I was just stuck in the house with his mother who criticized everything I did and said that I was a spoiled American girl; she said she would change all of that. It all sounded stupid, so I didn't keep quiet, I told them what I thought of them too. That made them angry, and they started telling me that I'd never see my family again, that I was there to learn how to be a real mother. I felt like I was being held hostage. All three of us were in one room in the back of this farmhouse that was way out of town. Most of the time I was in that room crying alongside my baby. I didn't know how I was going to call my mother or even my grandmother, so I used the excuse that the baby had the right to know my other grandmother, too, and that I had to visit her, too, because I didn't feel well. José bought the story and took me to my grandmother's. I sneaked into the living room when everyone was eating, and I called my mother. Grandma didn't know anything, and I couldn't tell her with José there.

"Mom got into action, only I didn't know what was going to happen until it happened. My uncle went to the farm to talk to those dumb people. They pretended that there was no problem. But I told him right there in front of them that the baby and I needed to leave with him because I was afraid of them. My uncle convinced them that they had to release the baby and me to go stay with my grandmother. I think I remember that he said that the baby and I were American citizens, that if I complained that they were treating me cruel or refusing to allow me to return to the U.S. that they could be in lot of trouble. At that point, José said that if I left he never wanted to see me again. I didn't care. I just wanted to be safe with my baby."

Getting freed from the clutches of José and his family was all that Celia wished for; the rest would have to be resolved later. She tells of the departure, "The baby and I went with my uncle. I cried most of the way to grandma's house. It felt like my world was falling apart again. I had screwed up so many times before, and here I was again trying to get out of another mess. But I had a child now that I had to protect, so I had to find the answer. I don't even remember how many days I spent at Grandma's, and although I loved her and she was very caring to me and the baby, I couldn't wait to get back to my home."

Back in Carpinteria, Celia once again needed the help of her mother to put things in perspective. "When I arrived home, I made all kinds of promises to myself and my mother that I was going to work hard to support my son. But then I got very sad and felt awful that I couldn't have my husband with me—that he didn't want to be with us. Sure, I knew that he wanted to live in Mexico. He had changed his mind since we first got together.

"Mom helped me to get my head back in order. She talked to me about getting back in school. I wanted to do that, too. I was ready to finish now. I had less than a year to complete, and I could do it in night school. Except for taking care of the baby at the same time, I actually enjoyed getting back to studying. It was still hard because my sleep was interrupted a lot and I had lots more home responsibilities."

Celia decided to do what many girls don't do after having a baby, return to finish high school. Much of her decision to continue was credited to her mother's support on all levels—emotional, psychological, and with child care. Celia began a new phase of her education when she went back to complete high school. "One of the best parts of returning to night school was reconnecting with some of my friends and making new ones. These were girls who had difficulties at home, too, even if they didn't have children, so we talked and listened to each other. I didn't have time to go out much because my family helped me with child care while I was in school, but I couldn't ask them to do it if I went out to have a good time.

"I finally finished high school. My plans were to go into nursing or medicine. My dilemma was leaving my baby to go into the army to study because they would pay all of my education and I'd also get a salary. I didn't know what to do. My mother helped me to think about what I should do as a mother, since it would be hard to take the baby to another state and have to find sitters and help. Besides I think Mom has become so attached to little Anthony. I want so much to get a good education, and if I stay home and work and go to school, it just seems impossible to ever earn enough money to go to finish college. But on the other hand, it seems like the most reasonable thing to do because my parents have been so helpful to me and I do need my family near me. Even my brothers have helped to baby-sit a lot when I need to study. I have a while before I have to decide since applications aren't due until the winter and school begins next fall. Anyway I'm really looking forward to it and getting on with my career." With a gleam of resolve in her eye, Celia smiled as she finished her comments.

By fall 2000, Celia had dropped out of the community college nursing program to enroll in a trade school, majoring in computer and business management. Her decision to change career plans was influenced as she tells, "My father began a small copying and computer repair business and is doing quite well. His business is growing, and I can help him in his two offices until I finish my courses and get my degree. After that, I'll find a job that pays more because I have my son to raise. For now living with my parents helps us to make it financially. And my son is so close to all my family now that I don't know what would happen if we moved out. Everyone helps with child care and once my son starts school next year, he'll get lots of help from my mother, since she's still a teacher assistant."

Although Ramona felt disappointed about Celia's pregnancy, the baby became a source of joy which led to forgiveness. Ramona made the emotional transition, which made it possible for her to give unconditional support to Celia and her new family. Ramona was spared having to raise Celia's child, at least for the time being. Celia's decision to attend the local community college, which provided low-cost child care for students, allowed Ramona to return to work full time and hold on to her dreams of one day completing her own schooling and becoming a teacher.

Adolescent pregnancies often deter young girls from completing their education. Sometimes girls do not have the support from their parents or the community that would help them go back to school to complete their education. However, in this household, Ramona held constant the parameters that steered her daughter back in the direction of school. Ramona's expectation for her children was relentless where education is concerned. In spite of Celia's choice to become a wife and mother before graduating from high school, her choice to return to school and continue her education was largely influenced by her mother.

Despite the generational differences that divide these three women, a strong bond beyond age and place of residence unites them. They turn to each other for support and guidance. In the three generations of Ramona's family, education played a central role in getting what they wanted, whether it was a comfortable place to live or preparation for a career, both in Mexico and the United States.

A collective effort undertaken by Latino families in Carpinteria on a family level as well as a community level, as in COPLA, made it safe for them to reach out to others beyond their limitations and to discover new resources. They built on their faith and caring to expand their potential. Together they identified resources for their children and their families and inevitably discovered a deeper sense of personal strength.

That people change when they immigrate to a new society goes without saying. Cultural change is inevitable, and immigrant families adapt to a new society to the extent that their local communities recognize their social and economic potential. Latino families have had more support in their dealings with social institutions, including the school, than did Chicanos who lived in Carpinteria when the schools and the community were more segregated. Although personal change occurs as a part of life, cultural shifts take longer, but through collective effort with those who share a common history and experience, cultural beliefs and values can change. COPLA provided a safety net for learning new practices in households, workplaces, and the community, empowering Latino families in the process. The organization has been an important context for growing, through criticism and conversation. Antonia Suarez explained, "Participating in COPLA has helped me not only to better understand how the school functions and to help my children, but COPLA has helped me to have more confidence in myself."

Like many Spanish-speaking Latinos, Antonia expanded along with COPLA. When she first became involved with the organization, she felt shy about speaking up at meetings. Although her attendance was consistent, she remained quiet. However, she was not inactive in her associations with others, including her neighbors and her family. Antonia talked with parents of students in her children's classes. Her reaching out to them kept her busy teaching them everything she learned at meetings. Other parents were not her only objective—her own family, too, benefited from her knowledge of the educational process. She began communicating with her children more directly and honestly, which compelled her daughter and son to trust her and seek her out for guidance. At the end of every COPLA meeting, parents, one-by-one, commented about the meeting. Antonia appreciated how strong her family communication was becoming because of what she learned at COPLA. She was convinced particularly that her strength in working through problems with her family also helped other families in the community who came to her for guidance and advice about their children and their education. Antonia acknowledged the value that she gained by being a part of a group like COPLA. Her communication skills were enhanced to the point that five years after first getting involved in the COPLA leadership, she became the president.

Rodrigo Reyes, activist, also felt that the communication skills had been enhanced in his household as a result of his involvement with the Latino parent organization. Sitting in his living room, Rodrigo pointed to his children's photos on the bookshelf, as I walked around the room looking at the family photos. Smiling with pride, he talked about his sons and daughter, all of whom were in the intermediate grades. Rodrigo felt especially proud that his children were receiving the education that he and his wife didn't get. Among the benefits he claimed of participating in COPLA was the communication between him and his children. Rodrigo spoke of the invaluable lessons he learned as an activist, "My participation in COPLA has taught me to value the opinions of others. I accept criticism as something positive, and sometimes it helps me move forward. Now, I appreciate and listen to everyone because I believe that they have something good to teach me. In COPLA I have learned a great deal from other parents on ways to motivate my children to stay in school. Additionally, I have learned to communicate with my children in a more effective way. I also have much better communication with my children's school when they have problems."

Rodrigo's assessment of what COPLA has accomplished confirms the protean development in his personal life and that of his family that permits him to impart his knowledge to and affection for his coworkers and other families. "In COPLA, I have learned to develop goals. I have learned that I don't need to feel like a victim. I know that even if we have difficult goals to achieve they have given me more confidence to be able to reach them with my effort. I feel happy to participate in this organization and hope that I have something to share with other parents. I have become aware of the importance of sharing my conflicts with other parents and teachers. I have also noticed that the majority of us have similar conflicts and that we struggle with the same objective—to provide our children with a good education."

His worldview changed to encompass a more promising vision and positive approach to working with other families for accomplishing mutual ends. Rodrigo explained, "Another thing I have liked about COPLA is the optimistic way we have launched our various tasks. Actually, for me it has been very important to be in this organization. I have changed a great deal in the relationships with my family, with my community, and with my children's school. Another of my changes has had to do with the way that I see things more objectively. Now I look for the best in each person instead of looking for defects."

Steadfastly, Latino parents confronted distress in their households and workplaces, but they adapted wholly to the strident changes, learned to think differently about themselves and others, and overcame hardships. People's belief system is the foundation of their transformation. Families transcend the adversity in their daily lives by uniting with supportive social networks.

Sometimes we hurt, and other times we triumph. Families in Carpinteria changed their isolation by thinking differently, thus empowering themselves. Thinking differently about ourselves and creating the needed changes in our family systems requires an inner strength that sometimes only comes through action.

# CHAPTER SIX

∽

# Knowledge as Power

Seven-year-old Monica tugged on her father's arm. "Papi, you said you would read me my favorite book tonight."

Standing in the living room, he smiled at her. "You got me. Where is this favorite book of yours?"

"Here, it's this one."

"Let's sit down on the couch so we're both comfortable."

Mom called to the two older boys who sat watching television. "Boys, turn off the TV and get ready for bed."

"Papi, don't forget to show me the pictures when you read the story."

"OK!" Holding the book, he began reading *The Pink Elephants* in Spanish. Monica's father read the story of the elephants that liberated themselves, and he showed the illustrations, one page at a time.

At this home, Monica and her father shared a story time that evening while the older boys read their own books in their rooms, like they did every other night since storytelling had become a regular event. On oc-casional Sundays, the entire family got together to hear the parents tell stories about growing up in Mexico. After several observations in this household, I brought in the video recorder. The family was comfortable performing their storytelling.

Storytelling at home is often thought to be one of the most edifying events involving children and parents. The most important people in children's lives are their parents and teachers, although these authorities sometimes find themselves at odds about what's best for children. But storytelling at home is one activity that teachers and parents believe is critically important to the language and literacy development of children.

Enthusiasm for parent involvement in schooling appears to be more widespread among Carpinteria's primary grade teachers, kindergarten, first, second, and third, although the upper grade teachers mentioned various ways they involved parents in their classrooms.[1] Overall, the underlying theme that prevailed among COPLA parents focused on the home–school relations. Communication was considered very important, but the consensus was that some changes were necessary in order to create "ideal" parent and teacher relationships.

## School Talk

Teachers and parents have traditionally communicated through well-established events like back-to-school nights and parent-teacher conferences. Both bilingual and nonbilingual teachers agreed that home–school communication was important in some way. Without initially providing parents with a connection to the school, it would be very difficult to maintain communication. Many teachers said that holding parent-teacher conferences and doing back to school nights were their most successful efforts to communicate with parents. As a teacher, Javier Torres had a great deal of experience with students who were much like he was when he was a young student in the Carpinteria schools. "I'm a little bit unorthodox; maybe it is the right word in the way I communicate with them. I grew up like them. I was a Spanish-speaking child, and I can identify with them. I think of the process or the adventure they are going to embark on. So, I tell them that the school district does not see them as individuals. It sees them as a collective group. If they want to make the system work for them, then they have to be better. They have to make more of an effort, they have to make the district stand up and notice, they have to be exemplary, the parents have to put a little bit more time with their kids, they have to read to them, they have to always be there for their kids. I tell them that in any school system there are good teachers, excellent teachers, mediocre teachers, there are bad teachers. All children are going to have all these teachers, but they always have their parents. During the good years, when you have a good teacher with whom you can communicate very well, take advantage of it and get into the classroom as much as possible and really make it a good year for them and for your children. And in the years when they have those teachers that are mediocre, or that do not care as much, or are just plain bad, then they have to carry the ball. And there will always be those times because that's the way schools operate."

According to Javier, teachers are important cultural brokers to students who speak other languages. He explained, "I strongly believe that some of the teachers of the language students, have got to come from the culture, they have to be Mexican American teachers who bridge the English-speaking world and the Spanish-speaking world. That's not to say that we should not have Anglo teachers that work with these children. They need to have those models too. But I think that those of us who have come from the community are powerful examples for them that they can succeed in the system, because we have succeeded in this system. If the children or their parents don't see that there is a place where they can see their culture, then they are going to grow up in the dark, and it is going to be a kind of blind walk through the school system. If they see that this teacher is there and that he lives in a decent house and makes pretty good money, is content with his life, is integrated in the system, is successful, then there is light at the end of the tunnel, the model is there."

More conventional teachers were quick to point out that mandatory events like back to school nights and parent-teacher conferences, were ways to establish some kind of relationship if the parents attended. Next to meeting personally with parents, teachers noted specific activities that they used to communicate with parents. Most often teachers sent home weekly letters or individual notes on each student, while phone calls usually meant negative reports of student behavior. If parents are illiterate or do not have phones, this activity would serve little purpose. More creative methods of contacting these parents would then become necessary. Assigning homework that must involve the parents or other members of the family was an activity mentioned by both bilingual and non-bilingual teachers. Parents' volunteering in class was most popular with nonbilingual teachers.

Teachers expressed their concern for what kind of time parents spent with their children at home. Many teachers, especially those who had taught for longer periods of time, believed that parents did not work at home with their children to the extent needed.[2] The lack of parenting skills or the lack of time to spend with their children was described as a problem. Those teachers believed that parents should be clothing, feeding, bathing, talking to, and providing necessities for their children. Many children come to school hungry, dirty, and ill. "They come from places that could not be defined as homes and arrive at school very unprepared to learn or behave properly," said Brenda Stone, a teacher.

In recent years, teachers in Carpinteria have become more vocal about their belief that parents, in general, have relinquished much of their parenting to the school. In fact, some teachers felt indignant about this. Teachers expected parents to provide children with basic needs such as food, health care, emotional and psychological support, and academic preparation.[3] Along with having parents supply children's physical needs, teachers also expected parents to support children in their homework and acquire primary literacy skills prior to entering school. By defining parent expectations, they limited their role as teachers to imparting information.[4]

Demarcating school and family roles suggested a curriculum that separated the home from school interests. In interviews conducted with forty-five bilingual and nonbilingual teachers in the primary grades kindergarten to sixth, 98 percent indicated that parent involvement was, in their terms, "very important, vital, critical, most important, crucial, and a strong need in the curriculum."

Teachers commented that communication between parent and teachers is most active in the earlier years. Kindergarten teacher Elisa Vaca, a bilingual teacher who works with Latino parents, believes in extensive contact between teachers and parents. "Weekly letters, phone calls, positive notes home, eighteen parent volunteers in the classroom, and help from parents at home are some of the ways I establish and keep home school relationships. Parents also have my telephone number and they know they can call me until 8:30 in the evening. There is almost 100 percent participation at back-to-school night, and at that time I make a big deal about helping, and much positive reinforcement is given to the parents."

Good home–school communication makes the job easier for the teacher. If parents work closely with teachers, they will know the teacher's expectations, and the students will know that the parents and teachers are working together with consistency.

## Respecting Cultural Practices

Teachers and parents sometimes feared each other. Still they reached out to each other in ways they knew best. Culture is the bedrock upon which the classroom curriculum is based, and as such, it is the most critical aspect of family-school relationships. Just as Brenda Stone incorporated parents' diverse talents in her classroom, she also organized her teaching to reflect cultural diversity. "It is very important to incorporate the home culture in the curriculum so that parents and students feel good about who they are, where they come form, where their fellow students come from, and about the language they speak. We use star of the day and star of the week students, spotlighting books, songs, poems, and artwork from other cultures. We do the back-to-back program with two nonbilingual kindergarten teachers, so the children are integrated and exposed to different types of cultures. We also openly talk about issues that are happening at home, both the positive and negative ones. Respect for all cultures is a general theme in all areas of learning. If children learn to see the good in all people, they will most likely see it in themselves."

COPLA meetings, particularly at Marina School, which included preschool through second grade, brought together teachers and parents so that they could learn about each other. Many meetings have been held over the past six years of COPLA activism. Teachers and parents at Marina School have gathered to talk with each other about children's education. Early years of schooling have long had the attention of researchers because parents tend to participate more actively in their children's schooling during those years. Marina School's bilingual program, from kindergarten to second grade, has enjoyed years of Latino parent participation through the efforts of COPLA. Bilingual teachers who desired to work closely with parents initiated teacher-parent meetings. They were held in the respective classrooms, where teachers presented the class literacy curriculum to the parents. Parents interacted actively with each other and the teachers, as together they attempted to learn to resolve homework problems, which could result from miscommunication between the teacher and the students or from a lack of knowledge about the classroom curriculum.

In one teacher-parent meeting, Dana Jeffrey met with the parents of her bilingual class. It was a Thursday evening, and about thirty parents attended. The teacher read the book, *Salvador y Señor Sam* to the parents. She posed questions to them as she read the story to demonstrate question-asking strategies. After reading the story, she opened discussion about the story and invited the parents to raise any personal concerns they had. Parents critiqued the book and asked where they could find more books in Spanish to read with their children.

Elias expressed his appreciation for the meeting and for the information presented. He asked Ms. Jeffrey to explain why homework was difficult for some students like his son, Pablo, who was a very good student. Pablo's grades had been high in math, but he required more help in his literacy skills.

"I have a problem with my son, Pablo, who doesn't want to do his homework on reading."

"What problems do you have with Pablo, Mr. Muñoz?" the teacher asked.

He explained, "Well, every night when he should be doing his homework, he doesn't want to do it and then I get very strict and he begins to tremble. Then, I feel terrible because he, like he's afraid."

"It's possible that Pablo may not feel confident about his reading. Although he is a good student, he doesn't have a great deal of confidence in himself where that subject is concerned. And if you're very strict with him, he may feel anxious."

"Yes, it is possible that I'm overly strict with him because I too am anxious about reading. Math is not as difficult for me because I always liked the subject and I could compute, but where reading was concerned, I didn't excel."

"Pablo is also a good student in mathematics, and now I know why he's so disciplined in that subject. It's because you enjoy it and you can help him advance in that subject."

"You're right, Ms. Jeffrey. Maybe I'll just wait for him to ask for assistance rather than to insist that he read to me."

The exchange between Ms. Jeffrey and Elias Muñoz about Pablo encouraged further conversation among the parents. A lively discussion followed, in which so many parents chimed in that Ms. Jeffrey couldn't respond to them all individually. Parents' remarks seemed to affirm their interest in working with the teachers and acknowledged their need to meet and talk about ways to support their children.

Elias Muñoz said, "For me, the important thing is that this group of parents has always wanted good discipline for our children so they don't learn bad habits or vices. I've learned to communicate with my sons. I always ask to see their homework. I help them in whatever way I can, and I'm glad whenever I can help. In these meetings with you teachers and with the other parents I can express my ideas, and in the variety of themes presented here, I feel very supported."

Ruth Calavera said, "The most important thing is to learn the strategies to help our children in their studies. That way parents and teachers can agree with what is taught to our children. I would say that when we work together, the children have more support."

Mr. Sanchez added, "Our daughters have demonstrated some wonderful work in their studies ever since their mother and I have become more active in their schoolwork. Now they want to read, write, and do their math, which before they didn't even want us to help them. Now they seem to have more discipline because they know that we assist them by coming to these meetings to learn a great deal with their teachers."

Mr. Muñoz agreed. "My wife and I have learned how to keep our son's mind occupied. That way he stays focused in his schooling. In our meetings with you, Ms. Jeffrey, I've learned how to love and discipline my daughter when it's necessary. Apparently this balance seems important, because she continues excelling in her studies."

Sofia Aguilar also noted, "I appreciate that these meetings with you, the teacher, have helped me reclaim my rights as a mother of a child in this class."

If power is a neutral force exercised positively or negatively, this group knew how to share it and use it positively to influence others. Finding the core of power is not easy under stressful situations. But neither is isolation and feeling powerless. In an unfriendly or unfamiliar milieu, we're apt to forget our strengths. Parents new to COPLA often attended meetings expecting the leadership to solve their problems. One such case occurred where a parent told the COPLA leaders that they should investigate her son's teacher. According to this person, the teacher had allowed another child to hit her son in class. Christina Meza first reassured the parent that she was not alone in her frustration, then questioned her about the nature of the complaint. After hearing the parent's complaint, Mrs. Meza asked her, "Have you talked with your son's teacher about the complaints?"

"I've never done that—I don't know how to do that," responded the parent.

"That's the part that we can help you learn to do," said Mrs. Meza.

They instructed her to call the school and make an appointment, then get someone to go with her to talk with the teacher. Here the leadership took great care to first, understand the parent's needs, second, extend a caring hand to the parent, and third provide the appropriate direction for her to follow. The instructions to the parent in the meeting also served others who had expressed similar problems. One of the COPLA goals—"to teach each other"—was accomplished.

After the meeting, Mrs. Meza offered to accompany the parent who had the complaint to the school. Her presence was important, because the new parent learned the questions to ask at a teacher-parent meeting. They discovered that no one had been hitting the woman's son. Actually, the young boy was the one who had been creating quite a bit of upheaval in class. Both the parent and the teacher realized the importance of meeting face-to-face, not only to resolve the child's negative behavior, but to build stronger ongoing academic support for the student. At a later time, this particular parent extended the same support to other new parents. COPLA prided itself on not jumping to retaliate against school personnel before considering all sides. This alone set them apart from some of the other communities with which I've been involved.

Respecting cultural practices helps parents and teachers reach an understanding about communicating. While parents and teachers agree that they need to communicate with each other, both sides claim their share of limitations in their work—together and apart. Many Latino parents have learned to communicate with their children's teachers; many more parents, however, have yet to be drawn into the school consciousness. The reverse also appears to be the case where parents want teachers to learn about the home culture so that they respect their children. They also want the school curriculum to reflect their home culture. Teachers look to the administration to support their efforts to build the skills they need to expand their classroom curriculums through release time, use of community liaisons, and other means to support home-school connectedness. The Carpinteria School District administration has evolved in terms of the way it deals with the Latino community.

Transformations in families, schools, community, and individuals have been evidenced in numerous ways. Family members reported that parent-child interactions in all households had been enhanced. They were able to build collective family dialogue about common issues. Parent-child communication evolved in ways that improved their attitudes toward the school and toward relationships outside the home. The family unit was also supported through the family literacy activities in Morton School.

Schools in Carpinteria were transformed by establishing effective school-family communication. Another effort was put into the implementation of effective classroom curriculum, addressing cross-cultural diversity. But the parents' participation transformed the schools most strongly by establishing a gifted and talented program for Spanish-speaking students. This was a statement that Spanish-speaking children were just as intelligent as their English-speaking counterparts. This feat moved the issue of language beyond just the language; power was at the center of the dialogue between Latino families and the school.

In the community, power became the voice of transformation when community members recognized the increased participation of Latinos in the community. Businesspeople believed that this could only be good news for the development of the community, because participation of everyone meant less isolation for Latinos and less stereotypic beliefs on the part of Euro-Americans.

Power was also at the center of a community political struggle between Latinos and Euro-American council members who wanted to impose a law limiting the number of Latinos living in single-family dwellings in Carpinteria. COPLA and Latinos for Better Government united, and their efforts proved successful in defeating the proposed law. Ultimately, the community as a whole won because the Euro-American group realized the strength and conviction of the Latinos, and of course, Latinos won their freedom to live as they pleased in their own homes.

At the individual level, many have talked about their personal empowerment and about the ways in which their lives have changed through activism. While much pain has been endured during the psychosocial changes that occur in the lives of immigrants, Latinos in Carpinteria stretched their vision even further. On a personal, individual level, Latino activists in COPLA saw themselves changing their senses of self. Whereas before they may have felt isolated and victimized, collectively they changed their sense of personal identity to that of empowered individual. Feeling empowered enabled many Spanish-speaking Latinos in Carpinteria to reach out and change the conditions in their lives, but it also enabled them to assist others in their social networks. Some have talked about their improved communication skills within their family as well as in public. Better communication skills have helped them gain knowledge, skills, and personal fulfillment. In immigrant communities, continuity is critical for the students whose language and culture differs from that of the school. Students are the beneficiaries of a strong dialogue between parents and teachers.

## Books between Home and School

A family literacy project became one of the strongest bridges between home and school. As the researcher, I worked with COPLA and the school district to design a project that would assist parents whose children were underachieving in reading. The first year of the two-year Family Literacy Project (FLP) was dedicated to teaching the families a literacy program. The second year the parents practiced their reading in the home with their children, and my research team visited them periodically to examine how they were progressing. A specific feature of the project involved COPLA parents in leadership roles. Maria Rosario and Antonia Suarez were two of the parents who assisted with the planning of the family literacy classes.

Three major premises guided the Family Literacy Project, and were discussed at COPLA meetings as we talked about the issues and planned the project: (1) That all literacy is based on specific social practices; (2) that children become empowered through interaction with parents about story text, which uses their personal experiences, and (3) that intervention involving families must consider the home cultural niche.[5]

COPLA parents became convinced that the more that parents read with children, the better readers they become.[6] Many of the parents had participated in the preschool workshops when their children went through the Carpinteria Bilingual Preschool. They believed that during the reading activity with children, parents could teach cultural knowledge based on their own experience. "There's so much that I want my child to learn, and they don't sit still unless I have a book to read to them," said Nora Duran. Parents convey values, a worldview about their position in society, and a sense of confidence to their children that they are important enough to receive their parents' attention. Until parents openly discussed these issues with each other in COPLA, they were unaware of the sociocultural knowledge that they shared with their children through reading together. For example, in their conversations about books, parents discovered that they all strongly valued cultural roots, extended family, and caring for others. These were values they wanted their children to learn. "I like books that help me teach my children good values about being kind to others," explained Flora Morales.

In addition, parents discussed how their social status in Carpinteria and U.S. society in general encouraged them to talk to their children about the value of books. Understanding how to apply this knowledge meant knowing one's status in society. Adults wanted to examine the books before they approved them. COPLA parents concluded that they were more able to teach their children how to reflect on their own experiences in relation to literature if they read stories that were of interest to them, too.

We selected *Rosa Caramelo, ¿A Dónde Vas Osito Polar? (Where Are You Going, Little Polar Bear?), Historia de los Bonobos con Gafas (History of the Monkeys with Sunglasses), El Primer Pajaro de Piko-Niko (The First Bird of Piko-Niko), Tio Elefante (Uncle Elephant), El Perro Del Cerro (The Dog of the Hills), Mira Como Salen las Estrellas (Look at the Shining Stars), La Rana de la Sabana (The Frog of the Meadow),* and *Monty.* The books varied in length, and the project began with shorter stories and progressed to longer ones.

A variety of questioning strategies were taught to parent-participants in the eight class sessions. They learned how to discuss a book's content with their children. At the monthly sessions, held at Morton School, parents were given children's literature books and taught the four types of questioning strategies that would improve their child's involvement in reading. The questions were designed for parents to get children to compare, contrast, analyze, and to give their personal opinions and think creatively about changing something about their lives.

At each monthly meeting parents discussed the new books and, working in small groups, asked each other questions to model possible ways of interacting with their children. Maria Rosario had a great deal of experience in reading with children and in working with the COPLA parent group. She assisted in the literacy classes, while Antonia Suarez organized child care and children's story hour during the parent literacy meetings. Involving parent leaders in its organization and implementation strengthened the FLP program. The parents played a critical role in helping others to learn new ways to get involved in their children's schooling. Their participation helped strengthen the families who took part in the Family Literacy Project.

Parents and teachers met to discuss children's progress in literacy. Parents, as recommended by the FLP instructors, usually initiated the meetings. Children of the parents in the FLP project were in novice reading groups in their respective classes, and parents were encouraged to talk frequently with the teachers and report to them about what the children were reading at home and about how their at-home reading sessions were going. In addition to frequent meetings with their child's teacher, families were required to keep a calendar of the materials they read and to report on it at the monthly classes. Although the FLP class met only once a month, families had homework to do. They were expected to hold nightly reading sessions, meet with their child's teacher, record all of the materials read, and meet at least once during the month with the research team for an interview and videotaping of the parent and child reading together.

Videotaping of family literacy events was scheduled ahead of time. Usually, the preferred hour was after dinner or right after school, when the parent could sit down with their child to share a book. When we first began videotaping the families in their homes, they showed reluctance at being observed reading with their children. This was evidenced by the fact that initially parents and children sat farther apart than they did in the later months of the project. Nonetheless, interaction observed while the stories were being read revealed that parents felt increasingly comfortable reading with their children as the individual stories progressed. As

the months passed, their discussions grew more complex. Parents became more comfortable talking with their children about their own beliefs, perspectives, attitudes, criticisms, likes, and dislikes. In turn, the
children discussed their views about the stories they read. In a reading
session with his father at home, Sergio Olivarez, a third grader, shared
his ideas about the story they were reading. He said, "I liked the book
about the little polar bear who got lost in the North Pole. I got very sad
when the little bear lost his mother and by himself floated on a small
piece of ice in the ocean searching for her. It made me think how sad it
would be if I lost my mother or father."

Children expressed how the stories touched them emotionally. An example involved the book *Historia de los Bonobos con Gafas*, in which
the male monkeys made the female monkeys do all of the work, like
gather their food and feed them, while the male monkeys lived comfort-
ably in the trees. The male monkeys eventually went on a trip to learn a
new language and returned wearing sunglasses, and they positioned
themselves as the elite group, which included the use of new words. The
female monkeys didn't understand why the males refused to share with
them what they had learned. One day the females decided to take their
babies and move to another forest, which left the male monkeys needing
to gather their own food and do their own work. After exhausting their
resources, the male monkeys went in search of the female monkeys. Although no one knows what really happened, some people suggest that
the males reunited with the female monkeys and that they learned to
help them with the daily work so that they all lived happily ever after.
But, alas, that could just be wishful thinking.

Parents read the story with their children and discussed the issues related to gender role distribution of household tasks. Children responded
to questions about the fair distribution of housework between men and
women, about the elite behavior on the part of the "bonobos" who didn't
share the new language they learned, and about male aloofness toward
their children. Children's opinions were solicited. Yolanda Romero, a
fourth-grade student, commented about her dislike of the bonobos'
chauvinistic behavior. Her teacher had commented about the enormous
development that she had noticed in Yolanda's literacy skills since her
family began participating in the FLP. Her shyness came to be overshadowed by her critical thinking about the books she read. She had some
questions and comments about what she had read. "I don't know why
the male monkeys have to act like this. They didn't want to share anything with them [the female monkeys], and they had to do all of the work.

They did right by going to another forest. I wouldn't want them to make me do all of the work like the female monkeys had to do. Hopefully, the male monkeys will never find the female monkeys because they can live very happy without those monkeys who were so lazy. Dad, don't you think that it's unjust for them to do that?"

"Yes dear, it's unjust," her father responded. "What would you do in a case like that of the female monkeys?" he asked her.

"I would throw them with the fruit they made me pick," said Yolanda matter-of-factly.

Her father chuckled. "The important thing is that you would not allow them to treat you unjustly."

Our theoretical expectation was that Spanish-speaking children and their parents would feel empowered when they learned to interpret literature in relation to their own experience and reality.[7] Yolanda's exchange with her father illustrates critical learning. To achieve this, the research team and the parents of Spanish-speaking children planned not only to have parents read children's books to their children, but also to pose a hierarchy of questions designed to generate discussion between children and parents.[8] We extended the premise of what it means to become analytical readers and read for meaning by having parents and children decide their own questions and interactions during their story reading sessions. Four types of questions framed the interaction between adults and children: descriptive, personal interpretative, critical, and creative. Descriptive questions solicited factual recall. For example, "What did the female elephants wear?" Personal interpretative questions asked the reader to think about their personal experience in relation to what they had read. For example, "Have you ever felt that you were prevented from doing things that others had permission to do? How did that make you feel?" Critical questions revealed the child's ability to analyze the text in terms of a sociopolitical perspective. For example, "Could the male and female monkeys have divided the work and responsibilities better?" Creative questions made the reader think about ways that they would resolve similar problems to those described in the story. For example, "If you had been one of the female monkeys, what could you have done to improve the situation?" During the evening classes, parents practiced asking these questions of each other in small groups, led by COPLA parents and members of the research team. Discussions ensued, such as the following brief excerpt on gender differences in the book *Rosa Caramelo*.

A parent, Ana Vega, shared her observations. "I would say that Rosa Caramelo did what she had to do to liberate herself. The way that her father constrained her in the small garden with the other female elephants and did not allow her to play in the larger meadows where the male elephants played was wrong. The important part of this book is that Rosa didn't only liberate herself, but she also encouraged the other female elephants to liberate themselves."

Guillermo Sanchez said, "Well, I don't agree that we should give our children ideas about disobeying their parents. I don't think those are values which we want to give our children."

Ruth Calavera added, "But Rosa didn't rebel simply to disobey her parents. It was that there was inequality in what the male gray elephants were able to do as compared with the females who were the pink elephants."

Ana asked, "What do I do if my daughter decided to accept Rosa's position and I don't agree with her?"

"I would say that what we need to do is to help our children express their ideas even if they are different than ours," said Ruth Calavera. "We also have a right to our ideas, and we should explain to them why we have our ideas. We don't always have to try and convince our children of our point of view, but it is necessary to explain our reasons and at the same time help them express their own ideas and examine their conscience."

Results from the FLP intervention showed growth in parents' and children's literacy practices as they achieved closer communication between the families and the classroom. In spite of these successes, the questioning strategies that were taught to the parents in the FLP classes caused some confusion. The parents were apparently overly concerned with the academic aspect of the project, that is, with the labels used to describe the category of questions. Some parents were confused by the hierarchy of the questions and matching the labels with the types of questions.[9] For example, in the creative category the type of question might be, How would you end the story differently? Parents were unaccustomed to working with academic strategies most likely to be employed by teachers. In our final analysis, they might have benefited more by becoming aware of their own process and using their own frameworks of interaction to initiate discussion about the literature. Overlooking the families' native literacy ignored the cultural importance of the project. Put differently, families nurtured their children with stories, amplifying cultural integrity in this community. Criticism of the school curriculum in COPLA meetings had cited the absence of home culture in the school curriculum, and then the FLP also neglected this critical aspect. Comments from participating parents, however, confirmed the success of the project.

Although such observations were forthcoming from the parents from the beginning of the FLP, one frequent comment disturbed me. It had to do with the predesigned questions that parents were taught to ask their children. Several parents said, "I still don't understand how to ask my child those questions each time we read a book together." This pointed out the parents' confusion about the questioning categories we taught them in the FLP classes.

Mr. Guillermo Sanchez commented, "This program was very important for me, and it made me see the importance of reading more frequently with my children. It also reminded me of the necessity to talk with the teachers specifically about the daily reading assignments they give the children. Before I took the FLP class I used to wait until parent-teacher conferences to talk with teachers. But now, even if there isn't a problem, I go to talk with the teachers."

Folk stories, which children learn from parents or other relatives, are central to the families' organic literacy repertoire, which existed prior to the Family Literacy Project. Had the FLP incorporated family stories as part of the curriculum, the academic questioning categories could have been taught differently and minimized the conflict, which lasted for the adults long after the literacy classes ended. This is not to say that the parents could not learn the importance of the questioning categories, rather it means that the questions may possibly have been learned much easier had family literacy been used along with the commercial children's literature books. The power of story for children undergirds the dynamics of culture. Children just as much as parents learn through the favorite stories that are told to them, which impact their thinking enough for them to retell the stories to each other in the classroom and in their play. Without a doubt, children look to their teachers and parents as the predominant figures of authority. Parents and teachers are important custodians of children's minds, and part of that responsibility entails teaching them to think critically and make informed choices.

# CHAPTER SEVEN

ॐ

# Envisioning Possibilities

"I'll graduate from high school in the year 2000. That seems years in the future, but it's only two years away. Not much has happened in high school that would make me change my mind about what I want to do when I get out of school. I want to go college and become an architect. I know I've got a long way to go, but my parents always tell me it doesn't hurt to dream as long as you've done work you need to do to get you there. I think they were also thinking about what parents had to do to help their children, too. When I first began talking about my dreams with them, they didn't say much except that I should do what-ever made me happy. They didn't know what it was to be an architect, so they couldn't help me to get to my goals, but they've learned a lot. I'm really proud of them because they began attending lots of meetings at the school and in the community—whatever would help them to learn about my interests. You see, they didn't do that with my sister. She's married now, and she also has three kids and lives with us because her husband left her. Anyway, I don't think she blames them for the way her life turned out, but my parents told me once that they felt bad for my sister and what happened to her. They blamed themselves because they couldn't help her to get motivated about her schoolwork or to get some-thing in her life to keep her in school and to get a career. I don't know about that, but they've sure become different people. I've seen how much they've tried to help me. They helped me last year when I didn't know if I was going to make it through all of the hard classes. They went to talk to the counselors. I think it'll sure be different for my younger brother who still has lots of years of school left."

Amalia was one of three children in the Sanchez household. The parents didn't know how to help their oldest daughter when she began losing interest in school and got involved with boys. They blamed their lack of education for their inability to turn her life around. But they made a strong effort to get involved in community activities in the church and in the school. The parents felt that they connected with others who shared their difficulties and got information and resources to help them deal with their tribulations. This inevitably helped Amalia when she got into high school. Now Amalia looks at her strong possibilities for her future education and career as hopeful because as she tells it, she's got her parents on her side.

Creating opportunity is the job not only of the educators but of parents as well. It is the responsibility of all the adults in children's lives to harness every ounce of creative energy and to make children recognize their true gifts and possibilities. Whenever COPLA parents weren't being heard by the school administrators, inevitably someone would suggest, "We need to make an appointment to go talk with the superintendent." Just as parents want teachers to support them and vice versa, so do teachers expect their school administrators to support them as teachers. And school administrators, in turn, need support from the district administration. But teachers and parents also have a connection with the district superintendent. They perceived a superintendent as the person who enforces a vision that leads their schools forward. Latino parents and teachers, in particular, viewed the Carpinteria school district superintendent as a power broker who could open opportunities for Latino children. Teachers expected the administration to support their parent involvement activities and to endorse their community outreach through release time, community liaisons, and support of skills to work more closely in the area of home-school connectedness. Parents also expected the superintendent to build meaningful communication with the community on all levels. Guillermo Sanchez explained, "Teachers have limited power if the principal and the superintendent don't support them 100 percent. After all, they're the leaders, and what they say and do says a lot about they way that they really feel about the community."

Support from the central administration toward the Latino community evolved in the decade I worked in Carpinteria. But one of the strongest child, teacher, and community advocates was Superintendent Dr. Pablo Seda. He felt as comfortable addressing a group of hundreds of community members as he did meeting with a few in his office. His office told a story of a busy but organized person. Stacks of papers, manuals, and books were neatly set in a designated spot on his desk. His potted garden near the window gave the room a warm and welcoming feeling. Dr. Seda served in the superintendent's position from 1990 to 1994. He spoke openly to the community about the importance of working closely with parents and the community. Upon his arrival in the school district, he formed a council of parents representing various interests in the community. He met with the groups monthly. In those meetings he solicited parents' views on current issues, while he shared his own vision of education for the district's students.

Dr. Seda's background prepared him for this leadership position in Carpinteria. He taught Spanish in a high school and coached basketball before becoming an assistant principal, then a principal. During the time he was principal of Garey High School, he remained active as a community coordinator for the city's Hispanic Youth Task Force. After receiving a doctoral degree in education from the University of Southern California, Dr. Seda became assistant superintendent for secondary instruction in the Santa Barbara High School District. During that time he continued speaking in community agencies and conducting workshops to train parents to work more effectively with schools and to learn ways to help their children reach greater academic success. As a superintendent in Carpinteria, Dr. Seda remained connected with the community at large through his column in the local newspapers, in which he communicated his perspectives on education.

In his article, "What Do Children Learn in School?"[1] Dr. Seda commented, "In reality, children learn much in school about who they are. Their teachers and peers frequently reinforce the self concept they acquire somewhere between kindergarten and twelfth grade." Dr. Seda further elaborated,

> Children learn and/or acquire leadership skills, self confidence, empathy for others, appreciation for life, responsibility for their actions, self discipline, and such values as honesty, integrity and perseverance. They learn these traits, skills and habits from their teachers, peers, parents and other adults. However, sometimes children fail to learn these lessons, and instead, they learn that they are not able to learn.

In Carpinteria, learning in and out of school happened through extensive contact with adults and peers in the home, school, and community.

According to Dr. Seda, "A teacher is so important! A teacher relates to the child why learning and school are important. A teacher helps a child to make the connection between school and his future. A teacher is also an advocate for the child and believes in the child and convinces him/her that he/she can learn. The teacher is also available at the hard and difficult times when things just don't go right and love and protection and sheltering are necessary."

Like many observant educators, Dr. Seda saw the relationship between schools and society. "I look around and see where our society is going and it is somewhat frightening at times. And so my wish is that teachers always wish the best for their students and do all that's necessary to make sure they succeed."

Dr. Seda's wish for teachers to live and teach the essence of empathy for others reveals his beliefs that teaching should promote truth, courage, knowledge, work, stability, balance, and joy. His assertions about the teachers' place in children's learning leads into Dr. Seda's understanding of teachers' responsibilities in what he terms the *Greatest of All Professions*. "I am convinced, that if our society and our country are to maintain its excellence, it will be done by teachers who are committed to making a difference everyday. A child once asked Willie Stargell, former major league baseball player, for his autograph. Mr. Stargell turned to the child and said, 'You should instead seek the autograph of your teacher. He (she) will do more for you than I ever will.' Willie Stargell knew about teachers and the difference they make."

In his experience as a classroom teacher, Dr. Seda recalls that intervening in a student's life made a major difference in his life. He reflects, "As a teacher, I can think of nothing more exciting and satisfying than knowing that I have made a positive difference in a child's life. Recently, I saw a former student of mine whom I had in my class in 1971 in San Diego. It has been years since I had seen him. I spent a great deal of time with Kirk, but his parents divorced and later drugs contributed to his downfall. When I saw him recently he told me during all the bad times in his life he could always remember he could win and succeed. I taught and coached him for three years and it was that experience he kept going back to until he finally made it. Now he is drug free, happily married, the father of two beautiful girls and successful in business. That's what teaching is all about. It's about making a difference."

The pervasive and enduring influence of teachers remains in us even through our dreams and aspirations. Dr. Seda tells of how that impact lives in the events of our life. "Teachers touch hundreds, maybe thousands of lives in their careers. Sometimes even unknown to the teacher, a child may make a great discovery that will change his/her life because of something positive the teacher said or did. In the movie *The Boy Who Could Fly* a girl talks about her teacher, 'He made us believe in ourselves again; now when I feel like giving up and not trying, all I have to do is think of what he taught me.' Teachers know all children are special and that all can fly."

Much like people in other service professions, teachers are undercompensated and often don't receive thanks for a job well done. Dr. Seda comments on teachers' commitments to do their work because they care. "I recently heard of a judge who has saved over twenty men on death row from their execution and so far he has not gotten one thank you card. I am sure he doesn't feel appreciated, but he goes on anyway and does what he thinks is right. Teachers have the same problem. They touch hundreds, maybe thousands of lives in their careers and they receive little recognition for their efforts. Their salaries are low and they receive few incentives to continue to strive and make a difference, but they do it anyway. Because what is important is that each teacher knows he/she is doing all that is possible to have the students experience success."

Having support during the tough periods of our life can make all the difference in the world. In Dr. Seda's life, teachers have come in the form of loving family members. "I remember a few years back I was unhappy with who I was. I had sold myself short and given up on my dreams. I was just kind of going along. I was living, but nobody was home. So I decided to take a look at myself and see who I was and where I was going. I decided that as hard and painful as it was I was going for the finish line and I was going the distance. Anytime we look at ourselves and work at expanding our experiences we experience fear. I choose to say that I experience fear, but I will not give in to say that I am afraid. I now live in the present and I enjoy every moment of my life and live everyday as if it were my last. Every night before I go to bed I can look at myself in the mirror and say. 'Today I made a difference in this world. Today I made a difference in someone's life.' I have this experience because I had some great teachers in my life. Alice, Mitch, Jack, Mr. S., and Pricilla were all there for me. They made me their project. They believed in me and convinced me I was unique and special. They were my teachers and they made a difference in my life. I am a better person because I was their student."

Teachers do make a difference. Teaching is the greatest of professions, because it allows both the teacher and the student to reach for their potential and be the best they can be. A teacher can make a difference every day in the lives of children.

Dr. Seda's candid account of his teaching experience supports his belief in the importance of teachers in children's lives. His expectations about teaching and learning are further expanded in his article, "We Are Able to Overcome Expectations of Others."[2] Turning inward in search of life's meaning is a crucial process according to Dr. Seda, especially in the darkest of times. "During World War II, Victor Frankl, Jewish psychiatrist and author of the book, *Man's Search for Meaning,* was sent to a concentration camp. His parents, brother, and wife died there. Naked and alone in a room, one day he became aware of what he later called the 'last of the human freedoms.' Noticing a far away home he saw a light inside. He chose to see this light as a sign of God and that he was heard. From that day on, Frankl decided the Nazis could never take away his chosen freedom. Through that freedom he learned that he could decide within himself how his present situation affected him."

Taking charge of our lives is a strong affirmation. Using Victor Frankl as an inspiration, Dr. Seda continued his message. "Between what happened to him (his stimulus) and his response, he found a vast world he could control. He used visualization and his mind (imagery) to project himself lecturing after the camp experience was over. He, little by little, disciplined himself (mind and emotions). His tools were primarily his imagination and memory. Slowly he exercised his new freedom until it grew larger and larger, even larger than that of his Nazi captors. He told himself that no matter what they did to him he would always have his dignity, his integrity, and he would survive to tell about it. He did!"

We may not always have a choice about the way that our life events unfold. But, regardless of the circumstances in which we find ourselves, we always have a choice about the way we perceive the situation. "Frankl discovered that between stimulus and response, man has the freedom to choose. In our places of work and in our homes, we often face negative stimuli. Lack of money, demands from insensitive people (be it a parent, administrator colleague, spouse, or child), and complaints from people who lack empathy, contribute to the negative environment in which we often live. We can choose to react to these stimuli by being negative, angry, upset, sad, by giving up, blaming, by saying, 'If only I had more money' or 'if we had a commitment from the district' or 'if I had a different boss . . . a different husband . . . a different superintendent.' Or we can choose to be proactive, to stand and realize that we can create our own response. We have the freedom to choose. We can say, 'I choose, I prefer, I will, I can, let's look at the alternatives.' We, too, must accept the fact that we can change our environment and our perceived realities and accomplish anything we want if we believe in our power to overcome negative stimuli. All children can become whatever they set out to be and accomplish whatever they want if they learn to utilize the power that exists within them."

People's unique inner power was the focus of Dr. Seda's expectations for students, educators, and parents. Such were the expectations of Latino parents with each other in their COPLA organization. Cooperation is one of the values inherent in the empowerment process. The issues are further explored in Dr. Seda's article, "Winning Isn't Always Defeating Somebody."

The nature of competition in our society poses many hard questions about its effect on us as a society, how we think about our potential, about each other's ability, and how we relate to each other given the power of these values. Dr. Seda had strong feelings about the meaning of competition and cooperation. He believes that as a society we're pre-conditioned to compete, and people usually interpret that to mean that someone must lose. Too little attention is given to the concept of win/win. The notion is considered one of settling for less than we can have. Some believe that if we don't emphasize winning and losing, then we're not serious about the thing we want.

According to Dr. Seda, we're hooked on winning because it brings us happiness. "We jump, we cheer, we laugh, and our disposition improves. However, when we lose, the opposite occurs." But what happens when we lose? Dr. Seda talked about the general impulse to dismiss a loss by saying, "It is just a game anyway."

Labeling ourselves as winners or losers is commonplace and defines the way that schools classify students during their entire school career. Dr. Seda observed that after a loss we should reassess the situation so that we can turn our defeat into a future victory. "We want to rank ourselves so we can tell others we are at the top. Of course, when one is at the top, someone must be at the bottom. . . . It is OK to rank students when one is among the top, but how would we like to be 499th out of 500? Where does it say that we must have so many As, so many Bs, Cs, Ds and Fs? School is not a football game where for one to win, another one must lose! . . .

"School can and should be a place where all can succeed, where all can win. There should be nothing wrong with all students earning As. If we truly believe that education is the answer to our society's problems, then we would want all classes, all schools, and all districts to win. We all win in education when all students learn and reach their potential."

What students need is a different orientation to winning. According to Dr. Seda, "Schools need to teach children that life is not a game about winning or losing arguments, scoring points, winning games, or collecting toys. Winning in life is about living full out, going for our potential, reaching for the stars, being a good person, giving all we have to give, and loving everyone with all our heart and soul. That's really winning!"

Leadership, under Dr. Seda's administration, emphasized a commitment to motivate others to make the same promise to education that he brought to Carpinteria. His philosophy of education began with an appraisal of his own strengths and an acknowledgment of the value of working toward negotiation in a collective way. Collectivity, cooperation, excellence, and forthright communication and inclusion were values congruent with those of COPLA's organization and leadership.

Dr. Seda's educational philosophy was to be available to the community, but his critics claimed that it was just a philosophy. They were less than patient with his efforts to decentralize management responsibilities. For example, on the issue of parent involvement, teachers requested assistance from the district administration in order to establish closer communication with parents. Teachers felt they needed a parent liaison to help them reach difficult children whose families required frequent home visits. Additionally teachers wanted release time to meet with parents and to bridge closer partnerships with families, which included composing weekly classroom newsletters. The central administration felt that such requests were the responsibility of school principals; they claimed principals should be the ones to assess their own school curriculum and staff needs. Dr. Seda was able to appoint principals who initiated projects tailored to the specific needs of their school's population.

## In Community

Connections among children, parents, and teachers, which Dr. Seda promoted, were dynamic and real in people's lives. These sectors of the community exist interdependently with each other, and each had particular perspectives about the way they interacted and connected with others. Most important, as exemplified by the student, parent, and teacher profiled in this section, people share their inspirations, strengths, and visions for a community that supports and accepts humanity, diversity, and excellence.

## Student—Francisca Avila

My interviews and interactions with people in Carpinteria were delightful and moving, but few were as energetic as those I had with Francisca. Her enthusiasm and honesty revealed a young woman with great introspective ability. "This year has been just about the best I've had in school since I began. I started school here in Carpinteria. My parents had just moved here from Oxnard when I went into the bilingual kindergarten. So much has changed for me since I first got into high school. Up until now I hated school and rebelled against everything. My poor parents tried so hard to keep me interested, but nothing worked. Even my older brothers and sisters—I have four, three brothers and one sister—tried to do everything to keep me out of trouble, but I just couldn't stand school. Don't get me wrong I liked learning and reading and all that, but going to school was a big nightmare for me."

Through the good and rough times, Francisca's parents supported and guided her, but her defiance made a strong statement about her need for a school that challenges more creative minds. "The worst was one year in the fifth grade when I wasn't doing my homework and my parents met with the teacher who told them that I wasn't bringing in my homework. After the conference with my teacher, my parents came home and sat me down. They told me how disappointed they were for what I had done. Not only were they upset because of what I hadn't done, but they were also angry because of all the time that the family had spent helping me to do my schoolwork, and I forgot to turn it in. I'm not sure why I didn't turn it in, except maybe I hated school so much that I always found ways to do something wrong—you know, break the rules. I could find no reason for getting up so early to go sit in a hard wood desk where a teacher just gave me dirty looks when I talked to my friends to get the answers she wouldn't help me with. Oh sure I like recesses because my friends and I got to play kick ball or volleyball, but who needed to go to school for that? I could do that at the park. And we did on weekends. My friends and I went to the park, and someone took a soccer ball, and we had a great time. We still do it every once in a while. I have a friend who's half as tall as I am, and she can run faster than anyone I know. I loved playing with her just to watch her run and kick the ball. I can jump high, but that only helps in volleyball and basketball. So playing with my friends at recess was OK, but as for school, I was bored to death."

Fortunately, Francisca found a way to stay connected to her friends in school. But something deeper stirred in her and kept her questioning. It wasn't the defiance of rules that kept her connected; as Francisca tells it, her respect for her parent's authority prevailed in spite of the fact that she had to endure miserable boredom. She had to keep doing her best, regardless.

"There's so many rules that I was going crazy, and no one seemed to care or understand me. My teacher or my family or even some of my friends, they would just say, 'You just don't want someone telling you what to do.' That was part of it, but it was more. I hated having to sit in the same seat all the time. I hated having to stop working when the teacher said so even when I hadn't finished my work. I hated the boring books we had to read in school. I would tell the teacher, 'Why don't you just turn us loose in the library so we can get the books we want to read all the time. It would be easier on you.' My teacher would just smile and tell me to get whatever book I wanted to take home. Honestly, I don't know how I got through all those years of horrible boredom in school. Maybe it was fear of my parents, who told me that if I didn't do my best, I wouldn't be able to go out to play with my friends. I couldn't imagine not having fun or playtime, since school was so boring."

Francisca credits her siblings and parents for helping her to hold up her head in her earlier school years. Her opportunity to give back to her family presented itself at the time of a family crisis. Francisca's own strength and nurturing ways helped to hold her mother together during her grief. "Anyway between my parents and my brothers and sisters I did my best through elementary school, and my grades were fine until I got into junior high school. That was tough because my father died and we could barely make it on my mother's salary. He got cancer, but he wasn't sick long, then he died. My older brother worked, but they didn't get much money. Actually I wasn't as bored, just sad. But I couldn't show that I was sad because my mom was so sad that we all had to help her feel better. One bit at a time, mom stopped crying, and we started going out for picnics at the park on weekends. I remember she wanted us to move to Mexico where she was born, but when she stopped crying, she stopped talking about going back. I was sure glad because I didn't want to leave my friends. During that time I still hated school, but it didn't seem to matter as much. I think I was thinking more about my mother and trying to help her around the house."

School ceased to be Francisca's focus, as her family needed more of her emotional energy. She managed to find a quiet way to stay in school since she told her mother that she would stay in school. Maybe it was her way of relieving her mother of any worry that she might drop out.

"When I got into high school, the work was really hard, and I had to get a lot of tutoring in math because that was the worst subject. I still hated school because we had to take all of these dumb classes that I didn't like and had no need for them! But, of course, if we didn't take them we'd never graduate. And by then I had promised my mother that I would stay in school. That made her happy, and I liked seeing her happy. But all the bad times at school changed when I started my sophomore year. I got really great teachers in Spanish and in history. They were so nice, and they cared about all the students, and I really felt like they wanted me to learn because it was important to learn, not just so I could get a good grade. Another thing that made me happy was when one of my girlfriends dragged me to an audition for a school play she was in. She wanted to play the lead in the play, and I watched her read for the play and it was so exciting that I wanted to do it too. So I signed up to play the part of one of the ladies in the play. It wasn't the lead, but it was a speaking part. Wow that was the coolest thing I had ever done. I went to rehearsals after school, and finally opening night arrived. We sold out for the two nights of the play. I felt important being in the play. I also got to make new friends, and they were different. Like they were more mature."

Finding a kindred spirit who believed in her creative spirit made all the difference in the world for Francisca. She discovered an emotional part of herself, in that good feelings could be attached to her academic achievements in school because she believed in the work she was doing and her teachers believed in her ability. They cared about her intelligence, not only about her behavior.

"What made that year in high school really super was that my Spanish and my history teachers got interested in the writing I did in their classes; they told me that I should submit an essay to a high school student contest. I spent a lot of time working on the essay, and they helped me with it, and one of my brothers helped me too. I couldn't believe that I could be so interested in something like writing. Then when I sent it in, I actually wanted to win. I wanted to see myself win, and I hoped and prayed and dreamed how neat it would be to have my essay win the contest. I had never done that before; most of the time I didn't care about grades or schoolwork or stuff like that because it was so boring. But now this was fun. I did care. Well the awards were made, and I didn't make first place, but I did get second place, which was a small certificate. There was no money, but my name was written up in the newspaper, and a lot of people read it. Then my name was put up in big letters on the school bulletin board. That was neat. What was great about that contest was that I got to see that I could do something I liked and something that I cared about and that others cared about it too. And school had never made me feel like that."

Reflecting on her road from boredom to dreams, Francisca realized that she wasn't just bored with school but that in fact she had ideas and she had intelligence that her teachers supported. She also saw that with the right support from loved ones and from teachers, she could unleash her originality to envision a role in creating a more inclusive type of school. She describes her hopes and optimism. "I have this dream, and now that I know that dreams can come true, I know it'll happen. I'm going to have some career in science like biology, or Spanish, like teaching it. And I'm going to get married and have at least two kids. And when my kids go to school, I'm going to help them in every way I can for them to have fun in school. I won't make them go to boring schools. Maybe by then schools won't have bells, kids won't have to sit in one desk all day, they won't have stupid homework, and they won't have to take dumb classes just to graduate. That's going to be way into the next century. Things will be really different."

Francisca connected with her family, friends, and teachers, but most importantly, she connected with herself and discovered her talent and interests through the pain of feeling stuck in school, the loss of her father, and dealing with her mother's grief. Things are different for Francisca.

**Parent—Mario Cortez**

Mario Cortez also hungered for things to be different. I had spoken to him several times at meetings and had worked with his children in their schools, but for longer interviews I visited his home. On one Saturday afternoon, when I went to his family's house to interview him about his thoughts and his work in the community, the smell of fresh paint still lingered in the air. Before I arrived, he had painted his children's bedroom. During the interview, he talked about his appreciation for COPLA's accomplishments and challenges. Before we began to talk, Carolina Cortez entered with cold drinks on a tray and set them down on the table in front of the couch where we sat. "No one has been more surprised than me that I've been so involved with my children's schools and the Latino parents," Mario said. "You see, I only had a few years of school in Mexico. And when my wife and I immigrated here, we had our children. I had to work hard at two jobs, the nursery and other jobs, just to pay the rent and keep us fed; the last thing that mattered was having to attend meetings at school or doing homework with my children. Somehow I thought that schools should know what they're doing, but I've learned differently. It was my wife who convinced me that I should go with her to some meetings because they discussed important issues about Latino children in schools."

Mario became convinced that his children needed his involvement in ways he had never known about until he attended COPLA meetings, where others like him shared their feelings of frustration about parenting their children in a new language and culture.

"Although I didn't know about my children's schools and maybe at first I didn't care, I did feel frustrated talking with my children because they were speaking more and more English and I wasn't learning it as fast. COPLA has been a wonderfully positive organization here in Carpinteria. The thing that kept me going back and staying involved is that the leaders always made time in the meeting to answer questions that we as parents had. And the leaders knew what we needed to learn because they're Latino parents here too, struggling like the rest of us. That's what made the organization successful. We talk about ideas and ways to act on behalf of our children. As a result, I learned to communicate with my children at home and even with the schools sometimes. The COPLA parents helped me to believe that I was intelligent even if I didn't have much schooling. I felt like I was a good parent even if I spoke less English than my children. Working together with other parents, I got to figure out how to think about the schools differently and to see that as Latino parents we can help our children. I mean we don't have to be afraid of schools just because we didn't get as much schooling. I admit, however, that my wife still goes to the school more often than me. But I stay interested in my children's schooling and I never did that before."

The strength of any organization rests on the impact it makes. Mario Cortez is witness to the change that he has seen in his life as a result of his involvement with COPLA. He also observes that the simple things are sometimes the most effective. "The simplest thing we can do is to make sure that we communicate clearly to all our parents, to all our students, to all our teachers, and to the administrators. I think that we find a position of strength by making our meeting times during hours that many can attend. For example, Friday evenings are the best, because lots of people have second jobs on weekends and they go to bed very early on weekdays. So our meeting times, locations, and the language we used in the meeting opened up the process for many people to get involved."

Mario continued commenting on the benefits of Latino parents' connection to their children, other Spanish-speaking adults, and their children's schools. "The people who benefit most by the involvement of Latino parents are first of all the students of the Hispanic parents, but in a broad spectrum truly the whole of our community stands to benefit tremendously. All students benefit because of the enrichment that is brought into the process when we expand that communication in every direction."

Mario transcended his feelings of disconnect with his children and with the schools they attended. Through his involvement in COPLA, he learned that even with little formal schooling, parents are still the most important teachers in children's lives.

### Teacher—Ms. Juana Garcia

In a classroom packed with thirty-three students, teachers know what their primary purpose is and whom they need to address. Juana Garcia had taught second grade for ten years in the school district. Inside her classroom, wet streaks on the blackboard told of closure for the day, as she sat down with me to talk about relationships with parents. "The primary group to me is really clear; it happens to be the students of Latino parents. But even more important, I really believe that all the students in the schools, the teachers, the staff, the whole community, if you want to take that point, really benefit. It is really just one method of getting people to become more effectively involved in a part of the system. And the students most directly benefit. If we are an educational institution, then obviously parent involvement is based on knowing the needs of the kids and the support system that is necessary for the students to succeed."

Juana Garcia's approach to working with parents is to invite them to coteach with her so that they always stay informed. "I really believe they need to stay informed and involved in as many ways as possible. Parents have just as many questions, so it's a two-way street. I don't obligate parents to come and volunteer or work in the classroom, but I do expect regular communication with each one. I call them, or they call me, and we talk about not only the negative but positive."

There are many ways for teachers and parents to stay connected; it is the quality of the interaction that really matters. Juana Garcia explains, "Communication is a two-way street between teachers and parents. The major thing would be the particular needs that they have in terms of assisting their children to be successful, the concerns they have in terms of how their kids are learning in an effective environment. Just a general communication is a major thing they can share so there is a development of understanding about what needs to be done and a list would come out of that."

As a teacher, Juana Garcia sees a way to bridge the distance between the home and the school. "We really are trying to tackle the gap. I say 'we,' including all teachers and parents because it has to be system-wide. That has come out as a major question. Let me tell you what I think we can do to make sure that it happens. The major way we can facilitate that is to make sure that we make available convenient, easy, comfortable, secure environments for that communication to take place. Where people feel they have a common interest and a common higher goal about working together in that environment rather than one in which distrust and ill will is fostered. Some ways that we have done that within the school district have been, to provide a calendar for parents and try to create meeting times and locations and environments for those meetings. We wanted them conducive to the parents to be involved and to try to provide for teachers the release time to go and meet with those parents in that kind of situation. This offered a new opportunity, not doing it for example at one o'clock in the afternoon, as sometimes some parents traditionally meet. Then people complain why parents do not show up and meet with us. Well it's not very convenient for anyone, and there is an underlying message that it wasn't that important to them, otherwise they would set a time for more people to get involved. Also meetings need to be bilingual. To me language, although a major barrier, is not a major difference in people and should be looked at as an enrichment aspect, not as a negative aspect that someone carries into the scenario. That being the case, to me the way we cooperate both groups working together, is to identify the strength that lies within that diversity and the enrichment. All parents, not only Latino parents but non-Latino parents, Latino students, and non-Latino students, showing how in all societies the infusion of new groups can work together for a stronger society. So, I think that teacher and parent connection is a major issue. More important is the process, the outcome of that; the more important issue is that someone begins to sense that there is a sincere caring. In fact, it is real. It cannot be a phony process. People would recognize us being phony and in a short time they turn away from it."

Building an inclusive learning community requires the energy of every student, parent, and educator. The net has to be cast far and wide to support those involved in children's schooling because parents and teachers are also learners, so they, too, need an ongoing forum for communication and advocacy for children.

**Looking Forward**

Dr. Seda's leadership accelerated the building of leadership in Carpinteria. Consistent with his educational philosophy, Dr. Seda's response to teachers' needs allowed people the freedom to make decisions and choices for themselves, even if it took more time to accomplish. The process takes more time and requires more patience and work on everyone's part than would be expected if the decisions were made in a centralized fashion. As Dr. Seda commented, "One way to empower teachers is to welcome them in the decision-making process. They, too, are leaders and as such should be involved in the decisions affecting their future." The superintendent had, however, included an accountability feature in his evaluation of principals. "Beginning this first year of my administration, principals will be evaluated for their progress in establishing strong family-school connectedness."

Just as Dr. Seda believed in including teachers in the educational decision-making process, he was also interested in involving parents and staff. "Parents and staff members are also very important. They too must become part of the solution by being involved in the decision-making process and in planning the goals to form the strategy which will create a new structure to meet the vision and purpose of our schools."

In his article "Carpinteria toward the 21st Century,"[3] Dr. Seda writes:

> The 21st Century is about students and their performance. Excellence is achieved when all students reach the peak of their abilities. By identifying the levels of skills, abilities and knowledge desired for each student, we can ascertain our schools' level of success. Carpinteria—The 21st century is about all our students knowing they are capable of reaching their potential and every student being engaged daily in the learning process to make that potential a reality. It will take an effort by the entire Carpinteria community to make Carpinteria—The 21st Century a reality. It is not just the job of educators. All of this could happen, but only if we chose to take a stand and hold hands together to make Carpinteria—The 21st Century a reality.

Dr. Seda's vision for Carpinteria may still come to fruition, but it will happen without him as superintendent. As I complete this book, Dr. Seda has just left Carpinteria to take a superintendent position in Southern California. And so the spiraling motion of empowerment takes still another twist, as a new chapter awaits COPLA as they participate in the selection of a new superintendent. Paul Niles threw his hat into the ring and came up number two of five candidates. The newly selected superintendent was an outsider to Carpinteria, and new opportunities awaited the community. Pablo Seda had continued one area of parent education that Paul Niles had begun: the training for parent leaders by the bilingual counselor, whose goal was to train small cadres of parents who would, in turn, train other parents in areas of parent-child relationships. The intent is for parents to receive separate training, then come together and learn from each other.

When Dr. Seda left the superintendent position in Carpinteria, his vision for the dynamic community and school partnership continued through the support of superintendents that followed and the sustained efforts of the community. In claiming their rights, including both political and cultural space as part of the community, Latinos challenge old conceptions of American educational practices. They are attempting to participate fully in the process and are thus reshaping old concepts of education, of Latinos, and of family-school relationships, thus the making of new citizens demands consistent participation in a new, more equitable society. Declaring cultural space and political voice and having utopian visions do not by themselves address the rigid structures that propel inequity and sever family-school relationships. Nor can COPLA meetings alone address these challenges or replace the structures of power embedded in capitalism, but they provide reservoirs of hope, and they struggle for healthier communities and in general, a better society.

In open conversation, parents revealed to each other that they believed their true power resided within themselves. Their cultural ways of organizing taught me about the organic nature of teaching. Parents effectively used dialogue within the group and between the community and the schools—actualizing the power of the culture and the culture of power. The case of the "Free Breakfast Program" saw the motives, values, goals, and priorities of the parents and the school district converge. In 1993, the Latino parents first rallied around the idea of initiating a free-breakfast program for children from families with low incomes. But the school district resisted. They opposed the costs of changing busing schedules and keeping school kitchens open.

At one very long and intense COPLA meeting about the breakfast program, the Latino parents and school personnel outlined the areas where they agreed and where they differed. As parents and teachers explored which children really wanted a snack, when they needed to eat, how much they needed to eat, and what they would eat, both sides realized that maybe the 7:30 A.M. breakfast program would not address the children's specific food needs. Instead, a mid-morning snack at the discretion of the teacher made more sense. Some parents and teachers also felt that teachers should have the option to keep food items (healthy snacks like nuts and fruits) in the classrooms. Through mutual respect, trust, focus on the child's needs, and willingness to listen to different points of view, parents and teachers were able to arrive at a viable solution on an issue that had divided them for months. The free breakfast issue was addressed at a school level, but it did not entirely go away as an issue for parents. The parents continued to talk about it in COPLA meetings in subsequent years when they noticed that many Latino students, whose parents left for work at 5:00 or 6:00 A.M., arrived at school hungry and unable to concentrate in class. With the consistent and sustained attention on the subject, the school administrators relented, and in the fall of 2000, the elementary schools implemented a breakfast program.

**An Ongoing Process**
School district personnel have changed in the superintendent's office, principals' offices, and in the classroom. Families have also moved out, going farther south to Ventura and Oxnard, mostly because of rising rent prices. Yet some things have remained constant to the benefit of the Latino community. Parents continue to work collectively, illustrating the benefits of the ongoing process of negotiating power relations. That is, when I first entered Carpinteria, the Latino parent voice was relatively quiet, except for a couple of vocal individuals and the successful bilingual preschool. The schools largely controlled the schooling of Latino students. Over the years, the COPLA changed that power relationship to include the parents. At present, having COPLA as an integral part of the school structure presents a different power relation problem—creating an agenda that is not only the schools' or only the parents' but one that addresses issues of both groups. The schools that have been most successful are those whose administrators relinquish some of their power and accept the parents' leadership.

Both administration and parents agreed that they needed to do more in the early grades to prepare students to enter a four-year college. Although in the spring of 2000, more Euro-American and Latino students went on to college after graduating from Carpinteria High School than in previous years, most will not continue on to a four-year college after completing community college. Although more Latino students are staying in high school, few end up in classes for college-bound students. Latino students who do take advanced subject matter classes come from families whose parents have been active in COPLA. Parents believe that this speaks volumes about their collective accomplishments. Parents talked about the need to put this matter on their agenda. More specifically, parents expressed the need for the school district and parents to jointly initiate a campaign to systematically direct children toward college-bound careers. Clearly, this is a task that COPLA will not dismiss.

## Re-creating

Carpinteria educators and families lived empowerment through their efforts to make "the child" their fundamental purpose and by interacting cooperatively with one another. It is critical that we implement a reflexive assessment of our local conditions. Doing so compels us to acquire a new vision that is all-encompassing and creates the practice of inclusion, in contrast to what we generally experience in these modern and postmodern periods. The five points that follow are empowerment principles that undergird the collective work accomplished in Carpinteria.

1. Underrepresented groups included women, ethnic, linguistically different, and poor people who are assigned unequal status in society. A truly democratic society is organized to provide all people of diverse backgrounds choices and opportunities to exercise their power.
2. All individuals have strengths, and cultural change should emanate from that position.
3. An understanding of the history of a given community or group, including the knowledge of language, cultural values, and conventions associated with cultural meaning, are indispensable in determining appropriate strategies for involving people in learning.
4. Learning new roles provides people with access to resources, and the learning of those roles occurs through the use of those new resources.
5. Collective critical reflection is an integral process to participation and empowerment because it helps bring concerns to a conscious level.

The empowerment process manifests three dimensions of power, including a collective process, critical reflection, and mutual respect, which in turn expand the dimensions of personal and collective identity. Empowerment is an ongoing intentional process centered in the local community. The process of listening, caring, and participating in a group allows people equal access to valued resources and gives them control over those resources as they become aware of their social conditions and their strengths: they determine their choices and goals. Steps are taken to unveil each individual's potential to act on his or her own behalf. Implicit here is the awareness of and responsibility for one's own behavior and a willingness to shape it through a social process. In the Carpinteria research project we all learned to think of ourselves differently. I learned, along with the families, that what makes us look at our circumstances as different from those of others goes much deeper than mere political knowledge; it goes to our fundamental values. In my capacity as a researcher and facilitator in family, school, and community life, I collaborated with community members to form new inclusive contexts for Latinos and non-Latinos in their personal and public arenas.

Family interactions were enhanced, specifically between parents and children. Dialogue about educational issues opened up as parents learned more about schools and children shared about the events, conflicts, and successes they experienced in the schools. Together they built a stronger confidence in their possibilities of achieving a fuller education. Although parents have always been the children's most important teachers, through increased parent-child communication, parents have become even more effective advocates.

Schools are organizations designed to support the learner. They are effective to the extent that they benefit the members. To enhance their effectiveness, schools in Carpinteria have become more responsive to the Latino students and community members, who have traditionally had a history of isolation and underachievement. Educators have begun to implement effective school-family communication, for example, by establishing the GATE program for Spanish-speaking students in response to requests by the Latino community.

Efforts to involve the Latino community were observed when the Community City Council sought the voices of COPLA and other Latino groups so that they could fully assess the conflict of housing ordinances affecting the Latino community. Having representative voices in community issues has kept Latinos informed, although the housing conflict remains unresolved.

Individuals who are active in Latino organizations like COPLA participated in a collective empowerment process that critically examined their history in Mexico and in the United States. Their analysis of their experience as poor and underschooled individuals convinced them that even though they lacked formal schooling in the United States, they possessed the cultural power and strengths they needed to raise their children and they had a strong desire to help their children succeed in school. They dismissed cultural stereotypes, like they were "uncaring parents" or "always late for meetings," that were imposed on them by the community at large and school personnel, some of which they had previously internalized. Active COPLA leaders have reached out to assist and encourage family members, friends, and acquaintances to get an education and to summon each other's strengths, in order to move forward and create new possibilities for everyone.

Through conversations, meetings, interviews, and organizing efforts, we all grew and encouraged one another to collectively create new community structures for continued learning and growth.[4] The family, schools, community, individuals, and I were all changed through our collaboration.[5]

# CHAPTER EIGHT

❧

# Time, Place, and Power Relationships

As I was driving down to Carpinteria in 1985, the flood of questions that filled me about the children, their families, their stories and dreams differed from the questions I ask fifteen years later as I complete this book. Much has changed, and previous publications have addressed earlier generations of research questions pertaining to family and community literacy in Carpinteria.[1] And years after this book is published, I will still be asking questions about the complex relationships among my collaborators who gained their voices in the community and myself as a researcher and facilitator in Carpinteria. That culture is central to changing power relations between families and schools was the premise of my work in Carpinteria. The story here describes one perspective of the journey that I shared with my collaborators. When I first began working in Carpinteria, the Latino parent voice was quiet and the schools totally controlled the education of Latino students. Over the years, COPLA changed those structural relationships to include new parents in the decision-making process.

The innovative ways in which the Spanish-speaking Latino families related proactively to the non-Latino community, the English-speaking Latinos, to each other, and to myself, the researcher, is the point of this book. It was necessary to navigate different languages and cultures while negotiating power relationships. What enabled this transnational Mexican immigrant group to rise above their arduous objective conditions is something called resilience. Immigrants of Mexican descent in the United

States are part of the Mexican diaspora. Although Mexicans emigrate from various parts of Mexico, in the United States, Mexican immigrants and nonimmigrants alike are united by a strong sense of attachment to a common history and culture.[2] Asymmetrical power relationships are the product of historically structured interactions between dominant and subordinate nation-states where those in control influence the social, political, and economic institutions at all levels, from the national level to the community and family.

Diaspora, or dislocation, as Robert Lifton[3] calls it, often impairs the familiar systems that, in the place of origin, hold together the person, family, and community. Historical dislocation occurs in the breakdown of the social and institutional arrangements that ordinarily anchor human lives. Dislocation can be traumatic, as was the case for some of the Carpinteria immigrants forced by poverty to cross the border under the threat of harm by border patrols. Family, religion, and social and political authority provide an order to life. In Carpinteria, the discontinuity touched the lives of Alicia Rosario, Rebeca Cortina, Manuel Peña, Rosa Martinez, David Segura, Antonia Juarez, Juan Ramirez, their families, and their broader community. The incongruence between what these individuals and their families felt themselves to be and what a society, formally or informally, expected them to be, created for them a sense of isolation. Carpinteria was a community where geographical, social, and socioeconomic schisms existed between Latinos and non-Latinos up until the later years of the twentieth century. The Latinos of Mexican descent in this story arrived in Carpinteria as workers at a time of historical change. How to adjust and live in a new culture was their challenge, and collectively they learned that change might cause pain, but it can also help one learn. And one of the most necessary lessons they learned was the need to build networks with each other, which would create a power that would transform their lives. One of the best ways to empower people is to give them examples of people just like themselves who are actually making a difference.

When the Spanish-speaking Latino families of the generation represented in this story first immigrated to Carpinteria, the receiving community was controlled by predominantly White Euro-Americans. However, in the 1970s, the political climate began to open up, especially concerning language and educational policies. That was the post–Civil Rights Era that made way for the *Lau v. Nichols* Supreme Court decision, giving students with home languages other than English an equal opportunity to learn. Not only were students who spoke a language other than English able to participate meaningfully in their own learning, but their parents also had an opportunity and responsibility to support their children in meaningful ways. Stirring up the classroom curriculum was a critical accomplishment of the Supreme Court decision, but the inclusion of parental voice in their children's schooling played an essential part in the success of these children's education. With this historical landmark unfolding, Latino immigrants to Carpinteria were able to develop new relationships with the school and general community, which was something Latinos who lived there before had not experienced, having been relegated to a separate Mexican school.

The collective and individual stories of the people in the COPLA leadership, including Alicia Rosario, Rebeca Cortina, Manuel Peña, Rosa Martinez, David Segura, Antonia Juarez, and Juan Ramirez, which took center stage in this book create a portrait of fluid, multiple identities and relationships within the community. These people had a common history as immigrants from Mexico. That shared experience of economic distress in Mexico and in their immigration process became a bond for them in their new community. They forged what was once a drastic discontinuity into a unifying continuity, as they organized to create social and cultural support for shaping a political presence in Carpinteria. Sharing a common language, cultural values, and family ties in Carpinteria and in Mexico, these individuals transcended their hardships and reached out to others to expand their opportunities.

Community organizing is not a new phenomenon for Latinos. It has deep roots to a time in history when legal school, geographic, economic, social, and educational segregation were used against Mexicans, as discussed in the first chapter of this book.[4] Although Mexicans in Carpinteria did not demonstrate against the isolation at the time that it was imposed, desire for change lived deep in the minds and psyches of many that succeeded in spite of the injustice and became community activists. They gave voice to that generation of Latinos. As educators and other professionals in Carpinteria, this cohort of activists advocated the empowerment of later generations of immigrant workers from Mexico who began arriving in the 1960s and 1970s, and who continue to come to this day.

Now the school district personnel and the parents know more about each other and use COPLA as a bridge through which they can learn from each other and return home with a deeper sense of self. One of the most critical aspects of parent advocacy is for the parent to establish a strong communication with the child's teacher. Latino parents in Carpenteria have learned to exercise their agency on behalf of their children. Most significant is the way that parents now ask more appropriate questions concerning their children's schooling. Parents have learned how to ask more pointed questions about the actual learning process. Key questions have more to do with how the student is performing in the state curriculum standards. This kind of question prompts increased accountability not only for the teacher and the student but also for themselves as parents. Listen to the way Olga Sanchez talked to her son's fifth-grade teacher. It was a rainy afternoon when Olga Sanchez received a call at home to meet with her son Raul's teacher after school. When she arrived at the classroom, Olga said to Peter Baker, the teacher, "I'd like Raul to join our meeting if it's about him."

"Yes, of course," responded Mr. Baker. After Raul joined them, Mr. Baker began to explain to Mrs. Sanchez that Raul had refused to comply with the classroom rules and continued to waste his time and that of others when he should be working.

"Raul, why are you acting out?" his mother asked him.

"I don't know, I'm just kind of bored," he responded.

"I'm not condoning his behavior," said Mrs. Sanchez, "but, Mr. Baker, I need to know if the curriculum is challenging Raul."

"I believe it is, but, if he's being honest about feeling bored, I want to know what about the curriculum is so easy that it bores you?" Mr. Baker turned to Raul and tried to get him to talk specifically about the areas that troubled him.

Mrs. Sanchez pressed the conversation in order to get to the root of Raul's problem. She moved beyond the possibility of just disciplining Raul for misbehaving. Mr. Baker was also attempting to pursue the right solution by asking Raul to express his opinion. At the end of the meeting, which lasted an hour and a half, the three of them reached an agreement. Raul would try to work at a different level for a week. At the end of the week the three met again and determined that positive results had been achieved.

My research in Carpinteria did not begin with set theories about learning, literacy, or family-school relationships. I did, however, take into the research setting a number of specific notions about culture, literacy, families, learning, schooling, and liberation that had evolved over my years of collaborating with the people in Carpinteria. There are seven general principles that I believe explain the links among language, culture, literacy, and empowerment: (1) language and literacy unfold in a sociocultural context; (2) literacy is a basic tool that enables people to participate in society;

(3) we need literacy to gather information and to discover the alternatives available; (4) literacy extends beyond written text; it involves the competent use of innate power in socially constructed contexts; (5) through literacy, people gather information to make conscious choices regarding how to conduct their lives and participate in diverse cultures; (6) one's ability to participate actively in social contexts permits the expansion and development of one's cultural knowledge; (7) in a collective process, the learning of language and literacy is malleable, ever shifting and in perpetual motion. Literacy is achieved through an empowerment process.

Through community actions, parents and educators created their own road to empowerment. It is the possibilities that we perceive to be ours and the understanding of our objective conditions that make up the strengths of a group's cultural knowledge. Latino parents claimed many gains through their years of community advocacy. Yet, my collaboration with them also gave me entry to the painful areas of their lives. They lived through joblessness, alcohol abuse, teen pregnancy, infidelity, catastrophic illness, and burnout. Families did not escape these parallel realities, but they managed to merge their efforts toward change— ultimately creating the life experience of transcendence. The original COPLA leaders have moved on to other projects, including setting up community after-school programs involving students and parents. As their children began to graduate from high school, their priorities and types of investment in community organizations changed.

Families and educators active in COPLA didn't get lost in the battle. They maintained a vision that continues to this day, because education is not a single, one-time or short-term project; their vision requires an ongoing dialogue based on moment-to-moment assessment of the issues to be addressed. Negotiation has become their major focus.

To appreciate the personal, cultural, and political struggles that Latinos in Carpinteria have faced, we need to consider how the historical context helps to shape the educational outcomes and sociocultural opportunities that play a role in the personal and collective transformations that transpire.

The Carpinteria story speaks to the heart of continuity and discontinuity in people's lives. Issues affecting the lives of children, parents, educators, and the community at large follow a rhythm defined by those involved. The players in this story showed how culture and learning are integrally related. Similarities and differences were manifested in the classroom, homes, workplaces, and playgrounds. Parent and child interactions showed the power of language as much as did the adults' interactions with each other across institutions.

Children's knowledge comes through the language they speak. Before even stepping foot in a school, students live in a family, a community, and in a social network that certainly expresses attitudes, norms, practices, beliefs, experiences, and aspirations. Some have had opportunities to participate in the larger mainstream culture, while others have been afforded less inclusion as a result of their social history in the community, their ethnic differences, and their socioeconomic status.

Teachers' knowledge of the students' home culture is imperative, not as a relic to hang on the bulletin board, but as a means to provide a rich curriculum that allows students to express themselves fully and to participate fully in their learning. While children's affective expression may be influenced by their culture, it is important not to stereotype children from a given cultural or ethnic group as being the same because they belong to that group. Gender, social class, regional, and individual differences exist.

Being familiar with students' cultural backgrounds not only helps teachers know who the students are, it makes them aware of the skills they may have that could contribute to their learning. Also, knowledge of other cultures increases a teacher's ability to see things from different perspectives. To consider incorporating culturally different approaches in the instruction setting calls for an understanding of the cultures represented in the classroom and the ways in which children learn outside the home. Various cultural ways of learning—for parents as well as for children in the classrooms—involve using diverse means to reach goals. Central to this matter is a mainstream community that needs to create a learning environment that supports variance and change. That is, immigrants learning a new culture is only part of the equation. The Euro-American community in power also needs to change in its interaction with immigrants. We don't have a great deal of data on how the Euro-American community in Carpinteria has changed as a result of interacting with Latino immigrants, however, as COPLA mobilized, the Euro-American community began to take notice.

Culture is relational. In this complex society, culture is constantly changing. Culture is always being shaped and re-created as it expands and comes into contact with others. Groups are in constant contact, and although some aspects of traditional cultures are maintained, more often, aspects of individual cultures begin to interrelate and blend together. Patterns, beliefs, and attitudes are integrated in a meaning that is learned and shared.

Parents—life teachers—play critical roles in shaping their children's cultural environment. Teachers create a classroom culture, and students respond; they know to remain quiet when the teacher is giving instructions, they know to walk, not run, inside the classroom, to turn in their homework at the beginning of the day, and to use soft voices inside the classroom. Just as they do in their homes, students act out classroom cultural norms, depending on their interpretation of the rules.

Teachers, too, are culture bearers. They bring into the classrooms a multitude of ideas, beliefs, and knowledge based on their own experience. Classrooms are forums where open inquiry and diverse points of view can be expressed. Consistent with democratic values, the teachers can provide contexts where students are informed about a variety of perspectives, opinions, and beliefs. It takes a resourceful and knowledgeable teacher committed to cultural change to create an appropriate learning environment where democratic values and cultural variance flourish within a rigorous academic curriculum.

Involving the students' culture in the learning setting means that the teacher motivates students to understand human freedom, justice, and equality through diverse cultural values. Such ideals shape a democratic society through the instructional program. This is possible when classroom teachers present curriculum and perspectives that include and reflect values of students from diverse sociocultural and socioeconomic backgrounds. Positive attitudes about diversity in and out of the classroom also play an important role in influencing students' acceptance of all peoples in this society.

Family and school cultures now share a power that the school alone has typically dominated. What educators need to focus on is trying not to make poor or ethnically different families into a mainstream culture, but to attempt to create a common culture with the families—a culture based on conditions that allow everyone to participate and express themselves in meaningful ways. Cultural congruency mandates a democratic process in which all school officials, families, and community members have a voice about their common interest—children. Continuity between educators and students doesn't just presume that the students change their culture to meet the educator's expectation. Educators also have a responsibility to understand their role in the school culture. Before assuming the role of a teacher, a person needs to clarify his or her own cultural heritage and experience. It is imperative that teachers understand how their culture intersects with the experiences of their students' cultures. Clarifying one's own relationship with other cultural groups requires adopting positive attitudes toward differences. Contact with and knowledge about the complexity of people and about their lives and interests makes it possible to transcend one's limited notions about a specific group. In schools, teachers sometimes make the mistake of teaching curriculum that reflects only the cultural groups represented in their classroom. This is as much a problem as teaching only curriculum that reflects the White mainstream culture. Every person in the world is part of an ethnic group and belongs to a cultural group, or various cultural groups, depending on their heritage and the society where they live. To represent the universal nature of culture, teachers need to include as many groups as possible in their curriculum. This provides the students with an awareness of the global reality of humanity and allows them to understand people's commonalties and differences on a wide-scale basis, which is a fundamental premise of a multicultural curriculum.

Recognizing that all cultures have a historical, social, and economic bases demystifies the notion of differences. Teachers hold the power to open students' minds about differences by teaching the *real* basis of culture and making the connection with their own culture, as well as with those of the students. Building bridges between cultures through effective teaching both expands a student's world and at the same time, makes it a smaller one.

No fixed formulas exist for learning a new language, culture, literacy, or empowerment. What promotes these things are our understanding of the conditions in which we find ourselves and our perception of our ultimate possibilities. And through collective engagement, we find meaning and the potential to resolve whatever situations confront us. When we participate meaningfully in our families and community—if we find an emotional and trusting connection—we can change.

Interpersonal connections between immigrants and nonimmigrants in Carpinteria were made in public spheres. Growing into a new community and learning a new language and culture create stresses that are added to those of the constant ordinary life issues of employment, money, health, family relationships, teen pregnancies, and child rearing. How people handle day-to-day adversity or major crises varies greatly from family to family and from community to community. And it is no different for the Latinos in Carpinteria. Strength, faith, and resiliency have emerged to create new possibilities through face-to-face interactions and activities in people's daily lives.

Resiliency is the ability to return to an original form after being stretched, compressed, or injured. A person's ability to recover from adversity, be it physical, emotional, economic, or cultural, reclaims and restores his or her agency to act on his or her own behalf. Resilience is not an end but a process. How immigrants exercise their resilience is the real question in the Carpinteria story. Research has revealed the characteristics of resilient behavior.[5] Negotiating and problem solving are at the heart of the Carpinteria people's story. Readings on resilience are replete with various notions about the concept, but to help understand the process of change in Carpinteria, I will focus on four major perspectives, ways of seeing and operating in the world: (1) *optimism prevails even in the midst of hardship*, (2) people *reach out for support*, (3) people *perceive their lives as meaningful*, and (4) people *sustain a proactive perspective*. These areas define a path that leads to learning, transcending stressful conditions, and fashioning new meaning in people's lives.

## Optimism Prevails Even in the Midst of Hardship

Optimism usually coexits with uncertainty. Events in the lives of the Carpinteria families revealed their potential and the possibilities for expanding their access to the cultural and educational resources they needed. But for people to become inspired and optimistic is difficult to do when they feel isolated. Carpinteria Latinos were not spared. They underwent tough times and less burdensome ones. Their participation in the Guadalupeños (a religious society) in the Catholic Church, Sunday soccer teams, and COPLA connected them socially, emotionally, and even economically. Through these networks they found others who shared their experience. Some families transcended their conflict-riddled times through their participation in cultural organizations, which spoke highly of the importance of COPLA. Others needed more time and support to find a way out of their pain.

I also met and worked with numerous others who felt stuck in their pain and feelings of despair, which often resulted from unemployment. This forced them to live in crowded apartments with little hope of change. While the people perceived themselves as powerless in these situations, they did not remain fixed in a negative mind-set. Living under these conditions made many people put hope in their children's ability to get a good education and find ways to improve their lives.

Families tend to transcend oppressive difficulties and find sources of strength. The question is how to convince people to confront their stressful situations and to connect with a supportive person or group who will help them redirect their pain outward rather than inward. Sometimes families who are active in groups like COPLA can't always find their strength, especially when their lives feel out of control. The reality of psychosocial dynamics is that no simple formulas exist for becoming an empowered individual, family, or community. What is certain is that strength resides in everyone, regardless of color, religion, socioeconomic standing, place of residence, ethnicity, or educational attainment. But, as COPLA families learned, a person's experiences of isolation and oppression can be mitigated when they are shared with others. Collectively our potential for changing our lives increases. Families in Carpinteria tapped that potential through family, social, workplace, religious, recreational, and educational networks. This makes grassroots organizations like COPLA imperative because they help people gain a sense of control over their lives, making them aware of their capacity.

Latinos in Carpenteria harnessed their ability to confront stressful situations related to their children. By connecting with others in a supportive situation, they redirected their pain outward rather than inward. By being active in the COPLA group, parents found support in dealing with the problems of schooling their children in an unfamiliar culture.

## They Reach Out for Support

*Child* was the most frequent word spoken at Latino parent meetings. It defined COPLA's efforts from day one. Latino parents established a dialogue with other parents and with the schools. The life of the organization as well as the lives of many of its activists have been transformed. Establishing a sociopolitical power base, making structural changes in the organization, and redefining and redesigning COPLA created a new community of Latinos and non-Latinos united in achieving one goal— improving the education of the children. Through their work, COPLA members, parents, and educators developed an ethic of respect, listened to each other, and addressed mutual concerns.

Collectivity these individuals challenged each other on a family level and on a community level through COPLA and made it safe to reach out to others and to discover new resources. They built on their faith and caring and expanded their potential. Together they identified educational access for children and families, and inevitably they discovered a deeper sense of personal strength.

## They Perceive Their Lives as Meaningful

When their children succeed in school, Latinos feel that the sacrifices involved in immigrating to a new society were all worth it. They are also proud to see themselves growing, especially as leaders in COPLA. Many who participated in COPLA were inspired to new ways of thinking—about themselves, about their families, and about the community. They were committed to learning about the system, supporting others, and uniting Latinos. Their newfound political and social consciousness was often spurred by a personal desire to learn and make the most of their life, goals that began early in their lives in Mexico. That very courage and tenacity that carried them across the Mexican-U.S. border propelled the innate leadership they displayed.

Although learning a new culture adds new layers of responsibilities and stress, Latinos in Carpinteria also found living in a new culture an opportunity to discover new meanings. New social networks served to make them realize that they were not alone. Their many abilities became assets in managing the changes in their lives, while affecting growth in the members of their families and in their workplaces.

## They Sustain a Proactive Perspective

Social networks provided opportunities for people in Carpinteria to become connected with others around common issues and to learn that they were not alone in dealing with their problems, as overwhelming as they seem at times. Joining with others we gain a different perspective and learn new ways to address problems, which motivates us to become proactive.

Against the instability created by threats of hunger, illness, separation, unemployment, confusion, and self-doubt, the people in Carpinteria have shown resilience. Together they found themselves evolving a self that had many possibilities, and collectively they achieved a goal that alone seemed difficult to envision.

The stories of the people of Carpinteria show that cultural change and adjustment, which the parents underwent on behalf of their children, require political education and grassroots mobilizing efforts. Untapped Latino potential is great across the United States and specifically in California, where Latinos now make up a majority of the state's population.

Some people question whether a more cooperative, progressive society, whose goal is the preservation of the species at both human and ecological levels, can be achieved solely through community and family-level empowerment efforts. One thing we do know is that transformation cannot occur without such efforts. Although COPLA is not a panacea in the development of the Carpinteria community, it has been like a pebble in the water and has produced ripples moving outward to create opportunities for people to expand in the face of dissonance.

Community-based educational organizations like COPLA link family, schools, and community, accessing social networks to improve socioeconomic, cultural, and educational resources. Through the COPLA effort, the Latino parent group challenged themselves and others to look beyond their singular personal needs and to unfold their potential for the benefit of everyone. Their strides may seem small, but they are giant steps in the creation of their complex cultural, political, and personal tapestry. Pain and hope undergird the daily work of these families, who hold children's educational and economic future as their inspiration.

# CHAPTER NINE

ༀ

# The Story and the Storyteller

The researcher's autobiography is an important piece of the story we tell about the communities we study. All research conducted by human beings inevitably involves the multiple lenses of the researcher. As researchers we need to reflect on the aspects of ourselves that most importantly influence our perceptions of the world and in particular the issues being studied. To account for the subjectivity throughout the research process we must consider ways in which our emotions, feelings, and life experience are a source of insight into the area of study.

In earlier publications I have reported on aspects of my personal history that influenced my professional and research orientation.[1] Much of what has moved me to work in the communities where I have taught and conducted research is located in my formative years. My parents' voices ring strong in my heart as I recall how influential they were in laying the brick and mortar for my educational and career achievements.

Carpinteria, more than any other community in which I have worked, has led me to examine the fluid boundaries between the self, the family, the school, and the community as well as the open border between researcher and the community. No longer are the researcher and the community ethnographically dichotomous. The question is which boundaries should be permeable and which should not be crossed. The demonstration of empathy with a community is one permeable divide that researchers need to be able to cross, but we must resist stepping over the bounds regarding the level of respect that we extend to the people in the field.

Power has been a leading force in my academic and personal concepts of education. The ways in which the Carpinteria families and I collaborated were significant for what we were able to accomplish and how we changed in the process. We made our differences and similarities our strengths in improving the family, school, and community for the children.

The people in Carpinteria and I related to each other with great respect and trust. The years I worked with the people in Carpinteria led me to question my academic assumptions more deeply, making it easier for me to understand my collaborators' perceptions about their lives. The lessons I learned in Carpinteria enlightened me professionally and personally. I encountered a serious health problem with a systemic debilitating disease five years after I started my fieldwork in the community. And during the tough times of recovery, I was inspired by the people's stories of strength, resilience, and change. Through courage, hard work, and willingness to learn, they transformed their lives before my eyes. I held on to those examples as I forged through the fear and faced the changes and challenges thrust upon me by a weakening body. I deepened my resolve and hope for the possibilities open to me, joining with others, as they had done, to form a supportive community.

My familiarity with working-class patriarchal family relationships, as well as my knowledge of the psychosocial adjustment required to learn a new language, culture, and school profoundly resonated with elements of the life stories I observed in Carpinteria, especially those where a value for education defined daily life.

My childhood in Mexico holds special memories. If I close my eyes, I can still smell the musty old school building and hear my friends' lively voices singing *naranja dulce* (sweet orange) and other popular circle games and jingles. The Spanish alphabet letters pinned neatly in the front of the classroom above the blackboard formed a background behind the young teacher, whose warm smile greeted us every day. By the time I was in second grade in my Mexican school I was reading history books. When we moved, I missed my days in Mexico, where the language and books were familiar and where my friends understood me. I was a star student before we immigrated legally to Los Angeles, California. Yet here, in my American school, despite improvements in my reading of the English language, threats from Mrs. Brown, my teacher, to keep me in during recess until I learned to read in English to her satisfaction, kept me fearful and anxious. I hated school when I first arrived; my teacher's insensitivity was almost unbearable.

On my first day of school, the teacher immediately handed me a book and expected me to read the first page. I heard my heavy Spanish accent, "Di bois guent too deir jawus," as I tried to read it phonetically (The boys went to their house). I stumbled painfully, trying to read aloud all the way to the end of the page. Then thankfully the recess bell rang. But as the girls' line walked out the door, my teacher took hold of my shoulder and said, "I'm sorry, Concha, but you must stay in during recess. You cannot read English, so you cannot play." This saddened me greatly, since I was looking forward to seeing my sisters, with whom I could speak Spanish during recess.

Months passed and the extent of my English conversations with classmates increased. I could say, "I like playing with my sisters and I like to eat in the cafeteria." But my teacher was still unimpressed by my progress in English. Spending my recess with my head on my desk had become a daily event. Although I couldn't speak English fluently, I could understand quite a bit. One classroom golden rule was, "Do not copy your neighbor's work." This meant that I was not to look at anyone's paper when the teacher asked us to answer questions in our books. My teacher threatened to tell my parents that I was not doing well in school. I was humiliated. I felt so alone. Intimidated by her warnings, I feared that until I learned English, she would continue to separate me from my sisters.

One day, the teacher instructed the class to fill in the answers to some questions in the reading workbook. I stared at the words on the page, but they meant nothing to me. Walking up to the teacher's desk, I told her that I didn't understand the questions. She looked at me and responded, "I've already explained it. If you have read the story you can answer the questions."

Embarrassed, I returned to my desk and looked around the room as if I expected to find the answers written on the children's foreheads. Instead I saw a sea of blond heads tipped forward reading their books. I was lost for answers, and my frustration got the better of me. I glanced across the row of single desks to my neighbor's paper, which was clearly exposed. But before I could copy anything, I felt the teacher's presence. She stood by my desk. "Let me have your paper," she demanded. I handed it to her. My eyes warmed with tears as I watched her tear up my clean sheet of paper that had only my name on the top right-hand corner. I felt my child-like spirit fleeing the classroom that afternoon, hiding with shame, leaving only my empty body sitting alone at the rigid desk. Mrs. Brown never knew that years later when I became a teacher I would think about her and know that I had to do everything opposite of the way she had done. The most important thing she taught was what not to do. The loneliness of the shame I felt for not knowing the answers left me winded. I wanted to escape, but my feet felt like they were set in cement.

School traumatized me. Most of the time I felt nervous just walking onto the grounds, and it only got worse once I was in the classroom. I wanted so much to show Mrs. Brown that I was trying the best I could. As she walked toward me, my eyes fixed on this older woman with salt-and-pepper hair pulled tight in a bun. Her eyes dulled with harshness. I felt like her captive, fearing that my parents would find out I was not a good student. Fearing that I would be forever stuck in these feelings, I was determined that I would not let her get the better of me. I thought to myself, "I know how to read, I'll show you, lady." Right then and there I promised myself that I would successfully brave that unfriendly place called school. Eventually I did.

Chocolate cupcakes compensated nicely when on Fridays Mom occasionally showed up at my classroom with armfuls of them. Although Mom spoke little English, she became a room mother and helped the teachers at every class gathering. My mother, Maria, was a very kind woman, and everyone loved her. Her visits to the classroom were important to my sense of belonging in this foreign school.

Susie, one of the girls in my class, especially liked Mom's cupcakes. She begged the teacher for a second one, something I wanted to do, but didn't dare. Mom would frown on that. She would think it was bad manners. Susie befriended me because she liked to correct my English. We made it a game. I pointed to things and she told me the names "That's a shelf. That's a closet." "Klozet." "No, it's closet." Eventually, I considered the possibility that this place called school might hold some fun for me, after all. Susie had a five-foot plunge pool in her backyard and invited me to her house to watch her dive. These were scenes from my fantasies about rich people. I had never imagined that I would actually ever know someone so rich.

I remember in the 1950s construction work paid well, if you didn't mind being unemployed half of the year because of weather conditions and labor union problems. Supporting a family of seven on a construction worker's salary required apt financial management and lots of faith! My father, a bricklayer, was frequently passed over for work because he spoke very little English. Few words were spoken about unemployment, shortages, or worries about "making it." My parents didn't have to tell us when things were tough; their silence said it all. I dreaded coming home after school and finding Dad's gray blue Dodge parked in the driveway.

It meant that he hadn't gotten work that day. Standing outside the screen door, I saw my mother's sullen face, holding deep her disquiet. Standing over the sink washing the day's dishes seem to distract her from the burden. Dad sat in the room with her, looking out the window, his black metal lunch pail on top of the table next to him.

"Hello, Mom," I'd kiss her on the cheek.

"¿Cómo te fue?" (How did it go?), she asked.

With an eye on dad's black lunch pail, I asked if we could have the untouched lunch he'd brought back home. "As long as you share it with your sisters." The bologna, mayonnaise, and lettuce sandwich temporarily helped me forget the uncertainty I shared with my parents over the persistent money shortages we faced. As much as my parents tried to shelter us from worry, Dad's lunch pail served as a stark reminder.

I was consumed with worry for my parents, on whose faces I read the same questions that were churning inside of me. How would Mom and Dad take care of us? What would happen to my sisters and me? I felt so badly that my father's limited English prevented him from getting a job. The fear that percolated within me was all too reminiscent of the dread I felt at those times when my teacher castigated me for not speaking English correctly. My father couldn't buffer my fear of not knowing English, but in later years I would know that Dad knew much more than "correct" English. Without any formal education, he would be my geometry and trigonometry tutor in high school. It occurred to me that maybe he didn't push school as much as Mom did because he had taught himself what the rest of us had to go to school to learn.

My mother was quite strict, but her loving style of parenting balanced my father's authoritarian role in the family. Her words on the importance of *educación* made a strong impression on me. It had a much broader meaning than the English word, *education.* One's comportment with others had to include respect, good manners, and a willingness to cooperate and coexist peacefully. I worked masterfully to avoid being caught behaving selfishly because she would say, "Asi no se comporta una persona con educación." (That's not the way an educated person behaves.) This cultural ethos shielded me from the sting of discrimination when classmates ridiculed me because I was Mexican. I aptly dismissed unfriendly comments in school and just stayed open to friendships that nurtured me.

Not all of my elementary school teachers were as insufferable as Mrs. Brown. I spent three years with Mrs. Clark who was my home-teacher when I was ill. She sat on the couch, and I sat in a tall, wooden-back, antique-looking wheelchair, which had been donated to my parents for my use. It reminded me of the one I had seen in the book *Heidi.* Mrs. Brown would have been shocked that I could read complete books. Heidi befriended a young disabled girl, whom she inspired to walk again. When I could walk again, it was time for junior high school. From the door I watched the tall gray-haired Mrs. Clark walk to her car, and I bade her good-bye. Her quiet manner made learning special, but I welcomed being able to walk into a real school building with real students.

I entered South Junior High School happy to have a place to belong. But anxiety overcame me when I received my first grade card and saw that I had all *C*s and even one *D.* I was particularly upset that the *D* was in drama! I had taken drama because I wanted to act in school plays. That I did, and I also spent long hours writing critiques on the plays we performed. This was one time when hard work did not pay off, and after getting the poor grade I questioned whether I even had fun acting in the school plays. To some people the *D* might represent a pretty average student who just needs a bit of motivation. But to me this was unforgivable! My years out of school were showing, and I had plenty of motivation; now it was time to get down to serious studying. I called on some fellow students, but I got a lot of cold shoulders. This didn't help to heal the gap I felt between the junior high school and me. Socially I felt awkward, so I launched myself into various school clubs, such as drama and choir, in the hopes of meeting new friends. But sometimes one can try too hard. In this case, my sadness overshadowed my unsuccessful attempts to fit in. I tried, but with little success. At times getting good grades just didn't seem like it was worth it. I felt friendless and alone. Maybe it was that I looked different—one of those kids from the other side of town who was bused in to desegregate this white neighborhood. Looks were most important, looking pretty, looking slim, and looking blond and white. And then there was the look of rejection. My first year of reintegrating into a social and academic setting taught me that I could survive academically and socially even if I didn't have close buddies. Yes, my grades improved after lots of dedicated studying; I had nothing better to do. I found comfort in books. Studying was the best way to stay out of the trouble that seemed to follow other Mexican kids who rode the bus with my sisters and me. Junior high had taught me one sure thing; that hard work had important payoffs.

At home I recalled that my mother enjoyed reading the daily newspaper and short stories in magazines. Her storytelling took the form of *platicas* (conversations) with me at the kitchen table on rare occasions when the household fell quiet. Mom told of her days as a child migrant worker with her family who worked the avocado, apricot, and lemon groves. She spoke fondly about a teacher at a school in Lompoc, California, who had taken an interest in her and taught her to love learning. Mom worked very hard with her family in the fields and attended school the few days of the year she could after the crop season ended; this was the era before migrant education began in California. Her love for learning about people in other parts of the world was conveyed in our *platicas*. Hard work and discipline were my parents' ways, but achieving in school was my mother's strongest expectation for my sisters and me.

Both of my parents missed out on formal schooling beyond the early years because they worked to help support their families. On their own, they pursued education to learn English and new skills for employment in the United States. Their experience manifested explicit and implicit messages of encouragement, especially from my mother, to study, travel, learn as much as possible, and above all, to respect myself and others. My identity as a Mexican woman was shaped in a household where the Spanish language and Mexican cultural traditions such as love for family were valued, along with new rules established by my mother. She expected her daughters to break the confinements of poverty and dependence on patriarchy.

After school, Mom made sure we completed our homework before dinner. After dinner we were expected to help wash dishes. After household chores, reading was the nightly pastime for years before we got a television. Although my second-grade teacher may not have thought that I could read the textbooks well enough to play during recess, I was an avid reader at home and loved reading everything, including books, magazines, and even can labels, when nothing else was available. Reading liberated me.

I took advantage of the school library to borrow books. At home, one of my greatest pleasures was to crawl up in a corner of the living room and absorb myself in adventure and fantasy books in English. In the *Courage of Sarah Noble* I got acquainted with living in the wilderness and the courage of a young girl even though she was afraid most of the time. Then there was *Charlotte's Web*. Charlotte was a much nicer spider than the one that bit me and put me in the hospital. The loyal friendship between the spider and the pig still warms my heart. I was impressed; she was a literate spider and used her intelligence to save her friend the pig by weaving words on her web. These and many other books stirred in me the notion of limitless possibilities; no matter how tough things seemed in the stories, they enlivened my imagination and fantasies. My real joy was reading about new people, new cultures, and uncharted places. Actually, reading any book in English gave me a peek into a culture different from what my family and I shared at home.

At nighttime my sisters and I had no problem falling asleep without the traditional bedtime story that many parents read to their children. But we often sat up in bed reading our books by the dim glow of a streetlight that shone through the small window in our room. Our reading in bed often turned into an untimely playtime for my sisters and me. We broke into fits of uncontrollable laughter playing tickling games, but it usually met with stern reprimands from my parents, who needed as much sleep as possible. The squeaky floorboards announced Mom coming toward us. We knew to quiet down or get our books and pretend to be reading in the dark. Mom stepped quietly into our room and pointed the flashlight at us, whispering, "Put away the books and go to sleep."

In high school, Mrs. Nichols was my counselor. She didn't know what my life dreams were, but she cared enough to make sure that I persevered against a system that only cared about the statistics on the standardized Iowa Tests of Educational Development (ITED) we had to take every spring, which determined where we were placed in our academic subjects.

When Mrs. Nichols called me into her office to inform me that I was in the top ten of my graduating class, I didn't really know what it meant except that I was crazed with learning. So it sounded great. To my surprise, the winning streak had just begun. I won a gold seal and a fifty-dollar cash price from the PTA. I also applied for a five hundred dollar scholarship from the scholarship society, which my best friend won. My friend felt bad for me and asked me if I was okay. I told her that I was happy for her and that I felt confident that God never closes one door without opening another. My mother had recited this refrain whenever the going got tough. I was sure that my faith could carry me through this and other disappointments. Two weeks later, I received a letter from the University of the Pacific, where I had applied for admission to their Inter-American Studies Program. UOP offered me a four-year scholarship, which covered tuition and fees. This was a great deal, even though I still had to work for my room and board.

My parents cried with joy and sadness all at once. Although they supported my going to college, they wanted me to attend one closer to home. My oldest sister had gone away to school in Massachusetts to earn her doctorate degree. My other sisters also lived away from home but attended local colleges. The fact that most of my sisters studied locally made my parents question why I had to go to a university in Stockton. I've often since thought about how, in my excitement to live away from home,

I was callous to my parents' feelings of loss. Perhaps they understood; eventually they stopped asking when I was going to come back home.

In college, I initially wanted to go into international service, working on issues of the world's children. But working in the community convinced me that my first career would begin in my backyard. My teaching elementary school and becoming a principal was influenced by my political work with the United Farm Workers. Later the Third World Women's Alliance and work in community centers shaped my career interest and my approach to work. I worked in a collective with other women of color, and we created a strong bond that sustained us through our work in communities, raising political awareness on women's issues in working-class communities and society. I would remain lifelong friends with many of the women in the organization.

I felt invigorated by our community work, and the energy of it spilled over into my teaching. In a community south of San Francisco I was assigned to a kindergarten. To see all of those children absorb every word, idea, and smile around them helped me release some of the trauma I suffered when I first began school in the United States. The small school building was surrounded by a neighborhood of tract houses all resembling each other. Some people owned their homes; others rented. It was a hyphenated American community—African-, Mexican-, Filipino- and European-Americans. Adults worked in nearby factories and businesses. Their jobs were temporary, with small salaries. The fresh smiling faces of those thirty, five-year-olds made my 6:00 A.M. wake-up call bearable, and sometimes I was even awake before I got to the school at 7:30. For a night owl like myself it was quite a feat to stand in front of a group of energetic children, lead them in song, and interest them in reading that early in the morning.

It was my quest for new challenges that led me to leave the classroom in order to head a large elementary school in San Jose as principal. Although I learned a great deal in that position, I always had more questions that I never seemed to have time to address as long as I was in charge of the school. I knew that I had to return to school to replenish my mind, and Stanford was the right place to immerse myself in the study of what I always enjoyed—children's folkways and oral narrative.

While working on my doctorate at Stanford, the pace I followed was exhausting, but I loved having time to study, read, and write. I stretched intellectually in directions I had not imagined were possible. For the purpose of researching family rituals concerning community lore, I gained entry into communities by introducing myself as a former teacher and school principal. I was willing to tutor their children in schoolwork in exchange for being able to record their children's games, songs, and stories. My love for people's oral and written traditions expanded me and moved me into new communities as a researcher. Although I loved studying and working with people's oral and written traditions, the most important lesson I learned about work first became known to me while I was finishing my dissertation. Before I had my own computer, I had a small electric Corona typewriter. Day after day I sat typing from noon until midnight. But on the days when I pulled back to reflect, think, analyze, I was anxious and frustrated that I hadn't worked at all. Aware of the notions about work that lived in me, where hourly factory assembly-line production ruled, I was at a loss as to how to change my thinking. It would take a future major health crisis for me to shift my thinking about how we construct our notions of work.

After Stanford I began conducting ethnographic fieldwork with families and communities, and I did so in Texas, southern and northern California, Colorado, the Central California Valley, and later in Alaska and Carpinteria. Influenced by Paulo Freire's writings on literacy, I deepened my understanding of how people can obtain their freedom through literacy. Years earlier when living in Berkeley, I met Freire when his book *Pedagogy for the Oppressed* was published in the early 1970s. At that time I was introduced to his concept of *concenticasao,* raising people's consciousness about their position in society as part of their literacy. Far different from Mrs. Brown, my second-grade teacher, Freire's ideas on changing people's conditions through literacy moved me profoundly. The power behind Freire's thoughts and theories were visible in every word he wrote. At the time that the Brazilian philosopher, educator, and visionary visited the Bay Area, he had been exiled from his homeland and was traveling the world to carry his message of empowering the oppressed through literacy. A professor whose class I was auditing at UC Berkeley hosted Freire at his home, and, among many others, the members of our seminar were invited. More than fifty people were crammed into the living room of the professor's huge, two-story Berkeley home, several long blocks from the campus. The Portuguese-speaking man sat in a maroon antique chair that seemed to swallow him. The professor mediated the questions directed to Freire, who answered each one with calm and ease, pausing frequently in search of the exact English word. We all hung on every word he spoke. One man at the rear of the room called out, "How can we use your notions of change to help those who are poor, illiterate, and oppressed here? They're hurting and need homes, jobs, education, and freedom from this oppressive system."

"You begin where they are," began Freire. "What is it that they know? Everyone knows something. You sound very angry, and before you can help others, you must put aside your own anger. That is very destructive when you're trying to help others to build their life."

A pregnant pause followed, but Freire's words to the angry young man rang so loud for me that little else has made as much impact in the way that I think about my work. I had heard this before when working for the Farmworkers' Union. Leaders espoused Cesar Chavez's philosophy that we should be impatient with the problem but not with ourselves. I interpreted Freire's words to mean something similar—that to empower others, we need to operate from a position of hope, not despair. Unbeknownst to me, the next time I was to see Freire I would be a professor at the University of California, Santa Barbara. That time I had the honor to serve on the same panel with Freire to discuss my work with families and communities based on his notions of literacy. After the panel discussion, a few of us were invited to have dinner with Freire and his wife. Of the people who have shaped the principles of how I work with communities, Freire was pivotal. For this more than any other reason I appreciated the opportunities I had to talk with him personally.

That everyone is a whole person, in spite of the fact that they might live in impoverished conditions is one of Freire's perspectives that inspired my work. His concept of conscientization, the practice of revealing and transforming reality, has been central in my work. He put into words what I felt deeply when conducting my family and community research and writing about oral and written traditions in people's lives.

After receiving my Ph.D. from Stanford I took a postdoctorate research position at the University of Colorado, Boulder. The one winter I spent there froze my eyelashes shut, when my eyes watered, and the nicks and dents on my car were getting so costly from my inability to drive in the snow that I welcomed any opportunity to return to California.

Thanks to my colleague and mentor, Henry Trueba, who at the time was a professor at the University of California, Santa Barbara, and Larry Iannaccone, who at the time was acting dean, I was invited to assume an assistant professor position at UCSB. Delighted at the opportunity of staying in California, I accepted. My penchant for work made it easy to fit into the lifestyle of an academic, where the few time limits that exist are those that the professors set for themselves.

Getting tenure in a research university is no small feat, but once again, my relentless work ethic rewarded me. During my fifth year at the university, I qualified for an accelerated promotion, two years earlier than the normal course of promotions for assistant professors. I became an associate professor.

As an associate professor I spent as much time as possible in Carpinteria with the children and their families. By this time, exciting things were taking place that involved me as a researcher in the community. I became more and more engaged in the lives of the families who participated in my research study. The people in Carpinteria challenged me to remain conscious of the relationship between who they were and who I was and what we had in common. We shared a Mexican immigrant cultural experience and the Spanish language, but our separate social and educational standings created a divide. The degrees of privilege available to us respectively translated into voice. Together, however, we, the researcher and community collaborators, discovered a new perception.

My ethnographic work is an extension of my interest in children, families, communities, and cross-cultural perspectives. My ways of observing, interviewing, and perceiving life stories were both learned and inspired. At Stanford, three renowned anthropologists made up my dissertation committee: Shirley B. Heath, George Spindler, and Sylvia Yanigasako. But it was my father's natural aptness for observing life and his keen storytelling ability that inspired and taught me up until his last days.

After my mother died, this man, then in his mid-eighties, decided to sell the home where they had lived for more than thirty-seven years. He chose to move into a retirement home in the same community and was the only Spanish-speaking man in the building. Life was quite different for him in a small apartment surrounded by neighbors who spoke only English. Initially, the new setting was overwhelming. But within days, he began telling life stories about other residents whom he had befriended and with whom he ate meals. He shared humorous anecdotes about the workers in the building. Dad had everyone's routine memorized and could describe the rhythm and movement of his new home and everyone in it. His acute level of listening, observing, and retelling of stories is something I still work at achieving.

Call it drive, inspiration, or a demanding workload, but I was too involved in research, teaching, writing, traveling to conferences, and giving lectures to preoccupy myself with setting time limits on my work. And so I approached my new position of associate professor with the same skills that had allowed me to succeed all my life—intense work, long hours, and total investment. Self-imposed time pressures greatly reduced any semblance of a life I might have had with my family and friends. Reminders were ever present that my investment in my career was out of control. Straddling university work, family and personal life wasn't easy, but it kept me sane. I kept work in perspective. Or so I thought. By the end of my second year as a professor, I was clocking in more hours a week than two people working full time.

"You need to slow down," my family and friends cautioned me.

"I can't," I replied. "I have too much to do."

I worked energetically and played equally hard. This was the norm for me; anything slower made me worry that I wasn't being productive enough. Secretly, however, I just wanted the world to stop so that I could jump off, even if for just a minute. Surviving the academic culture demands long hours for any professor, and I was no exception, investing my time without restraint. Whenever I was feeling overwhelmed, I'd hear the words of George Spindler at Stanford, who upon my asking, "Will this work pace at least ease up after my dissertation?" laughed and said, "You must be joking, Concha. It only gets worse." But even his warning didn't prepare me for how I would feel after years of program development, writing and publishing research articles, endless hours of sitting in meetings, teaching classes, and writing research proposals for funding. But I plunged deeper into my teaching, writing, and field research in communities with poor and underrepresented families.

An unexpected surprise came my way in 1990. A university in northern California offered me a position as one of three new faculty members with an anthropological background invited to develop a doctorate level Sociocultural Studies Program. I didn't hesitate. I welcomed the opportunity to build a new program and again work with my colleague Henry Trueba, and of course to return home to the Bay Area.

Shortly after I returned to the Bay Area, my life began to unravel. I was falling apart from the inside out. Physically, I felt weighted, tired, debilitated, exhausted, depleted, weakened, expended, listless—just plain inert and with pain the intensity of a third-degree burn all over my body! Before long I was using a cane, then crutches, and finally a power wheelchair, disabled. I was diagnosed with systemic lupus.

I stubbornly continued to teach and attend meetings full time at the university as well as travel to my research sites in southern California, Alaska, and Mexico, while presenting keynote addresses at human development symposia at Cornell University, the University of Cincinnati, and UCLA. For every invitation to speak, I found some reason for accepting. Work kept me focused, but the reality was that I felt the need to balance my life differently.

Reduced traveling increased the time I spent at home, because I needed all my strength to combat the persistent respiratory complications that debilitated me in the winter. I spent the entire month of December 1994 sleeping sitting up at night. Breathing hurt. It was an exhausting challenge to manage my daily physical therapies, university work, and family responsibilities. I rested as much as possible during the day, then I sat up with my laptop to write a few minutes on the chapter for the volume on women's research before I lay down again.

In 1996, two years after becoming a full professor at the university, I left academia. Leaving the university, I could heal and commit to a new career, with my health as top priority. I am grateful that I was able to complete this volume covering fifteen years of one community's work and transformation.

Why the researcher's life story matters to the reader is that the story and the storyteller are interdependent. The research community and the researcher are two parts of the whole. By telling this thread of my life I do not apologize for, justify, or idealize my role as researcher and facilitator in Carpinteria. But I do believe that in ethnography we bring much more than academic skills to the research site. Just as immigrants bring their culture, language, and values to a new society, so do researchers bring their values, beliefs, and life experiences to fieldwork. Our life lessons form lenses through which we see the world. And in our research communities we create an arena where biography and autobiography meet. That was my experience in this community.

Of all my work in communities and research, Carpinteria's children's stories speak to me the loudest. One in particular is entitled, "Planting Seeds Together." Seven-year-old Maria Vargas told her favorite story. She smiled sweetly, and her eyes danced during her storytelling. "Once there was an old man who had one seed to plant in the earth, and it delayed in growing. Then a little boy watered it, and it grew and grew, and the old man needed help. The young boy told him that he would help him prune the tree that had grown so big. He told him to cut it with a saw. When they finished taking care of the tree, the tree produced apples. Then children gathered to help the man. When all the children collected all of the apples, he gave each one a dollar. Later the old man said, 'Thank you,' and all of children became friends with the old man. And the old man went home happy." Convinced as I am that stories about our lives provide continuity for humankind to relate to, I believe Maria's *cuento* has an important message. To me it symbolizes our common ground, the place where the story and the storyteller's work intertwine.

# CHAPTER TEN

❧

# Reflections

Sitting at the kitchen table, I could see out the window. The dense avocado groves surrounded the Garcias' small two-bedroom house. They lived on the property where Samuel Garcia worked as the head gardener. The comforting smell of fresh perked coffee filled the kitchen area where I sat listening to Samuel and Teresa Garcia's stories. Nibbling on the *pan dulce* (sweet rolls) between questions felt quite familiar. Talking with people in their home and community settings had not only been a part of my other ethnographic research studies, but was central to my earlier work as an elementary school teacher and school principal. In Carpinteria, being with the families was edifying. It connected me to my past, to the families, and taught me about new possibilities for field research and change.

In 1985, I entered the community by invitation from a graduate student who wanted me to observe their bilingual program. My visits to the classrooms in grades 1 through 3 revealed children's interactions with peers and teachers. After observing the classrooms, I wanted to learn about their literacy practices in the home and in the community at large. Initially I didn't have a multiyear plan for the research. Literacy practices in the households provided a point of entry to family life. This opened up a multitude of questions, including, "What is the meaning of education in Latino families? What oral and written traditions do they value? How do family members talk with each other about their work, play, and dreams? Research questions built upon each other, creating new generations of issues to study. The question on how parents deal with school matters led me to the classroom to follow the children in that learning environment. How do they communicate with their families in Mexico? What literacy do they practice in the workplace? Spanish-speaking children were placed in different reading ability groups beginning in the first grade. Educators, including some classroom teachers, suspected that the students who were in advanced reading groups had parents who read to them and were more attentive to their schoolwork than parents of children who were in the novice reading groups.

To get a deeper understanding of cultural change in Latino families and community at large obligated me to present my data of the home literacy activities to a larger group of Latino families, who also lived in Carpinteria. Parents participated in ethnographic analysis and, in the process, became aware of the variance of knowledge that parents had about schools. More questions emerged when the Latino community at large reflected on the literacy data that I collected in the twenty households. In the open community conversations, Latino parents discovered an opportunity to discuss and learn from those involved, resulting in the formation of the Comité de Padres Latinos (COPLA). Its purpose was to support each other as they learned how to better help their children in school. In large community meetings, they discussed issues of parental responsibilities in their children's education. Parent leaders recognized the absence of Latinos in school and community activities. Even when they were present, most felt invisible. COPLA leaders knew from their own experience that this did not mean they were uncaring or incapable. They understood that "learning how" required a knowledgeable support system.

The European-American community recognized the value of COPLA in Carpinteria. It was evident that the Latino group's activism had reached the mainstream community. Without specifically naming COPLA, *The Carpinteria Herald* ran an article in May 1990 that acquainted the community with the benefits of the organization. The article, entitled "A Brighter Outlook" read as follows:

> The Carpinteria School district and the Hispanic parents and students it represents have made tremendous strides in recent years. Other school districts having difficulty motivating their Hispanic communities would do well to study what has happened here.
>
> As recently as three years ago, school officials say, you couldn't get Hispanic parents involved in their children's education. They rarely, if ever, came to board meetings and seemed intimidated by teachers and administrators. Worse

yet, there seemed in some Hispanic circles to be an inbred opposition to students distinguishing themselves. A teacher of Hispanic students once said that if one student excelled academically, he would be accused of trying to show up the others.

But all that is changing. It is as if an element of American society that has until now stagnated is starting to jell. In Carpinteria, Hispanic school-parent meetings are so popular that as many as 100 parents attended in one night. Sometimes they draw adults who don't even have children in the classes.

The realization that education is the key to Hispanics moving up in American society seems to be sinking in. . . . Carpinteria is a place, which is a tribute to those now in charge. The Carpinteria school district, from the superintendent to the school board to teachers and principals, is bending over backward to provide Hispanic students with an enlightened education. . . .

As demographic studies show the Hispanic minority in Carpinteria, Santa Barbara and other communities may one day be the majority, we applaud Carpinteria school officials for having made such vital progress in the bilingual field of education.[1]

A research team of graduate students accompanied me to conduct ethnographic observations and interviews. Although the individuals changed almost year to year, depending on their graduate student status, all research assistants mastered the ethnographic tools of working on the project. The first three years of the Carpinteria study were especially taxing because the research team, particularly myself, were comprehensively immersed in the community. For the first five years of the study, I was a professor at the University of California, Santa Barbara. I observed family interactions in literacy events as well as classroom literacy activities. This opened the door to more questions about other aspects of family life in and out of the home as I followed the adults into their workplace, including nurseries and factories.

When I moved north and could only travel to Carpinteria a couple of times a month, I trained a couple of teachers and parents to collect some children's stories and interaction data on audiotape at specific meetings.

The case studies of the original group of twenty families generated volumes of data about literacy in the home and raised a new generation of questions about the nature of parents' participation in their children's education.[2] I examined family interaction in the home and at student-teacher literacy activities in the school and made observations from community events involving family members of the original case studies. Twenty families were the focus of the daily visits, usually by me, but other times by one of the assistants in the research team pertaining to practices involving literacy. I observed adult-child interactions as well as those among siblings and extended family members. Video, audio recordings, and fieldnotes captured the family engagements as they carried out daily chores. Usually, only the children were home after school and managed the household tasks until their parents arrived from work. Activities involving written text were examined. Educational personnel participated in the study throughout the various phases. Teachers of children in the case studies were interviewed, as were principals and district administrators.

Data collection in Carpinteria included ethnographic observations and interviews, case studies, and selective surveys. My participation as a critical ethnographer in the collective community organization in Carpinteria determined my research strategies for each step of the study.[3] Reflexive thinking between the researcher and the collaborators in the community raised additional research questions about their relationship to the community. How do Latino families participate in the school and the community? How do members of the Latino community galvanize to support each other?

To provide a comparison between Latino and Euro-American parent participation, I interviewed a group of English-speaking parents in the largest school-parent group in the largest elementary school. Through personal interviews of the parents and observations of their meetings, I was able to study issues involving Spanish-speaking parents more directly.

What began as a conventional ethnographic study on family and community literacy turned into an intervention study. That is, when my research role shifted into one of facilitator and resource person, I ceased being strictly an observer and interviewer. At that point my role became more complex as I collaborated with the families in organizing activities while I observed and studied the process. Several of the families who participated in the initial literacy and critical reflection phases of the ethnography subsequently organized COPLA. Together with other Latino families they met to support each other in their interactions and to provide for their children optimal support with their schooling. Five women and seven men were the initial COPLA organizers. COPLA formed a school district-wide group that met weekly for about two months, at which point they organized school-site committees. Literally, COPLA was composed of all Latino parents who had children in the Carpinteria schools.

As data collection expanded, so did the pounds of equipment I carried. Weighing heavy on my shoulder were a video-camcorder, audio recorder and laptop computer to document parent meetings and all community and school activities that parents attended. COPLA, the focus of the research, helped me to understand how parents taught themselves to work with their children and the schools while struggling to negotiate a different culture. Essentially, parents in Carpinteria organized themselves for the purpose of supporting each other, and "in conversation" they shared historical experience—in their former country, in Carpinteria with their families, and with the schools. Through the conversation process parents shared their cultural knowledge. This was the rich inheritance they shared with their children. The intent was to explore how Latinos shaped the organization and reciprocally how the organization influenced their lives and in general, the cultural community.

The district COPLA group met monthly, and together with school-level committee meetings, there was a minimum of one large Latino group meeting per week. Other meetings were spawned as parents met together and with school personnel to plan the larger meetings. Meetings were audio recorded and many were also video recorded. COPLA members carried their learning to their homes, which raised more research questions about the impact that COPLA had on the leaders and their families.

COPLA grew in size and meaning, intensifying its work with the schools and directly and indirectly impacting the daily lives of Latino families. Data on Latino families in all five schools necessitated survey strategies to understand their participation in the schools as a result of COPLA. Two years after the inception of the district-wide COPLA, a survey of 515 Latino parents was conducted to ascertain the extent of parent involvement in COPLA. The research team designed a questionnaire in Spanish and administered it to parents who attended the COPLA meetings at the respective schools. We wanted to learn the extent of COPLA in helping Latino parents to understand the school system and support their children. Care was taken not to duplicate surveys for parents who may have attended meetings at more than one school as a result of having children in different grade levels. A problem in the survey was a result of the low literacy level of many of the adults. This necessitated conducting the survey in person and instructing the parents on how to respond to the survey, making this an enormously labor-intensive project. Members of the research team read each of the questions to all of the parents present at the meeting. The respondents included all Latino parents who attended a meeting on the particular day we had designated to take the survey. As one assistant read each of the questions with the parents, another assisted some parents in marking the appropriate response. The task was complicated by the fact that one of the items called for an open-ended response. The onerous part of this survey taught us that we could obtain a large set of data through survey when working with a Spanish-speaking population. Without prior experience in responding to survey-type formats the research team spent long hours collecting the data in person with adults who were unaccustomed to school-like curriculum. In spite of that, the results of that questionnaire were invaluable in understanding how Latinos participated in COPLA.

COPLA's concern with the underachievement of Spanish-speaking readers in the upper elementary grades prompted the design of the Family Literacy Project (FLP). Parents' frustrations centered around their children's lack of motivation and the unavailability of reading materials for those who were motivated. Parents discussed students' literacy performance results, which showed that by the time Spanish-speaking children reached the third or fourth grade, parents felt intimidated by the language barrier that homework presented. English caused fear and distance in the parent-child relationship, a crucial source of support for children's school success.

These concerns emerged as parents and educators negotiated their needs to improve education, not only for Latinos but for all students. The goal of the FLP was to have third and fourth graders read with their parents at home and as a family. Parents were to report back to the classroom teacher, and together they evaluated the child's academic literacy performance.

Three of the active COPLA parents were selected to assist as teachers in the FLP. They were trained by the research team to perform three major tasks in organizing eight monthly family literacy sessions. Third- and fourth-grade teachers identified underachieving Spanish-speaking students in Weaver and Morton Schools. When the project began, another issue surfaced in the FLP study. Because homework consumes most of the children's time at home, parents found little time to do leisure reading with their children. As parents became aware of their literacy practices in the home they expressed an interest in increasing their reading at home with their children; parents who had children who did not excel in reading were especially interested.

Fifty books were screened intentionally for topics that were culturally sensitive and would generate discussion in families in this community. Eight books for the project were nonsexist, nonracist, and nonclassist stories. They received major consideration. Parent-participants were observed reading to their children in the natural home setting on five different occasions. A recording was made during each of these periods.

These occasions provided the researchers with observation and interview data on parent-child interaction regarding literature content. More
important than what and how they read to their children were the meaningful interactions between parents and children. That part was documented in interviews and observations.

As a critical ethnographer, I played a dual role as an ethnographer and
facilitator. By critical, I do not mean I gave a negative account of those
involved; rather critical is a way of understanding the circumstances,
making meaning of experience, and re-creating their lives through open
conversation. When community members asked me to assist them in
their organization, I made it clear that I could assist them in raising the
important questions but that they were the leaders, not me. My role
evolved day by day throughout the decade it took to compose the
Carpinteria story. One of the most enjoyable parts was working with the
community's members in reflecting on their family life experience in
Mexico and Carpinteria and their family stories and relationships with
each other as they involved themselves in their children's schooling.

The intersection between ethnography and social issues calls for the
researcher to assume an interactive position with the people in the research setting. My participatory relationship with the people in the study
taught me that my ethnic identity, gender, class ethos, and personal history influence the ethnographic process of research. It also influences the
activities in the field. These things also shape the way that I as a researcher interpret what I observe and how I write about it.

During the years I worked in Carpinteria, I was invited to make many
public presentations in many cities across the United States, in Mexico,
Spain, and France. In every case, there was an individual in the audience
who wanted to know how much the Latino children in Carpinteria improved their grades as a result of their parents' involvement in their children's education. When asked questions like this, I usually explain that
over the years that I knew these families, many students received better
grades after their parents got involved in their schooling. But in some
cases students had a very difficult time in school even when the parents
were very involved and supportive. Some feel unsatisfied when I take
more than a few words to remind them that the relationship between
families, communities, and schools is not a straight line linking parent involvement and grades on a student's report card. More important to me
is reinforcing the point that what we have learned from the families in
Carpinteria is that learning is a lifelong process and that grades had to be
understood in the specific context, not as a fixed categorization. Higher

grades on a student's report card or declining test scores hide the bigger story of the complex parental role in children's education in this Latino community. Often the finger is pointed at the parents when the question of parent involvement is raised, especially if students are not high achievers. Simplistic blueprints for parent involvement also minimize the importance of the students' learning process as well the teacher's role. The findings in the Carpinteria research represent the intricate relationships negotiated day by day that impact continuities and discontinuities back and forth from home to school to community. First, parents do care about their children's education. But how we document cultural change and its meaning makes all the difference in the interpretations of the shifts that occur within the family and the community. While the language spoken, the numbers attending meetings, the books read, or the jobs obtained are visible forms of cultural participation in a community, the invisible meaning of those activities is what drives the cultural changes from the inside out. How these people changed their perception about their lives from being one of deficit to empowerment led to the cultural changes in the family, the community, and in their personal lives.

My job as an ethnographer and writer is to honor these people's stories about the meaning of language, culture, and literacy in this community where people used their power to learn new directions through mutual support. In the process, the parents expanded their support networks and opportunities. Together Carpinteria families and I discovered that power is not a tangible commodity to be given or withheld, rather it is a process. Empowerment is not a hierarchical position or status of a given person; empowerment is a process, an exchange of power that occurs through the process of sharing, reflecting on, and learning from our stories. We served as mirrors for each other in trust, respect, and common goals—in order to achieve in our respective lives and to form a united group, COPLA. Important cultural values were and are the heart of the COPLA endeavor. Their mission of support and change embraced all who were encompassed by this issue.

Even immersed in the life of this community, I was not sheltered from my academic training. Their approach to organizing was contrary to what I imagined should have been done in forging a new organization. Conventional wisdom suggests that the group would have to draft bylaws and elect a president, vice president, and secretary. And, of course, Robert's Rules of Order would govern interaction at meetings. It was times like this that my academic interpretations interfered with their meaning. Years after they formally organized as COPLA, the group adopted bylaws. But they did not adopt Robert's Rules of Order as a way to control interaction at meetings. More people can join in a conversation when respect is the tradition guiding the exchange.

Families and school personnel have claimed many gains through their years of community advocacy. The mantle of leadership has been passed on. The original COPLA leaders have moved on to other projects, including setting up community after-school programs, involving students and parents. But other Latino leaders have stepped up to the challenge. By focusing on strengths and confronting perceived deficits, parents and school personnel created a culture with a common language, "the child." Hard, slow and deliberate, this process mobilized a community and offered a language of possibility defined through focused interaction.

When I entered Carpinteria, being in a community, but not of it, posed dilemmas for me—the researcher. As much as I wanted to belong and to blend into the community, my position as a university professor and researcher defined me as an outsider, and I automatically, became thought of as the "other." So, I found a way to straddle both identities. Since collaboration is only possible through trust, respect, and honesty, year after year, I found it necessary to abandon preconceived notions of who these Latino families were and how they identified themselves and related to each other. I have learned that although educational and economic status isolates a community socially and politically, it does not incapacitate it. Social scientists and educators have promoted cultural deficit myths by equating differences with inferiority. But a person is not defined by objective conditions. And to transform the burden of one's adverse environment requires full participation of those who experience it subjectively. Presently, fifteen years after their first meeting, the COPLA community remains mindful of the shared history, culture, and commitment to children that initially mobilized them.

Carpinteria families and school personnel went to school, got married, had children; they laughed, cried, and loved like everyone else. Their humanness made us resonate with them. And their commitment and actions to improve children's lives empowered those involved and taught us to make our voices heard. Daily, our own complex problems defy simplistic, formulaic answers. The Carpinteria project holds many lessons. Most salient are the complex processes that teach us, both community collaborators and field researchers, to expand our inner and outer worlds. By working collectively, listening, engaging in open conversation, and discovering our internal and external resources, we connect theory and practice to the research and the researcher.

~

# Notes

## Chapter 1

1. See U.S. Census Bureau 2000, *The Foreign Born Population in the United States, 2000,* Stockton 1960, *La Carpenteria,* and U.S. Census Bureau 2000, *Population Projections of the United States by Age, Sex, Race, and Hispanic Origin: 1992 to 2050,* Washington, D.C. Two scenarios for Latinos in California in the twenty-first century appear in Hayes-Bautista, Schink, and Chapa 1988.

The U.S. Census Bureau has projected statistics for Latinos in the twenty-first century. Research on immigration now more appropriately travels under the theoretical concept of "transnational migration." Numerous references develop this perspective (see for example, Bodnar 1985, Rouse 1989, 1992, Schiller, Basch, and Blanc-Szanton 1992). The concept of transnationalism casts the study of migration in a global perspective. Only by understanding the world as a single social and economic system can we comprehend the implications of the new patterns of migrant experience that have been emerging from different parts of the globe into the United States as well as those occurring *in* different parts of the world. Simultaneously, we can understand the individual and collective strategies of adaptation of international migrant people, which enables us to observe the migrant experience in process. By expanding the theoretical perspective of immigration to include ethnicity, class, gender, and identity in both the homeland and the new culture, we can comprehend the cultural practice and agency of the immigrants. The Carpinteria study, however, is limited by the fact that it does not examine the immigrants in their Mexican homeland other than through ethnohistorical interviews. For other examples of work on migration from Mexico and adaptation in the United States, see Achor 1978, where Achor uses the term *Mexican American* as the ethnic identity of the group.

2. Lifton 1993 depicts the United States as a protean nation in that it has continued to change and expand, yet it has a legacy and history of racism and oppression of many peoples who need to be included in the fabric of democracy.

3. A more culturally democratic society is at the heart of a study done by a team headed by Henry T. Trueba. The publication, *Healing Multicultural America* (Trueba, Rodriguez, Zou, and Cintron 1993), chronicles a group of Mexican immigrants to a Northern California community who, in spite of obstacles, learned to participate in the U.S. democratic system to obtain access to the educational system.

4. Historically, we have seen that immigrants whose culture of origin most resembles that of White Anglo Americans have traditionally had the warmest reception in this country. By contrast, immigrants from countries whose culture is less known to Americans have always had less access to the sociopolitical and socioeconomic systems. See Cremin 1957, Ehman 1980, and Spring 1991 for a discussion of the social and political purposes of education in the United States. Delgado-Gaitan and Trueba (1991) presents research on the education of immigrant families in a Northern California community. The research presents the accounts of the home and community life of the Spanish-speaking families and the school they attended. We describe the human resource potential, as children and their parents undergo cultural and language changes, while maintaining fragments of their Spanish language and Mexican and Latino values and attempting to incorporate new cultural and academic knowledge in order to obtain socioeconomic and political access. Ultimately, we note the commitment that is required to live and participate in a democracy in spite of tremendous economic burdens and social isolation from the mainstream community.

5. Lina Avidan of the Coalition for Immigrant and Refugee Rights and Services, as stated in her testimony to the Select Committee in the California Assembly as reported in the Summary Report Prepared for Assembly Select Committee on Statewide Immigration Impact—Assembly Member Grace Napolitano Chairperson—prepared by Assembly Office of Research—#0501-A. Robert L. Bach and Doris Meissner, *America's Labor Market in the 1990s: What Role Should Immigration Play?* (Washington, D.C.: Library of Congress, June 1990).

6. Simon 1989. The National Immigration Law Center, Guide to Alien Eligibility for Federal Programs, 1992, reports that undocumented immigrants are eligible for only the following programs: emergency medical services, WIC, school lunch and breakfast, Head Start, federal housing, and social services block grant. The Report on the Legalized Alien Population, 1992, published by the U.S. Department of Justice, Immigration and Naturalization Service, provided statistics on immigrants who legalized their residence during the 1987–88 Amnesty program. At the time of application, the legalized alien population had used fewer taxpayer and employer-supported social services than had the general U.S. population. The study found that less than 1 percent of the legalized alien population had received general assistance, social security, supplemental security income, workers compensation, and unemployment insurance payments. Economist Marta Tienda (1983) found that immigrant family income was less than that of native family income by $1,700 to $3,800, except for Black and

spouse-absent White families. One would expect significantly higher participation by immigrants in public assistance programs than natives; however, immigrant family participation in such programs does not exceed their native counterparts' participation rate by more than 5 percent. Immigrants are less likely than natives to become dependent on welfare. Recent immigrants do not use welfare at a higher rate than immigrants who have already been in the United States for some time (except for refugees who receive cash assistance from the federal government when they are resettled from abroad).

7. I discuss the various principles of empowerment in numerous publications, Delgado-Gaitan 1990, 1992, 1993(a), 1994(a), 1994(b), 1994(c), 1994(d), 1994(e), and 1996, and Delgado-Gaitan and Trueba 1991. Each of these publications emphasizes and explores in detail particular aspects of empowerment as it involved families and educators in Carpinteria.

8. Protean-like resilience and malleability are the essence of Lifton's (1993) work, but the background for these concepts was drawn in his earlier books. Lifton's brilliant and provocative writings have intrigued me for years, including, in addition to his 1993 book, his work on the Vietnam War (1973), Hiroshima survivors (1967), the the Nazi Holocaust and the nuclear threat (1990). Each of these books (out of his sixteen published) explores the psychological dimensions of totalitarianism, social change, nuclear weapons, and more generally, death and the continuity of life. As a psychological investigator Lifton develops new theories and methods for applying psychological principles to historical events. His long-standing interest in the interplay between individual psychology and historical change led him to investigate the psychological effects of dropping the atomic bomb in Hiroshima. The assertion and establishment of the self, which Lifton so intricately and passionately pursues, results in his unique formulation of the self. He envisions it as a protean self, developing into an elaboration and expansion of self, culminating in the twentieth-century tendency toward inventing the individual self by means of the protean pattern of radically imagined extensions, re-creating, and mocking caricatures of actual experience.

9. Lifton's (1993, 5) point is that undergoing continuous change and transformation is a central tenet of what he calls proteanism. According to Lifton, proteanism is also a struggle of ideas and beliefs. Shifts in individual or collective ideas and beliefs occur constantly. Says Lifton, "one is likely to hold a variety of ideological, political, and religious positions in a lifetime, not to mention one's aesthetic values and revisions in personal relationships as well as life style modifications." Given these tendencies, the protean self evolves, accommodates and transmutes obstacles and pain, and remains fluid in a form. Proteus was a minor-aged character in Greek mythology, capable of changing his form from sea dweller to land creature at will. He was a prophetic man healer, a sea God, herder of Poseidon's seals. He would foretell the future if anyone could catch him at noon and keep him from changing his form. Whenever anyone pursued him to give prophesies, he changed his form to avoid prophesizing the future, and when he was caught, he told the truth. In Homer's *Odyssey*, Menelaus held on to Proteus until he told him how to return to Sparta.

10. Minimal education for children who speak limited English has long marked the educational system. *Lau v. Nichols*, as discussed in Donato, Menchaca, and Valencia 1991, *Lau v. Nichols* 1974—414 U.S. 563,566, and Roos 1978, was the landmark case that dramatically changed the delivery of education to Spanish-speaking children. Although these authors do not discuss other language groups, the 1974 federal mandate, *Lau v. Nichols*, has affected the education of limited-English speakers from all language groups. The lawsuit was initiated against the San Francisco School Board by the parents of a Chinese student, whose last name was Lau. The decision held that public schools had to provide an education that was comprehensible to limited-English proficient (LEP) students. The Supreme Court recognized that limited-English-speaking students had historically been denied "meaningful" access to education as a result of having been taught their entire curriculum in English. The decision prompted federal funding for school districts to design bilingual education programs in cases where members in any one language group per grade level numbered more than twenty. Other limited-English-speakers whose language group did not constitute more than twenty people per grade level were provided instruction according to individualized plans.

11. Joseph (1993) writes extensively about one's relationship to society, in particular about issues of connectivity and patriarchy and personhood. Her message is summarized in this quote: "As scholars begin engaging these complex and contradictory junctions of self and science more critically and reflectively, relational conceptions of knowledges may take shape. It is increasingly clear, however, that we need alternatives to the Western binary of autonomy/relationality, self/other. We need vocabularies for talking about autonomous selves who are relational, relational selves who sustain autonomy. We also need to investigate the intersections between relationality and structures of domination, as well as conditions of relative equality. Such constructs and experiences of personhood are woven throughout the most basic processes by which we observe and analyze. Therefore, they become an integral part of the fabric of knowledge. If we are to weave science out of stronger cloth, we must understand how the threads are both separate and mesh" (30).

12. For concepts of cultural continuity interweaving culture and education, see works by Spindler 1955 and Spindler and Spindler 1994. As key figures, "parents of Anthropology and Education," they are credited with recognizing that learning is a process of acquiring a culture and schools are entrusted with imparting the culture. Their notion of cultural transmission and continuity and discontinuity has enlightened the field of education by recognizing the critical importance of culture in the learning process.

In the 1970s, the analyses of schooling expanded to account for an economic perspective of schools, teaching, curriculum, and policy, according to class theory. Bowles and Gintis (1976) were major leaders in this new framework. They argued that the educational system was a product of the Capitalist economic system that also governed the social order of the country. Their work, along with that of Carnoy and Levin (1985), formed the springboard for the new ideological direction that followed.

Resistance ethnographic research by Everhart 1983, and Foley 1990, as well as by McLaren 1986, showed that the struggles of working-class students in urban schools stemmed from their lives in social isolation and exclusion from participation in the mainstream curriculum of schools as a consequence of their poverty. Curriculum is the focus of critical theorists, including Apple 1979, 1993, and Giroux 1992. Feminists, including Lather 1991, Ellsworth 1989, Grosz 1988, and Luke 1992, have extended the critical pedagogical discourse to include women.

# Chapter 2

1. I use the term *Latino* to refer to recent Mexican immigrants, Mexican Americans who have been long-term residents in the United States, and Chicanos who are of Mexican decent and usually born in the United States. I chose the term *Latino* because that is what Mexicans in Carpinteria call themselves when referring to the group as a whole. The same people who refer to the larger group as Latinos also call themselves Mexicans when referring to the individual or the nuclear family unit. By this I mean to point out that the identity of Latinos in Carpinteria is complex in that they identify themselves by language use, migratory practice, ethnic, and class categories. Most of the people I collaborated with in this study used the term *Latino* to refer to themselves and sometimes used *Latino, Mexicano,* or *Chicano* to refer to others in their community (see Delgado-Gaitan 1990).

Writings on Latino and other immigrants have shown the power and strife of the community. Among those publications are Suarez-Orozco 1998, Trueba 1989 and 1999, and Goldberg 1992.

2. *Santa Paula Chronicle,* 5 October 1929, sec. 6B, cited in Menchaca and Valencia 1990, 240.

3. Exclusion of Mexican/Chicano students from school dates back to the late 1800s. Gonzalez 1990 reports that Mexican children were separated from Anglo-American children, and by 1920 most schools actively practiced "separate but equal" policies. The concept of Mexican schools, as existed once in Carpinteria, was prevalent in communities where Mexicans/Chicanos lived. Segregation of Mexican/Chicano students in schools led to the 1947 landmark case *Mendez v. Westminister,* which was the first case ever argued on the 14th amendment, taking the position that the premise of "separate but equal" is unconstitutional.

A participant in my research study in Commerce City, Colorado, concerning Latino students who succeed and those who drop out of high school (see Delgado-Gaitan 1988 and Delgado-Gaitan and Segura 1989), related the following firsthand experience to me. Lucy Olivarez, a parent of one of the young girls who dropped out of school, told of her early schooling days in a Colorado school, where half of the school population was Mexican. "I was about six years old, and I had just begun school, and I loved going to school, because my mother braided my hair so pretty, and I wore long beautiful ribbons, and my grandpa used to walk me to school everyday. All my friends were Mexican because that's the way our school was divided and in my classroom—we were only Mexicans or "Spanish people" as many called us here in Colorado. So, one day I remember getting to school, and as soon as the bell rang we went to be filed in line and went into the classroom. Immediately, the teacher asked all of us to line up again, because we had to go to the auditorium, because the nurse wanted to see us. So all of the students were there, and they asked us, the Mexicans, to go stand against one wall, and they asked the White kids to go to the other wall. Then they went out of the auditorium, and we were left standing against the wall, and the nurse came around and untied all of our pretty braids, and they proceeded to pour kerosene on our hair. All the [Mexican] boys and girls had this done to us because there was a breakout of piojos (lice) you know those hair bugs, and they thought that the Mexicans were the only carriers. This happened many times through my schooling there. The humiliation and anger we all experienced still haunts me."

Desegregation made "separate but equal" illegal, however, what remained intact was the practice of tracking, which maintained exclusion and academic segregation (see Rangel and Alcala 1972, and Uribe 1980). Volumes have been written about tracking. Jeannie Oakes (1990) writes about the benefits of heterogeneous groups on the school curriculum and examines the injustices and travesties in education under organized tracking. Her findings are consistent with what Robert Slavin (1990) reports in his review. And in an edited volume, Oakes and others (2000) describe how schools in different states struggle to make a difference by attending to the conflicting demands of equity and excellence.

4. San Miguel (1984, 1987) discusses the historical discourse of bilingual education, while Zentella (1985) debates the fate of Spanish-speaking people in the United States by analyzing language policies, and Merino, Trueba, and Samaniego (1993) present the theoretical framework for maintenance of the home language in language-minority students.

5. School district statistics were supplied by Carpinteria District administrators; it was usually Paul Niles who collected statistics on the students and projects.

6. Parental knowledge about the school system is seen as an essential ingredient to effective socialization. The impact in the home provides a powerful link between the family setting and social institutions (Berger 1991, Blakely 1983, Clark 1992, Cochran and Dean 1991, Coleman 1987, Comer and Hayes 1991, Delgado-Gaitan 1991a, Epstein 1990, Klimer-Dougan, Lopez, Nelson, and Adelman 1992, Lareau 2000, Phelan, Davidson, and Cao 1991, Torres-Guzman 1991). Immigrant families were the focus of the first part of my study in Carpinteria, beginning in 1985, which found that Spanish-speaking families experienced isolation from the school because they lacked information about its operations and expectations. This phase of the study occurred prior to the organization of the parent group and helps to explain the changes in family interaction after the family's participation in a community organization. The distance between many of the families and the school created problems for children's schooling.

Research has shown academic gains on the part of students when families and schools participate in term projects for a finite period of time to forge strong contact between parents and educators (Davis 1982, Diaz 1992, Dornbusch, Ritter, Leiderman, Roberts, and Fraleigh 1987, Gotts and Purnell 1986, Jordan 1990, Kohn 1959, Levy and Wildavsky 1975, Morrison 1978, Stevenson and Baker 1987, Walberg 1986). School reforms contribute to improved academic results for the period in which they operate but usually stop short of criticizing the conditions that created the inequity of resources in the first place.

7. This topic is also discussed in Delgado-Gaitan (1996), which places an emphasis on literacy learning.

8. Americanization has long been the goal of public education and public programs in the workplace. Gonzalez 1990 writes that special teachers were hired to direct Americanization programs and to go into the homes to help immigrant families with their "inferior" lifestyle. As one home teacher stated, Mexicans had a "tendency to wander and live in a shiftless way, which was not checked by the economic conditions in which this type of family finds itself here" (Vera Sturges, "Home Standards among Our Mexican Residents," *Los Angeles School Journal* 9, no. 4 [1925]: 13. Cited in Gonzalez 1990, 54).

In schools the Americanization programs attempted to eliminate the "dirty, shiftless, lazy irresponsible, unambitious, thriftless, fatalistic, selfish, promiscuous, and prone to drinking, violence, and criminal behavior" (see Garcia 1978, and Gonzalez 1990). School principals dictated classroom and school programs based on the "culturally deficit" hypothesis. An example of this is provided in the following quote by a Phoenix, Arizona, school principal. "Much more classroom time should be spent teaching the [Mexican] children clean habits and positive attitudes towards others, public property, and their community in general. . . . [The Mexican child] can be taught to repeat the Constitution forward and backward and still he will steal cars, break windows, wreck public recreational centers, etc., if he doesn't catch the idea of respect for human values and personalities" (Jessie Hayden, "The La Habra Experiment in Mexican Social Education," [master's thesis, Claremont College, Claremont, Calif., 1934], 27. Cited in Gonzalez 1990, 37).

# Chapter 3

Portions of this chapter appear in some of my earlier publications: *Protean Literacy* (1996); *Crossing Cultural Borders* (with Henry Trueba 1991).

1. High rents for families with low incomes has been a contentious issue in Carpinteria on more than one occasion. The local nurseries have been the target of disapproving council members. A local newspaper wrote, "In Carpinteria, nursery housing projects become an exercise in politics when the Carpinteria City council and County Board of Supervisor (1st District) have thus far failed to provide leadership on the issue of affordable housing. The issue is one involving Edward Van Wingerden, owner of Ever-bloom Nursery in Carpinteria which employs about 25 Latino workers on a year-round basis, all of whom live in Carpinteria. Due to Carpinteria's lack of affordable housing, these workers are forced to live with extended family members who

can contribute to the rent. The idea of a nursery owner footing the bill to provide his workers with quality living conditions at an affordable rate is both honorable and worthy. This appears to be the ideal situation for both the city and the workers.

The plans for the housing project called for the northern end of Santa Ynez Road to be granted by the city. The neighbors along the Road rejected the project because it would increase the traffic as a result of twenty new housing units. Apparent was the fact that the Mexican/Latino community remained virtually silent. In essence, they have no active voting bloc exercising their rights against nursery workers who have no voting status which the politicians didn't overlook" (*Vos Popular*, July 1990).

2. The social change in the Carpinteria families, schools, and community is grounded in research and theory addressing social, cultural, and political assumptions leading to critical reflection and dialogue at a community level. The authors who have influenced my conception of empowerment include Allen, Barr, Cochran, Dean, and Greene 1989; Barr 1989; Delgado-Gaitan 1990; Freire 1970 and 1973; Lather 1991; Lifton 1993; and Williams 1989.

The respective concepts represented by these authors form a confluence that spotlights inequality in society and holds the individual central to the process of change. Change involves critical reflection both individually and collectively and also builds on the people's strengths and undergirds the full expression and participation of the individual or collective. Each of these theorists contributes an important principle to the process I term empowerment.

1. The critical reflection process enables people to envision their place in society and in their community and appraises their strengths and, through their continual reflection, can create a vision to expand their potential to learn (Allen et al. 1989).
2. Conflict reinvents power to a win/win position as opposed to a win/lose situation (Barr 1989).
3. A critical ethnographic approach is essential in understanding literacy and how empowerment operates in ethnic and linguistic communities that have been underrepresented and isolated (Delgado-Gaitan 1990, also Delgado-Gaitan 1996).
4. Literacy is a process of not only reading written text but of experiencing one's social position in the world in which we live. Through literacy we learn critical consciousness (Freire 1973 and 1995).
5. The concept of proteanism helps to understand the individual's resilience and ability to continually change (Lifton 1993).
6. Education means "giving to the ordinary members of society its full common meanings, and the skills that will enable them to amend these meanings, in the light of their personal and common experience" (Williams 1989, 14).
7. In response to the question, "What is to be done?" Theory nurtured by action is the premise of praxis, which leads us to take action in the world and become creative through our activity (Lather 1991).

# Chapter 4

1. Redirecting one's pain outward rather than inward is a concept that has been explored in Lifton 1993.

A different form of outward expression in dealing with one's pain has been documented in the resistance movement. Resistance is a way of confronting and dealing with the hopelessness of oppression and can serve as a way out of oppressive conditions. See Willis 1977, McLoed 1987, and Foley 1990.

Resistance often creates negative thinking on the part of Chicano students. This behavior is often the only resort available to a community when their culture is denigrated (see Delgado-Gaitan 1988, 1991b. Foley (1990) has also noted that resistance is the only option available to Chicano students when Capitalist forms of education undermine their language and culture in the midst of poverty. Unjust blaming of immigrants for the economic decline of the U.S. economy is explained by Simon (1989). This is a seminal study that helps us understand the political dimension of immigration serving Capitalists interests.

2. Delgado-Gaitan 1990, 1991a, 1992, 1993a, and 1993b discuss the position of power in Latino families, including the researcher's role in the process. My research on immigrant families, including Latino, Russian, and Indochinese, has departed from the premise that poor families are "culturally deficient" and uncaring about their children because they lack formal education and are therefore unable to raise their children. My position on empowerment begins with the rejection of the "deficit theory." Although I do not have the space here to name the extensive list of publications on this topic of social networks related to Latinos, I need to mention the seminal work on the question of Mexican social networks by Vélez-Ibañez 1983 and 1988. The social networks reported by Vélez-Ibañez differ from the nature of the COPLA organization, but the informal networks offered social and economic support for the Mexican communities in Arizona. The "Funds of Knowledge" concept is a response to cultural deficit perspectives of Latinos.

3. Latino parents are criticized for not "pushing" their children into careers, thus creating underachievement in a generation when students require all of the direction they can get to achieve the most in this society. However, the parents in this study have shown that they encourage their children as strongly as possible to work toward a career—to the extent they are knowledgeable about resources that permit their children to enter a specific career. A discussion of the underrepresentation of Latinas in education is noted by Baca Zinn 1980 and Delgado-Gaitan and Segura 1989.

4. Accountability for homework is examined in schools that Latino children attend and in households where Spanish-speakers interact around the question of education. Delgado-Gaitan (1992) describes the strengths of the families examined in their daily interactions in both household and community contexts. The way in which homework assignments place many students at a disadvantage because of their socioeconomic status is supported by Kralovec and Buell (2000). They aptly document how homework creates a greater gulf between students and the school.

5. Documenting details of a family in the privacy of their home requires that the family trust the researcher and calls for extensive and triangulated strategies as well as a constant critical perspective on the part of the researcher when dealing with participants' self-critiques (see Delgado-Gaitan 1993a).

# Chapter 5

1. Parents in Carpinteria who were active in COPLA expected both their daughters and sons to be educated. Poor immigrant parents are criticized for having lower expectations of their children. Such critiques do not take into account the socio-economic and historical context or the particular community in which the children live (see Delgado-Gaitan 1990 and 1996).

2. Anthropologist Dorine Kondo (1990) specifically argues that selves are crafted in the processes of work and within the practices of power. This reflects the position that experience and practice are inseparable.

# Chapter 6

1. Parent involvement has been a focus of extensive research, which requires much more space than I will take here to list all of the publications that merit acknowledgement. I must, however, recognize a select few references that are important studies because they are theoretically grounded in a way that offer us the opportunity to engage in the discourse of "parent involvement" issues beyond a mere portrayal of strategies for involving parents in the school, which I regarded limited in its understanding of the complexity of the subject. On that note, see, for example, Allexsaht-Snider 1991; Bronfenbrenner 1978; Cochran and Dean 1991; Coleman 1994; Comer 1984; Delgado-Gaitan 1994a; Delgado-Gaitan and Allexsaht-Snider 1992; David 1989; Epstein 1994; Levin 1987; Lareau 2000; Phelan Davidson, and Cao 1991.

2. Many teachers know that if a child is underachieving, parents cannot bear the entire responsibility. I would not presume to imply that teachers, categorically, blame parents when children underachieve. In fact, in my research, I have taken care to describe those cases where teachers are knowledgeable and professional in their relationship with families and in integrating home culture into the curriculum. As I have written in this book and in numerous other publications, the relationship between parents and schools is too complex to simplistically point the finger at either the school or the family when children face learning problems. When I first began my study in Carpinteria in 1985, I observed in many classrooms and I was told by most of the teachers that bilingual children had learning problems in reading because their parents did not care. Some of the teachers were careful to note that most Latino parents worked hard and long hours and could not read English, which made it difficult for them to read with their children. As my study progressed over the years I documented how teachers actually dealt with Latino parents differently and that as the

COPLA organization became more active, many of those same teachers who once criticized parents now began to reach out to the Latino parents and to recognize that they did and do care about their children and schooling and found ways to better communicate with these parents.

3. Realistically, parents should provide their children with all of the basic needs. No one can argue with that, but blame cannot be hurled at families as if they are isolated from society's power over a family, which includes economic, political, and cultural influences. A common wish expressed by many educators and the public in general is that families should return to what has been referred to as the "traditional family." In Stephanie Coontz's 1992 book, whose title is in response to the popular wish to be "the way we were"—*The Way We Never Were: American Families and the Nostalgia Trap*, the author presents an excellent historical study examining two centuries of American family life and shatters the myths that so often burden modern and postmodern families. Pressures ranging from dwindling resources to families compound intrafamily interactions and organization. Studies by Baca Zinn 1983; Baca Zinn and Eitzen 1996; Saragoza 1983; Segura 1988; Williams 1990 and Ybarra 1983 on Mexican/Chicano families adequately examine these questions.

4. Most parent involvement efforts are intended to endorse the schools' policies with little regard for the parent's understanding of the schools.

5. In the reading, interactions between parents and teachers teach more than bare mechanics and strategies about reading. See Ferdman, Weber, and Ramirez 1994.

6. The need for frequent reading by parents to children is studied in emergent literacy research, involving families in linguistically diverse communities. See Delgado-Gaitan 1994b and 1996; Heath 1982; Pease-Alvarez 1991; Ramirez 1994; Schieffelin and Cochran-Smith 1984; Scollon and Scollon 1981; Taylor 1983; Trueba 1984; Trueba, Jacobs, and Kirton 1990; and Vasquez 1989. Here again the list of exceptional research in emergent literacy in culturally and linguistically different communities is enormous. By selecting these few, I by no means intend to ignore the multitude of other excellent, critical, and cross-discipline research on literacy.

7. Following Paulo Freire and Donaldo Macedo's (1987) concept of liberation with his work on literacy with Brazilian peasants, Alma Flor Ada attempted to have parents learn how to motivate their children to practice four questioning strategies. The questions were intended to teach their children how to read a story by reflecting on their own personal experiences.

My research team departed somewhat from the recommendation of Flor Ada's curriculum. Our opinion of some of the books Flor Ada used in the Pajaro Valley project was that they were inadequate for use in our parent group because they were presented in cursive and were therefore unclear to children. We felt that some of the illustrations (e.g., a partially naked mermaid) might also be offensive to the parents. In addition, some of the themes were not interesting enough to generate discussions. We did overlap with Flor Ada's recommended list when our criteria fit.

8. Flor Ada (1988) designed a series of questions for teachers to use with Spanish-speaking children.

9. Part of what my research team and I learned in our work with the FLP was that the hierarchy of questions designed by Flor Ada was effective where the project involved classroom teachers as the key teachers in the reading program. However, as we designed the project to focus on parents as the key educator relative to reading with children, we should have allowed the "question" classifications to emerge from an etic perspective. In the FLP classes we observed that parents had keen insights about their relationship with their children, not only where reading written text was concerned but also in the sharing of oral stories with their children. Parents also had strong opinions about topics and themes surrounding the stories we read in each class. Therefore, I had to intervene during the second—"follow-up"—year to explain to the parents that the most important part of their learning was not the category of the questions they taught their children to ask, but the close interaction they experienced through reading with their children.

# Chapter 7

1. Dr. Pablo Seda, "What Do Children Learn in School?" *The Carpinteria Herald,* 21 January 1993. Portions of this and other articles cited in this chapter also appear in Delgado-Gaitan 1996.

2. Dr. Pablo Seda, "We Are Able to Overcome Expectations of Others," *The Carpinteria Herald,* 17 September 1992.

3. Dr. Pablo Seda, "Carpinteria towards the 21st Century," *The Carpinteria Herald,* 27 November 1991.

4. COPLA is certainly not a magic remedy for either restructuring a school's educational format or initiating a social change at the community level. I have learned a great deal from a group of professors at Cornell, who began researching and writing about empowerment in communities during the early 1980s. The collective project is no longer ongoing, but the results of some of their efforts remain and their writings continue to be instructive examples of what is possible. Numerous comparable empowerment efforts, nationally and internationally, corroborate the success of this type of empowerment process. One case study that demonstrates such a success was carried out in Annie Strack Village, a private, nongovernmental residential facility that serves sixty children and has a staff of thirty. The educational level of the child-care workers varies between standards six and ten (grades 8–12). Basic qualifications, in-service training and National Diploma, are mandatory standards for all child-care workers.

Prior to the empowerment model, the village functioned on the "family-system-model," in which the role of the child-care workers was that of substitute parent, or what often resembled "glorified nannies." The village had a high staff turnover and tired, frustrated, and low-paid workers who had no autonomy. During a general staff meeting, it was decided to conduct an evaluation.

During the evaluation process, the staff identified the problems, brainstormed alternatives, and made decisions about actions and implementation of those actions. The evaluation report was presented to and discussed with the management board.

Mutually accepted plans were implemented and revised as specified. This developed into a refined and very effective participatory decision-making process and service-review model. The most significant outcome of this process was the empowered people that it "generated." In addition to many concrete changes (such as staff structure, improved salaries, and goal-directed intervention programs), the village's "glorified nannies" were transformed into primary intervention agents. That is, they became full partners in all the decisions that affected their own lives and the lives of the children in their care. Once more, individual voices were heard, and this enhanced the efficacy of the service professionals (Allen 1990).

A different empowerment experience can be cited as an exemplary effort in the fight against crime and drugs in the Mattapan neighborhood of Boston. Residents have lobbied for and succeeded in retaining an abandoned building for use as a recreation center. The success thus far can be attributed to the five-year involvement of a core group of tenants to mobilize broad-based support within the community.

International community empowerment efforts have been documented in Barbados, by the Women and Development Unit (WAND), in the School and Continuing Studies Department of the University of the West Indies. In this instance, women have helped empower other women to take control of their lives by launching an ongoing adult education program based on curricula defined by the community and providing income-generating projects and a pre-school and day-care center (Cochran 1991).

Barbados's endeavors have been duplicated by communities in other countries, including the Black Health Center in Cape Town, South Africa, the Department of Social Studies and Organization in Ålborg, Denmark, the Community Health Center in Hamilton, New Zealand, the School of Child and Youth Care in Victoria, British Columbia, Canada, Centro de Educación y Comunicación in Managua, Nicaragua, and the Home and Day Care Education Project in Joensuu, Finland. The principle common to the empowerment processes in all of these communities has been the inclusion of those who had previously been isolated; indigenous and subordinate cultures have been valued. Further, it is believed that educational communities should support the goals of the communities they serve through continued collective thinking and cooperative dialogue that is committed to enabling personal and structural change (Barr 1992; Cochran 1991).

    5. See Delgado-Gaitan 1993b.

# Chapter 8

    1. See Delgado-Gaitan 1990, 1993b, and 1994b.

    2. Cohen 1996, Portes 1996, and Rumbaut 1997.

    3. See Lifton 1993.

    4. Gonzalez (1990) reports that Mexican children were separated from Anglo-American children, and by 1920 most schools actively practiced "separate but equal" policies.

    5. See Lifton 1993 and Trueba 1999.

# Chapter 9

1. Anzaldua 1987, Delgado-Gaitan 1993a, Delgado-Gaitan 1997a, and Delgado-Gaitan 2000. Anthropologists whose work on subjectivity has been influential in my writing include Kondo 1990, Joseph 1993, and Behar 1997.

# Chapter 10

1. This article appeared in *The Carpinteria Herald,* 13 May 1990.

2. The term *literacy* has been the subject of extensive research, and of importance here is the how the concept is defined. Literacy here is framed as Hymes (1974) described it, an interactional structure. The event is often centered on relationships between oral and written language strategies and how they are used for general use by participants in order to play, work, and communicate. Literacy as a conceptual tool in the sociocultural context has been studied in more references than I can possibly mention here, but I will list a few significant works that have shaped my thinking about the practice of literacy as I studied it in Carpinteria: Abrams and Sutton-Smith 1977, Anderson and Stokes 1984, Botvin and Sutton-Smith 1977, Devine 1994, Freire 1970 and 1995, Freire and Macedo 1987, Heath 1983, Hymes 1974 and 1996, Lankshear and McLaren 1993, Leichter 1984, Reder 1994, Schieffelin 1986, Schieffelin and Cochran-Smith 1984, Scollon and Scollon 1980, Scribner and Cole 1981, Shor and Peri 1999, and Vasquez, Pease-Alvarez, and Shannon 1994.

3. Two articles, Delgado-Gaitan 1993a and Delgado-Gaitan 1997a, describe my subjective interface with my research topic and the people and my shift in conceptualization about my observations and myself as a researcher. Behar (1993) and (1997) verifies the importance and natural part of ethnography to engage the ethnographer's emotions.

# Bibliography

Abrams, Davis M., and Brian Sutton-Smith. 1977. "The Development of the Trickster in Children's Narratives." *Journal of American Folklore* 90: 29–47.

Achor, Shirley, 1978. *Mexican Americans in a Dallas Barrio.* Tucson: University of Arizona Press.

Allen, Josephine. 1990. "Experiencing the Empowerment Process: Women and Development." *Networking Bulletin* 1(3): 1–17.

Allen, Josephine, Don Barr, Moncrieff Cochran, Christiann Dean, and Jennifer Greene. 1989. "The Empowerment Process: The Underlying Model." *Networking Bulletin-Empowerment and Family Support* 1: 1–12.

Allexsaht-Snider, Martha. 1991. "Family Literacy in a Spanish-Speaking Context: Joint Construction of Meaning." *The Quarterly Newsletter of the Laboratory of Comparative Human Cognition* 13(1): 15–17.

*America's Labor Market in the 1990's: What Role Should Immigration Play?* Washington, D.C.: Library of Congress.

Anderson, Alonzo B., and Shelley J. Stokes. 1984. "Social and Institutional Influences on the Development and Practice of Literacy." In H. Goelman, A. Oberg, and F. Smith, eds., *Awakening to Literacy,* 24–38. Exeter, N.H.: Heinemann Educational Books.

Anzaldua, Gloria. 1987. *Borderland—La Frontera: The New Mestiza.* San Francisco, Calif.: Spinsters/Aunt Lute Book Co.

Apple, Michael W. 1979. *Ideology and Curriculum.* Boston: Routledge.

———. (1993). *Official Knowledge: Democratic Education in a Conservative Age.* New York: Routledge.

Aronowitz, Stanley, and Henry Giroux. 1991. *Postmodern Education: Politics, Culture, and Social Criticism.* Minneapolis: University of Minnesota Press.

Baca Zinn, Maxine. 1980. "Employment and Education of Mexican-American Women: The Interplay of Modernity and Ethnicity in Eight Families." *Harvard Educational Review* 50(1): 47–62.

———. 1983. "Ongoing Questions in the Study of Chicano Families." In A. V. Valdez, A. Camarillo, and T. Almaguer, eds., *The State of Chicano Research in Family, Labor and Migration Studies*, 139–47. Stanford, Calif.: Stanford Center for Chicano Research.

Baca Zinn, Maxine, and D. Stanley Eitzen. 1996. *Diversity in Families*. New York: Addison Wesley.

Bach, Robert L., and Doris Meissner. 1990. *America's Labor Market in the 1990s: What Role Should Immigrants Play?* Washington, D.C.: Library of Congress.

Barr, Don J. 1989. "Critical Reflections on Power." Cornell University Project, Department of Human Services Studies, College of Human Ecology, Ithaca, N.Y.

———. 1992. "Understanding and Supporting Empowerment: Redefining the Professional Role." *Networking Bulletin* 2(3): 3–8.

Barrera, Mario. 1979. *Race and Class in the Southwest: A Theory of Racial Inequality*. Notre Dame: University of Notre Dame Press.

Behar, Ruth. 1993. *Translated Woman: Crossing the Border with Esperanza's Story*. Boston: Beacon.

———. 1997. *The Vulnerable Observer: Anthropology That Breaks Your Heart*. Boston: Beacon.

Berger, E. H. 1991. "Parent Involvement: Yesterday and Today." *The Elementary School Journal* 91(3): 209–19.

Blakely, M. 1983. "Southeast Asian Refugee Parents: An Inquiry into Home-School Communication and Understanding." *Anthropology and Education Quarterly* 14(1): 43–68.

Bodnar, John. 1985. *The Transplanted: A History of Immigrants in America*. Bloomington: Indiana University Press.

Botvin, G. J., and B. Sutton-Smith. 1977. "The Development of Structural Complexity in Children's Fantasy Narratives." *Developmental Psychology* 13: 377–88.

Bowles, Samuel, and Herbert Gintis. 1976. *Schooling in Capitalist America: Educational Reform and the Contradictions of Economic Life*. New York: Basic.

Bronfenbrenner, Uri. 1978. "Who Needs Parent Education?" *Teachers College Record* 79(4): 767–87.

Camarillo, Albert. 1992. "California and Ethnic/Racial Diversity." *La Nueva Vision* 1(2): 1–11, Stanford Center for Chicano Research.

Carnoy, Martin, and Henry Levin. 1985. *Schooling and Work in the Democratic State*. Stanford: Stanford University Press.

*Carpinteria Herold, The*. 1990. "A Brighter Outlook." Editor's Section, 12 May.

Clark, Reginal M. 1992. "Critical Factors in Why Disadvantaged Students Succeed or Fail in School." In J. H. Johnstron and K. M. Borman, eds., *Effective Schooling for Economically Disadvantaged Students: School-Based Strategies for Diverse Student Populations*, 65–77. Norwood, N.J.: Ablex.

Clifford, Marcus, and George E. Marcus. 1986. *Writing Culture: The Poetics and Politics of Ethnography*. Berkeley: University of California Press.

Cochran, Moncrieff. 1991. "Child Care and the Empowerment Process." *Networking Bulletin* 2(1): 4–15.

Cochran, Moncrieff, and Christiann Dean. 1991. "Home-School Relations and the Empowerment Process." *The Elementary School Journal* 91(3): 261–69.

Cohen, R. 1996. "Diasporas and Nation-State: From Victims to Challengers." *International Affairs* 72: 507–20.

Coleman, J. 1987. "Families and Schools." *Educational Researcher* 16(6): 32–38.

Coleman, James S. 1994. "Family Involvement in Education." In C. L. Fagnango and B. Z. Werber, eds., *School, Family and Community Interaction: A View from the Firing Lines,* 23–38. Boulder, Colo.: Westview.

Comer, James P. 1984. "Home-School Relationship as They Affect the Academic Success of Children." *Education and Urban Society* 16(3): 323–37.

Comer, J. P., and N. Hayes, 1991. "Parent Involvement in Schools: An Ecological Approach." *Elementary School Journal* 91(3): 271–77.

Conway, Jill Kerr. 1998. *When Memory Speaks: Reflections on Autobiography*. New York: Alfred A. Knopf.

Coontz, Stephanie. 1992. *The Way We Never Were: American Families and the Nostalgia Trap*. New York: Basic.

Crawford, John. 1989. *Bilingual Education: History, Politics, Theory, and Practice*. Trenton, N.J.: Crane.

Cremin, Lawrence. 1957. *The Republic and the School*. New York: Teachers College Press.

David, Mirian D. 1989. "Schooling and the Family." In H. A. Giroux and P. L. McLaren, *Critical Pedagogy, the State and Cultural Struggle,* 50–65. New York: SUNY.

Davis, K. 1982. "Achievement Variables and Class Cultures: Family Schooling, Job, and Forty-Nine Dependent Variables in Cumulative GSS." *American Sociological Review* 47 (October): 569–86.

Delgado-Gaitan, Concha. 1988. "The Value of Conformity: Learning to Stay in School: An Ethnographic Study." *Anthropology and Education Quarterly* 19(4): 354–82.

———. 1990. *Literacy for Empowerment: The Role of Parents in Children's Education*. London: Falmer.

———. 1991a. "Relating Experience and Text: Socially Constituted Reading Activity." In M. McGroaty and C. Faltis, eds., *In the Interest of Language: Context for Learning and Using Language,* 150–69. Berlin, Germany: Mouton de Gruyter.

———. 1991b. "Involving Parents in the Schools: A Process of Change for Involving Parents." *American Journal of Education* 100(1): 20–46.

———. 1992. "School Matters in the Mexican-American Home: Socializing Children to Education." *American Educational Research Journal* 29(3): 495–513.

———. 1993a. "Research and Policy in Reconceptualizing Family-School Relationships." In P. Phelan and Ann Davidson, eds., *Cultural Diversity and Educational Policy and Change,* 139–59. New York: Teachers College Press.

———. 1993b. "Researching Change and Changing the Researcher. *Harvard Educational Review* 63(4): 389–411.

———. 1994a. "Consejos: The Power of Cultural Narrative." *Anthropology and Education Quarterly* 25(3): 298–316.

———. 1994b. "Parenting in Two Generations of Mexican-American Families." *International Journal of Behavioral Development* 16(3): 409–27.

———. 1994c. "Russian Refugee Families: Accommodating Aspirations through Education." *Anthropology and Education Quarterly* 25(2): 137–55.

———. 1994d. "Socializing Young Children in Immigrant and First Generation Mexican Families." In P. Greenfield and R. Cocking, eds., *The Development of Minority Children: Culture In and Out of Context,* 56–86. Hillsdale, N.J.: Lawrence Erlbaum.

———. 1994e. "Sociocultural Change through Literacy: Toward the Empowerment of Families." In B. Ferdman, R. M. Weber, and A. Ramirez, eds., *Literacy across Languages and Cultures,* 143–70. New York: SUNY Press.

———. 1994f. "Spanish-Speaking Families' Involvement in Schools." In C. L. Fagnango and B. Z. Werber, eds., *School, Family and Community Interaction: A View from the Firing Lines,* 85–98. San Francisco: Westview.

———. 1996. *Protean Literacy: Extending the Discourse on Empowerment.* London: Falmer.

———. 1997a. "Dismantling Borders." In P. L. Peterson and A. Neumann, eds., *Reflexivity and Research in Education: Self and Work in Academic Women's Lives,* 37–52. New York: Teachers College Press.

———. 2000. Incorporating Diverse Abilities in Academia: Irreconcilable Laws. In H. Trueba and L. Bartolomé, eds., *Immigrant Voices: In Search of Pedagogical Reform,* 167–86. New York: Rowman & Littlefield.

Delgado-Gaitan, Concha, and Martha Allexsaht-Snider. 1992. "Mediating School Cultural Knowledge for Children: The Parent's Role." In J. H. Johnston and K. M. Borman, eds., *Effective Schooling for Economically Disadvantaged Students: School-Based Strategies for Diverse Student Populations,* 81–100. Norwood, N.J.: Ablex.

Delgado-Gaitan, Concha, and Denise Segura. 1989. "The Social Context of Chicana Women's Role in Children's Schooling." *Educational Foundations* 3(1): 71–92.

Delgado-Gaitan, Concha, and Henry Trueba. 1991. *Crossing Cultural Borders.* London: Falmer.

Devine, Joanne. 1994. "Literacy and Social Power." In B. M. Ferdman, R. M. Weber, and A. G. Ramirez, eds., *Literacy across Languages and Cultures,* 221–39. New York: SUNY Press.

Diaz, Rafael M. 1992. "Research Takes a Close Look at Home-School Conflicts." *La Nueva Vision* 1(2): 5–12, Stanford Center for Chicano Research.

Donato, Ruben, Martha Menchaca, and Richard R. Valencia. 1991. "Segregation, Desegregation, and Integration of Chicano Student: Problems and Prospects." In R. R. Valencia, ed., *Chicano School Failure and Success: Research and Policy Agendas for the 1990's.* London: Falmer.

Dornbusch, S. M., P. L. Ritter, P. H. Leiderman, D. F. Roberts, and M. J. Fraleigh. 1987. "The Relation of Parenting Style of Adolescent School Performance." *Child Development* 58: 1244–57.

Ehman, Lee H. 1980. "The American School in the Political Socialization Process." *Review of Educational Research* 50(3): 99–119.

Ellsworth, Elizabeth. 1987. "Why Doesn't This Feel Empowering? Working through the Representative Myths of Critical Pedagogy." *Harvard Educational Review* 59(3): 297–324.

Epstein, J. L. 1990. "School and Family Connections: Theory, Research, and Implication for Integrating Sociologies of Education and Family." In D.G. Unger and M. B. Susan, eds., *Families in Community Settings: Interdisciplinary Perspectives,* 49–68. New York: Haworth.

Epstein, Joyce L. 1994. "Theory to Practice: School and Family Partnerships Lead to School Improvement and Student Success." In C. L. Fagnango and B. Z. Werber, eds., *School, Family and Community Interaction: A View from the Firing Lines,* 39–54. Boulder, Colo.: Westview.

Everhart, R. 1983. *Reading, Writing and Resistance: Adolescence and Labor in a Junior High School.* London: Routledge and Kegan-Paul.

Ferdman, Bernardo M., Rose-Marie Weber, Arnulfo G. Ramirez, eds. 1994. *Literacy across Languages and Cultures.* New York: SUNY Press.

Flor Ada, Alma. 1988. "The Pajaro Valley Experience: Working with Spanish-Speaking Parents to Develop Children's Reading and Writing Skills through the Use of Children's Literature." In Tove Skutnabb-Kangas and Jim Cummins, eds. *Minority Education,* 223–38. Philadelphia: Multilingual Matters LTD.

Foley, Douglas E. 1990. *Learning Capitalist Culture: Deep in the Heart of Tejas.* Philadelphia: University of Pennsylvania Press.

Freire, Paulo. 1970. *Pedagogy of the Oppressed.* New York: Continuum.

———. 1973. *Education for Critical Consciousness.* New York: Seabury.

———. 1995. *Pedagogy of Hope: Reliving Pedagogy of the Oppressed.* Trans. Robert R. Barr. New York: Continuum.

Freire, Paulo, and Donaldo Macedo. 1987. *Literacy: Reading the Word and the World.* New York: Bergin and Garvey.

Garcia, Mario. 1978. "The Americanization of the Mexican Immigrant." *Journal of Ethnic Studies* 6(2): 53–70.

Garcia, Pedro. 1991. "What Do Children Learn in School?" *The Carpinteria Herald,* 30 October.

———. 1991. "Teaching: The Greatest of all Professions." *The Carpinteria Herald,* 27 November.

———. 1992. "Carpinteria Reaches toward the 21st Century." *The Carpinteria Harold,* 17 September.

———. 1993a. "Winning Isn't Always Defeating Somebody." *Montecito Life,* 21 January.

———. 1993b. "We Are Able to Overcome Expectations of Others." *The Carpinteria Herald,* 18 February.

*Genocidal Mentality: Nazi Holocaust and Nuclear Threat, The.* New York: The National Immigration Law Center, Guide to Alien Eligibility for Federal Programs, 1992.

Giroux, Henry. 1989. *Border Pedagogy.* New York: Routledge.

———. 1992. *Border Crossings: Cultural Workers and the Politics of Education.* New York: Routledge.

Goldberg, Barry. 1992. "Historical Reflections on Transnationalism, Race, and the American Immigrant Saga." In N. G. Schiller, L. Basch, and C. Blanc-Szanton, eds., *Towards a Transnational Perspective on Migration,* 201–17. New York: The New York Academy of Sciences.

Goldenberg, Claude. 1987. "Low-Income Hispanic Parents' Contributions to Their First-Grade Children's Word-Recognition Skills." *Anthropology and Education Quarterly* 18: 149–79.

Gonzalez, Gilbert, G. 1990. *Chicano Education in the Era of Segregation.* Philadelphia: The Balch Institute Press.

Gore, Jennifer. 1992. "What We Can Do for You! What *Can* We Do for 'You'? Struggling over Empowerment in Critical and Feminist Pedagogy." In C. Luke and J. Gore, eds., *Feminist Critical Pedagogy,* 54–73. New York: Routledge.

Gotts, E. E., and R. F. Purnell. 1986. "Communication: Key to School-Home Relations." In R. J. Griffore and R. P. Boger, eds., *Child Rearing in the Home and School,* 157–200. New York: Plenum.

Grosz, Elizabeth A. 1988. "The Intervention of Feminist Knowledges." In Barbara Caine, E. A. Grosz, and Marie de Lepervanche, *Crossing Boundaries: Feminisms and the Critique of Knowledges,* 92–104. Sydney: Allen and Unwin.

Hall, Stuart, and David Held. 1990. "Citizens and Citizenship." In Stuart Hall and Martin Jacques, eds., *New Times: The Changing Face of Politics in the 1990s,* 173–88. London: Verso.

Hastrup, Kirsten. 1992. "Writing Ethnography State of the Art." In J. Okely and H. Callaway, eds., *Anthropology and Autobiography,* 116–33. London: Routledge.

Hayes-Bautista, David, Werner O. Schink, and Jorge Chapa. 1988. *The Burden of Support: Young Latinos in an Aging Society.* Stanford, Calif.: Stanford University Press.

Heath, Shirley B. 1982. "What No Bedtime Story Means: Narrative Skills at Home and School." *Language and Society* 11(2): 49–76.

———. 1983. *Ways with Words.* Cambridge: Cambridge University Press.

Herman, J. L., and J. P. Yeh. 1983. "Some Effects of Parent Involvement in Schools." *The Urban Review* 15(1): 11–17.

Hymes, Dell H. 1974. *Foundations in Sociolinguistics.* Philadelphia: University of Pennsylvania Press.

———. 1996. Ethnography, Linguistics, Narrative Inequality: Toward an Understanding of Voice. Portsmouth, N.Y.: Taylor and Francis.

Jordan, C. 1990. "Cultural Compatibility and Education of Ethnic Minority Children." *Educational Research Quarterly* 8: 59–71.

Joseph, Suad. 1993. "Fieldwork and Psychosocial Dynamics of Personhood." *Frontiers* 13(3): 9–32.

Klimer-Dougan, B., J. A. Lopez, P. Nelson, and H. S. Adelman. 1992. "Two Studies of Low-Income Parents' Involvement in Schooling." *The Urban Review* 24(3): 185–202.

Kohn, M. L. 1959. "Social Class and Parental Values." *American Journal of Sociology* 68: 471–80.

Kondo, Dorine K. 1990. *Crafting Selves: Power, Gender, and Discourses of Identity in a Japanese Workplace.* Chicago: University of Chicago Press.

Kralovec, Etta, and John Buell. 2000. *The End of Homework: How Homework Disrupts Families, Overburdens Children, and Limits Learning.* Boston: Beacon.

Lankshear, Colin, and Peter McLaren, eds. 1993. *Critical Literacy: Politics, Praxis and the Postmodern.* New York: SUNY Press.

Lareau, Annette. 2000. *Home Advantage: Social Class and Parental Intervention in Elementary Education.* Boulder: Rowman & Littlefield.

Lather, Patti. 1991. *Getting Smart: Feminist Research and Pedagogy with/in the Postmodern.* New York: Routledge.

*Lau v. Nichols.* 1974. 414 US 563, 566.

Leichter, Hope Jensen. 1984. "Families as Environments for Literacy." In H. Goelman, A. Oberg, and F. Smith, eds., *Awakening to Literacy,* 38–51. Exeter, N.H.: Heinemann Educational Books.

Levin, Malcolm A. 1987. "Parent-Teacher Collaboration." In D.W. Livingstone and Contributors, *Critical Pedagogy and Cultural Power,* 95–120. Westport, Conn.: Berin and Garvey.

Levy, F., A. J. Meltsner, and A. Wildavsky. 1975. *Urban Outcomes: Schools, Streets, and Libraries.* Berkeley, Calif.: University of California Press.

Lifton, Robert Jay. 1967. *Death in Life: Survivors of Hiroshima.* New York: Random House.

———. 1973. *Home from the War: Vietnam Veterans Neither Victims nor Executioners.* New York: Simon and Schuster.

———. 1987. *The Future of Immortality and Other Essays for a Nuclear Age.* New York: Basic.

———. 1993. *The Protean Self: Human Resilience in an Age of Fragmentation.* New York: Basic.

Lifton, R. J., and Eric Markusen. 1990. *The Genocidal Mentality: Nazi Holocaust and Nuclear Threat.* New York: Basic.

Luke, Carmen. 1992. "Feminist Politics in Radical Pedagogy." In Carmen Luke and Jennifer Gore, eds., *Feminist Critical Pedagogy,* 25–53. New York: Routledge.

Luke, Carmen, and Jennifer Gore. 1992. *Feminisms and Critical Pedagogy.* New York: Routledge.

McLaren, P. 1986. *Schooling as a Virtual Performance: Towards a Political Economy of Educational Symbols and Gestures.* London: Routledge.

McLoed, Jay. 1987. *Ain't No Makin' It.* Boulder: Westview.

Mead, Margaret. 1970. *Culture and Commitment.* Garden City, N.Y.: Anchor.

Menchaca, M., and R. Valencia. 1990. "Anglo-Saxon Ideologies in the 1920's–1930's: Their Impact on Segregation of Mexican Students in California." *Anthropology and Education Quarterly* 21: 222–49.

Merino, B., H. Trueba, and F. Samaniego, eds. 1993. *Language and Culture in Learning: Teaching Spanish to Native Speakers of Spanish*. London: Falmer.

Morrison, G. S. 1978. *Parent Involvement in the Home, School, and Community*. Columbus, Ohio: Charles E. Merrill.

Neumann, Anna, and Penelope Peterson, eds. 1997. *Lessons from Our Lives*. New York: Teachers College, Columbia University Press.

Oakes, Jeannie. 1990. *Multiplying Inequalities: The Effects of Race, Social Class, and Tracking on Opportunities to Learn Mathematics and Science*. Santa Monica, Calif.: Rand.

Oakes, Jeannie, Karen Hunter Quartz, Steve Ryan, and Martin Lipton, eds. 2000. *Becoming Good American Schools: The Struggle for Civic Virtue in Education Reform*. San Fancisco: Jossey-Bass.

Ogbu, John U. 1987. *Minority Education and Caste: The American System in Cross-Cultural Perspective*. New York: Academic Press.

Okely, Judith, and Helen Callaway. 1992. *Anthropology and Autobiography*. New York: Routldege.

Pease-Alvarez, Lucinda. 1991. "Oral Contexts for Literacy Development in a Mexican Immigrant Community." *The Quarterly Newsletter of the Laboratory of Comparative Human Cognition* 12(1): 9–13.

Phelan, P., A. L. Davidson, and H. T. Cao. 1991. "Students' Multiple Worlds: Negotiating the Boundaries of Family, Peer, and School Cultures." *Anthropology and Education Quarterly* 22(3): 224–50.

Portes, Alejandro. 1996. "Global Villagers: The Rise of Transnational Communities." *The American Prospect* 25 (March-April): 74–77.

Ramirez, A. G. 1994. "Literacy Acquisition among Second Language Learners." In B. M. Ferdman, R. Weber, A. G. Arnulfo, eds., *Literacy across Languages and Cultures*. New York: SUNY Press.

Rangel, Jorge C., and Carlos M. Alcala. 1972. Project Report De Jure Segregation of Chicanos in Texas Schools. *Harvard Civil Rights—Civil Liberties Review* 7: 310–19.

Reder, Stephen. 1994. "Practice-Engagement Theory: A Sociocultural Approach to Literacy across Languages and Cultures." In B. M. Ferdman, R. M. Weber, and A. G. Ramirez, eds., *Literacy across Languages and Cultures,* 33–75. New York: SUNY Press.

Report Prepared for Assembly Select Committee on Statewide Immigration Impact—Assembly Member Grace Napolitano Chairperson—prepared by Assembly Office of Research—#0501—A. Robert L. Bach and Doris Meissner. June 1990.

Roos, Peter, D. 1978. "Bilingual Education: The Hispanic Response to Unequal Educational Opportunity." *Law and Contemporary Problems* 42: 111–40.

Rosaldo, Renato. 1989. *Culture and Truth: The Remaking of Social Analysis*. Boston: Beacon.

Rosaldo, Renato, William V. Flores, and Blanca Silverstrini. "Identity, Conflict and Evolving Latino Communities: Cultural Citizenship in San Jose, California." Report to the Fund for Research on Dispute Resolution, November 1993.

Rouse, Roger. 1989. "Mexican Migration to the United States: Family Relations in the Development of a Transnational Migrant." Ph.D. dissertation, Stanford University, Stanford, California.

———. 1992. "Making Sense of Settlement: Class Transformation, Cultural Struggle, and Transnationalism among Mexican Migrants in the United States." In N.G. Schiller, L. Basch, and C. Blanc-Szanton, eds., *Towards a Transnational Perspective on Migration,* 25–53. New York: The New York Academy of Sciences.

Rumbaut, Ruben, 1997. "Ties That Bind: Immigration and Immigrant Families in the United States." In Alan Booth, Ann Crouter, and Nancy Landale, eds., *Immigration and the Family: Research and Policy on U.S. Immigrants,* 3–46. Mahwah, N.J.: Lawrence Erlbaum.

San Miguel, Guadalupe. 1984. "Conflict and Controversy in the Evolution of Bilingual Education Policy in the United States—An Interpretation." *Social Science Quarterly* 65: 501–18.

———. 1987. *Let All of Them Take Heed: Mexican Americans and the Campaign for Educational Equity in Texas, 1910–1981.* Austin: University of Texas Press.

Saragoza, Alex. 1983. "The Conceptualization of the History of the Chicano Family." In A. V. Valdez, A. Camarillo, and T. Almaguer, eds., *The State of Chicano Research in Family, Labor and Migration Studies,* 111–38. Stanford, Calif.: Stanford Center for Chicano Research.

Schieffelin, Bambi B. 1986. *How Kaluli Children Learn What to Say, What to Do, and How to Feel.* New York: Cambridge University Press.

Schieffelin, Bambi, and Marilyn Cochran-Smith. 1984. "Learning to Read Culturally: Literacy before Schooling." In H. Goelman, A. Oberg, and F. Smith, eds., *Awakening to Literacy,* 3–23. Portsmouth, N.H.: Heinemann.

Schiller, Nina Glick, Linda Basch, and Cristina Blanc-Szanton. 1992. "Transnationalism: A New Analytic Framework for Understanding Migration." In N. G. Schiller, L. Basch, and C. Blanc-Szanton, eds., *Towards a Transnational Perspective on Migration,* 1–25. New York: The New York Academy of Sciences.

Scollon, Ron, and Suzanne Scollon. 1980. "Literacy as Focused Interaction." *The Quarterly Newsletter of the Laboratory of Comparative Human Cognition* 2(2): 26–29.

———. 1981. *Narrative, Literacy, and Face in Inter Ethnic Communication.* Norwood, N.J.: Ablex.

Scribner, Sylvia, and Michael Cole. 1981. *The Psychology of Literacy: A Case Study among the Vai.* Cambridge, Mass.: Harvard University Press.

Segura, Denise. 1988. "Familism and Employment among Chicanas and Mexican Immigrant Women." In M. B. Melville, ed., *Mexicanas in Work in the United States,* 24–32. Houston: University of Houston Press.

———. 1993. "Slipping through the Cracks: Dilemmas in Chicana Education." In A. de la Torre and B. M. Pesquera, eds., *Building with Our Hands: New Directions in Chicana Studies,* 199–216. Berkeley: University of California Press.

Shor, Ira, and Caroline Pari. 1999. *Critical Literacy in Action: Writing Words, Changing World.* Westport, Conn.: Boynton/Cook.

Simon, Julian. 1989. *The Economic Consequences of Immigrants*. Cambridge, Mass.: Blackwell Publisher.

Slavin, Robert E. 1990. "Achievement Effects of Ability Grouping in Secondary Schools: A Best Evidence Synthesis." *Review of Educational Research* 60: 471–99.

Spindler, George D. 1955. *Education and Anthropology*. Palo Alto, Calif.: Stanford University Press.

Spindler, George, and Louise Spindler, eds. 1994. *Pathways to Cultural Awareness*. Thousand Oaks, Calif.: Corwin.

Spring, Joel. 1991. *American Education: An Introduction to Social and Political Aspects*. New York: Longman.

Stevenson, D. L., and D. P. Baker. 1987. "The Family-School Relation and the Child's School Performance." *Child Development* 58: 1348–57.

Stockton, G. 1960. *La Carpinteria*. The Carpinteria Valley Historical Society. Carpinteria, California.

Suarez-Orozco, Marcelo M., ed. 1998. *Crossings: Mexican Immigration Interdisciplinary Perspectives*. Cambridge, Mass.: Harvard University Press and J. D. Rockefeller Center for Latin American Studies.

Taylor, Deny. 1983. *Family Literacy: Young Children Learning to Read and Write*. Exeter, N.H.: Heinemann.

Tienda, Marta. 1983. "Market Characteristics and Hispanic Earning: A Comparison of Natives and Immigrants." *Social Problems* 31(1): 59–72.

Torres-Guzman, Maria. 1991. "Recasting Frames: Latino Parent Involvement." In M. McGroaty and C. Faltis, eds., *In the Interest of Language: Context for Learning and Using Language,* 111–32. Berlin, Germany: Mouton de Gruyter.

Trinh, Minh-Ha. 1989. *Woman, Native, Other*. Bloomington: University of Indiana Press.

Trueba, Henry T. 1984. "The Forms, Functions and Values of Literacy: Reading for Survival in a Barrio as a Student." *NABE Journal* 9: 21–40.

———. 1989. *Raising Silent Voices: Educating Linguistic Minorities for the 21st Century*. New York: Harper & Row.

———. 1999. *Latinos Unidos: From Cultural Diversity to the Politics of Solidarity*. New York: Rowman & Littlefield.

Trueba, Henry T., Lila Jacobs, and Elizabeth Kirton. 1990. *Cultural Conflict and Adaptation: The Case of the Hmong Children in American Society*. London: Falmer.

Trueba, Henry T., Cirenio Rodriguez, Yali Zou, and Jose Cintron. 1993. *Healing Multicultural America: Mexican Immigrants Rise to Power in Rural California*. London: Falmer.

Uribe, Oscar. 1980. "The Impact of 25 Years of School Desegregation on Hispanic Students." *Agenda: A Journal on Hispanic Issues* 10(5): 3–35.

United States Census Bureau. 2000a. 1999 Census Data for the State of California.

———. 2000b. *The Foreign Born Population in the United States*.

———. 2000c. *Population Projections of the U.S. by Age, Sex, Race, and Hispanic Origins.*

Vasquez, Olga. 1989. "Connecting Oral Language Strategies to Literacy: Ethnographic Study among Four Mexican Immigrant Families. Unpublished Doctoral Dissertation, Stanford University, Stanford, California.

Vasquez, Olga, Lucinda Pease-Alvarez, and Sheila M. Shannon. 1994. *Pushing Boundaries: Language and Culture in a Mexicano Community.* New York: Cambridge University Press.

Vélez-Ibañez, Carlos. 1983. *Bonds of Mutual Trust.* New Brunswick, N.J.: Rutgers University Press.

———. 1988. "Networks of Exchange among Mexicans in the U.S. and Mexico: Local Level Mediating Responses to National International Transformations." *Urban Anthropology* 17(1): 27–51.

*Vos Popular.* July 1990.

Walberg, H. J. 1986. "Home Environment and School Learning: Some Quantitative Models and Research Synthesis." In R. J. Griffore and R. P. Boger, eds., *Child Rearing in the Home and School,* 195–220. New York: Plenum.

Williams, Norma. 1990. *The Mexican American Family: Tradition and Change.* Dix Hills, N.Y.: General Hall.

Williams, Raymond. 1989. *Resources of Hope: Culture, Democracy, Socialism.* London: Verso.

Willis, Paul E. 1977. *Learning to Labor: How Working Class Kids Get Working Class Jobs.* New York: Columbia University Press.

Ybarra, Lea. 1983. "Empirical and Theoretical Developments in Studies of the Chicano Family." In A. V. Valdez, A. Camarillo, and T. Almaguer, eds., *The State of Chicano Research in Family, Labor and Migration Studies,* 91–110. Stanford, Calif.: Stanford Center for Chicano Research.

Zentella, A. Celia. 1985. "Language Variety among Puerto Ricans." In C. Ferguson and S. Brice Heath, eds., *Language in the USA,* 242–71. New York: Cambridge University Press.

# Index

∾

# About the Author

**Concha Delgado-Gaitan** has numerous publications on oral and written traditions in immigrant communities including: *Protean Literacy* (1996); *Crossing Cultural Borders* coauthored with Enrique (Henry) T. Trueba (1991); *Literacy for Empowerment* (1990); and *School and Society* coedited with Trueba (1988). In 2000 Delgado-Gaitan received the George and Louise Spindler award for her contributions to educational anthropology.